IN PLACE

D1737145

IN PLACE

SPATIAL AND SOCIAL ORDER IN A FAEROE ISLANDS COMMUNITY

DENNIS GAFFIN

SUNY College at Buffalo

WAVELAND
PRESS, INC.

Prospect Heights, Illinois

For information about this book, write or call:
Waveland Press, Inc.
P.O. Box 400
Prospect Heights, Illinois 60070
(847) 634-0081

Reproduction of pastel drawing on front cover and frontispiece illustrations by William Heinesen. Used with permission.

Parts of chapters 4 and 5 appeared in *Ethnos* 1–2 (1993): 53–72 and *Landscape* 32, no. 2 (1994): 20–27. Parts of Chapter 6 appeared in *Ethos* 23, no. 2 (1995): 149–72.

Maps appearing on pages xiii and 4 are reprinted with permission from *The Ring of Dancers: Images of Faroese Culture* by Jonathan Wylie and David Margolin (University of Pennsylvania Press, 1981).

Map appearing on page 14 is reprinted with permission from *Northern Mists* by Carl O. Sauer (University of California Press, 1968).

Map appearing on page 91 is adapted with permission from *Landscape* 32, no. 2 (1994).

All text photographs taken by the author.

Contents

Preface

Part of northern Europe, the Faeroe Islands illustrate how Westerners can adapt to a difficult environment and integrate their culture with it. This book investigates the ways in which Faeroese villagers have put boundaries around both their physical and social environments and the ways in which the environment influences culture and culture influences environment. A study in the conversion of physical space into cultural place, it generally falls within the anthropological discipline of cultural ecology.

The Faeroes are an isolated group of small North Atlantic islands about four hundred miles from Norway, three hundred miles from Iceland and two hundred miles northwest of the Shetland Isles. Inhabitants live on seventeen of the islands and speak their own Norse (West Scandinavian) tongue—Faeroese—one of the five Scandinavian languages. For a thousand years Faeroe Islanders have eked out a precarious existence, fishing, raising sheep, fowling, and hunting whales. Winds and stormy seas channel their lives. Occasionally a fisherman drowns or a fowler falls off a steep mountain cliff searching for fulmars, puffins, and other edible seabirds.

The historical remoteness of the islands, the seclusion of many villages within the mountainous terrain, and the careful attention necessary to harvest the dangerous waters and cliffs affect behavior and attitude. Faeroese culture emphasizes self-sufficiency, social independence, emotional self-control, verbal facility, and a strong sentiment of belonging to places. Their intimacy with the land and sea provides sustenance, but also a literal and symbolic embeddedness of the person, the community, and the culture in the surrounds. With multiple references and meanings affixed to particular and general locales, their senses of place are central to their survival and culture.

A modern visitor must either fly or sail to the Faeroes via Denmark or Iceland or take a summer-only passenger ship from northern Scotland, at the port of Thurso. The British built an airfield on the islands during World War II. Airplane passengers clap upon each landing, and the planes that fly there are especially designed to land and depart on the short runway of the rugged island terrain. Faeroese geography and travel time have their own logic: the largest town and capital, Tórshavn, only twenty-five kilometers from the airport, is two and a half hours away by car and ferry. With a population of about sixteen thousand, Tórshavn contains about a third of the islands' inhabitants. The majority live in eighty or so small villages.

My wife and I traveled to and from the Faeroes via ship over the notorious, stormy stretch of northern waters between Scotland and Faeroe. It was to save money that we went by sea, but the sea is the best way to go there. It is the method that most people have used to reach the Faeroes over the centuries. Approaching by sea, one has time to marvel at the islands' unexpected appearance and stark beauty.

I began twelve continuous months of fieldwork in August 1983. My purpose was to do ethnographic research on social control in a small village. I thought that an isolated, relatively unstudied Western context would be a good place to examine the daily workings of a community's regulation of behavior. It became apparent after awhile, however, that most facets of social and cultural life on the islands were interdependently related to physical and geographic aspects of the environs. Thus, ultimately the study came to embody social and cultural ecology.

I chose to live in a village distant from the most modern influences creeping into the two or three big towns of the islands. Villagers gave me, and I assumed, a few different but overlapping roles. They included that of ethnologist and folklorist, but also of American, student, writer, ornithologist, friend, and spy. They were all representative of my work in one sense or another and permitted me to move around more or less at will, although certainly under villagers' close watchfulness.

I spoke Faeroese as best I could. Despite some minimal study of Faeroese beforehand, it was only after several months of learning through extensive conversation and some language lessons from two local teachers (in exchange for teaching them English), that I came to understand and speak pretty well. After awhile I was conversing passionately and transcribing texts of tape-recorded interviews from Faeroese into English.

To earn living money and to become as much a part of the village life as possible, I worked with a municipal construction crew and intermittently in two privately owned fishline baiting houses. I also helped some men with their agricultural and shepherding chores, drank with friends and neighbors, and danced the Faeroese ring-dance. By the time I was about to depart, I felt that I could stay forever. I even had an offer to be trained as a full-time fisherman in a private cooperatively owned business and to gain the full equal earning rights of a crewmember. Such was the level of acceptance that the Faeroese give, even to some outsiders.

After months of thinking, writing, talking, reading, and churning about my experiences, and especially after living again in the United States, where people generally seem distant in space and in sentiment from nature and from each other, I more fully understood how environment and culture mold one another.

I want to acknowledge the support of people who got me to the Faeroes, helped me while there, and struggled with me in putting this book together.

I want to thank Tom Curtin at Waveland Press for his patient and judicious assistance with the manuscript.

Jonathan Wylie helped prepare me in Faeroese before my wife and I departed for the islands and has continued to provide me with intellectual support for working with Faeroese materials. The Fróðskaparsetur Føroya (Faeroese Academy), particularly Jóan Pauli Joensen, made it officially possible for me to do research in the Faeroes and for me to obtain a work visa. Upon request, while I was there, the Faeroese government was also kind in granting me research funds to continue my study.

I owe the largest debt of gratitude to the residents of Sumbøur. Gracious and giving, they accepted us and made us feel at home. There are too many to list, but I would especially like to thank Johan, Eli, Dagny, Pól, Anna Sofia, Hjartvar, Sjurður, Georg, Andrew, Anna, Daniel Johan, Alma, Maria, Johannes, Leivur, Arnfinn, Róland, and the Vestergaard brothers. I would also like to thank one other, special friend, Jaspur Midjord. I would hope that all men everywhere were as loyal and caring as Jaspur has been to me—and, I hope, I to him. It is to Jaspur that I dedicate this work.

I would also like to thank Raoul Andersen, Robert Paine, and Jean Briggs and others at the Anthropology Department and the

Institute for Social and Economic Research at Memorial University of Newfoundland for their support of my work on the Faeroes and the award of a Postdoctoral Research Fellowship (which I later had to decline).

I am also indebted to members of the anthropology department at the University at Buffalo. They have always supported me intellectually and financially. Without the Doctoral Fellowship in the Social Sciences, I might have never reached this point.

Marion Dickson and Jean Grela always helped me with their administrative and moral support. For intellectual support, fair treatment, and hours of encouraging discussion of some of the material in this book I heartily acknowledge the assistance of David Engel, professor of law and jurisprudence; Robert Dentan, professor of anthropology and American studies; and my major mentor Gerry Rosenfeld, professor of anthropology. Gerry's unflagging integrity as an anthropologist, and as a moral human being, has provided me with a role model for which I cannot imagine any better.

My own and my wife's family have always supported me, but my wife, Madelynn Fatelewitz, has, most of all, withstood the trials of several years of my work and has continued to support me in many ways, but most importantly, in her heart. Without her, and our joint adventure abroad and in our own incredible landscape at home, 'In the Hollow,' much of the meaning of this work, and of my life, would have long ago wilted away.

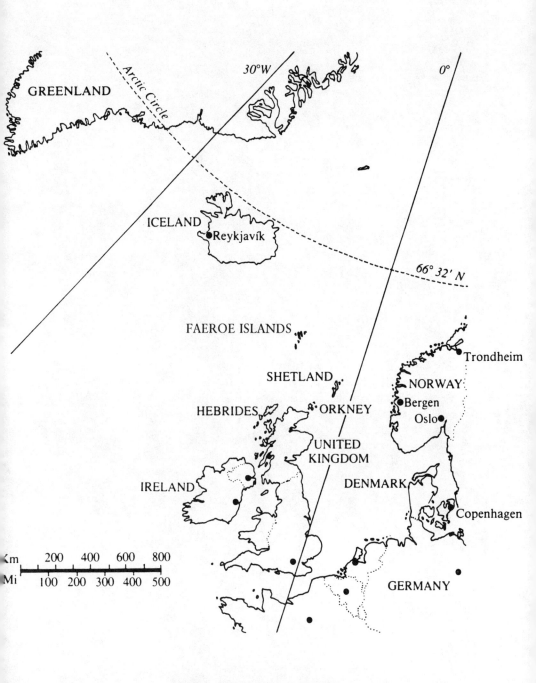

GREENLAND

Arctic Circle

30°W

0°

ICELAND
●Reykjavík

66° 32' N

FAEROE ISLANDS

SHETLAND

NORWAY
●Trondheim

HEBRIDES ·ORKNEY

●Bergen
Oslo●

UNITED
KINGDOM

IRELAND

DENMARK

Copenhagen●

Km | 200 400 600 800
Mi | 100 200 300 400 500

GERMANY

The Faeroe Islands
in the North Atlantic

Chapter One

Introduction

The Approach: Ecology and the Study of Place

Relationships between human beings and their environments are of interest to anthropologists, geographers, biologists, ecologists, and other scientists. Cultural ecology, the study and application of principles of ecological systems, is a major sub-branch of anthropology drawing on various branches of anthropology as well as biology, systems theory, and other physical and social sciences. Historically anthropologists have examined small-scale tribal settings to study ecology (e.g., Tsembaga of New Guinea, Rappoport 1967). Such non-Western contexts have provided relatively simple technological cultures to research the complex relationships between human beings and nature. European and North American settings have been studied less. The fact that the Faeroe Islands were isolated until the mid-nineteenth century, and that the islands are unmistakably set apart from the outside world by hundreds of miles of open, often stormy ocean helps to limit the ecological variables in this Western context.

Some ecologists have focused on the mathematical, energy flow, and caloric intake/output features of human, animal, and plant interactions or on the details of human natural resource utilization (e.g., Moran 1982). In contrast, the emphasis here is to link social behavior, spatial orientation, personality traits, values, aesthetics, and other abstract aspects of culture to environment. Gerald Pocius (1991), in a study of a Newfoundland outport, is similarly concerned with the meaning of space for the orderliness of a community, but his focus is primarily on material culture, the arrangement and patterning of artifacts. This work looks at how the Faeroese people situate themselves, their identities, and their

1

culture in spatial and geographic ways. It links ecology and the study of "place," now becoming central to a variety of disciplines.

I thus conceptualize place as socially constructed (Rodman 1992), place as sets of spaces converted into meaningful locations through people's ideas and experiences with them. Place is not simply a demarcated area, a physical setting, a subsistence niche, or a location for objects, but it also is an amalgam of social and cultural interactions and associations. Even Faeroese systems of giving names to place (chapter 3) and people (chapter 4) are ways of maintaining order and linking individuals and groups with geographic locations and characteristics of locations. People embody places, places embody people. Geographic names and associations ground the past, the present, and the future. Physical, social, and philosophical knowledge and feelings bind to landmarks and places: Faeroese villagers are inseparable from place.

This ethnography also builds upon studies of culture and social order in Scandinavian village societies. As in other Scandinavian locales, Faeroese culture is marked by a pervasive differentiation between (external) formal and (internal) informal levels of behavior and discourse. This occurs in various realms, in language (Blom and Gumperz 1972; Wylie and Margolin 1981), political and economic life (Barnes 1954; Wylie 1974; J. P. Joensen 1982), and in social control (Gaffin 1991, 1994; Hollos 1976; Yngvesson 1970, 1976). The lack of both open conflict and strong extrafamilial social alliances typifies the informality of Northern village life. In the isolated, insular topography of the Faeroes such informality, as well as typical Scandinavian concerns with language, nature, and the past (Wylie 1989), are especially apparent.

The Setting: The Faeroe Islands in the North Atlantic

Lying below the Arctic Circle at 62 degrees north latitude (see map), some twenty Faeroe Islands of various sizes total only 540 square miles. Myriad fjords, sounds, and mountains intricately divide them. The archipelago is volcanic in origin, with layers of tertiary basalt separated by layers of tuff, a softer reddish stone made from volcanic ash. Evidence indicates some prehistoric forests, but now even brush is rare, and the soil is so shallow that plants with long root systems cannot flourish. The winds are frequently so strong that plants that do not hug the ground cannot survive. The islands are virtually treeless, but a few small plantations endure in protected places.

With little foreshore, the islands are mostly sloping moorland and rocky terrain. The need for protection from winds and access to relatively calm sea made for a human settlement pattern of elongated or nucleated villages on fjords and bays at the base of mountains. The uninhabited areas between villages are remote, open, and desolate. If no hills block the view, one can easily observe a shepherd on a distant mountainside. But one must be wary of surprise endings: villagers often warn visitors about walking near cliff edges and in the hillsides in the fog. (Cairns, piles of rocks made by earlier inhabitants, still dot the slopes to mark paths between villages.) With various topographic features—promontories, gullies, ridges, chasms, and so on—the details of the coastlines and landscape provide a panoply of unique geographic experiences.

The islands' topographic features stand out not only because they are dramatic and present obstacles to transportation, but also because landscape is also highlighted in hundreds of place-names, which furthermore form parts of names for people. Moreover, Faeroese words for directions and "idioms of orientation" (Wylie and Margolin 1981), words and phrases for locating places in space, are complex and specific. Faeroese have a well-developed spatial vocabulary to refer to where others are, who they are, and where they are going.

The weather is mostly cloudy and overcast, in contrast to touristic photos. Average temperatures are 52 degrees Fahrenheit in summer and 40 degrees Fahrenheit in winter. The insulating effect of the Gulf Stream and surrounding ocean moderate the climate, despite its subarctic position. The winter weather is windy and rainy: snow remains on the ground only briefly, except on mountaintops. The other seasons are also windy and rainy, but less so, and summer can have several sunny days. Frequent fog lies low on the sea, in valleys, and in the villages. Winds and rainstorms can last a few days: sometimes fierce, they keep people inside talking to one another. Families may even temporarily sleep overnight in leeward rooms of their houses to avoid the pounding winds against their bedrooms.

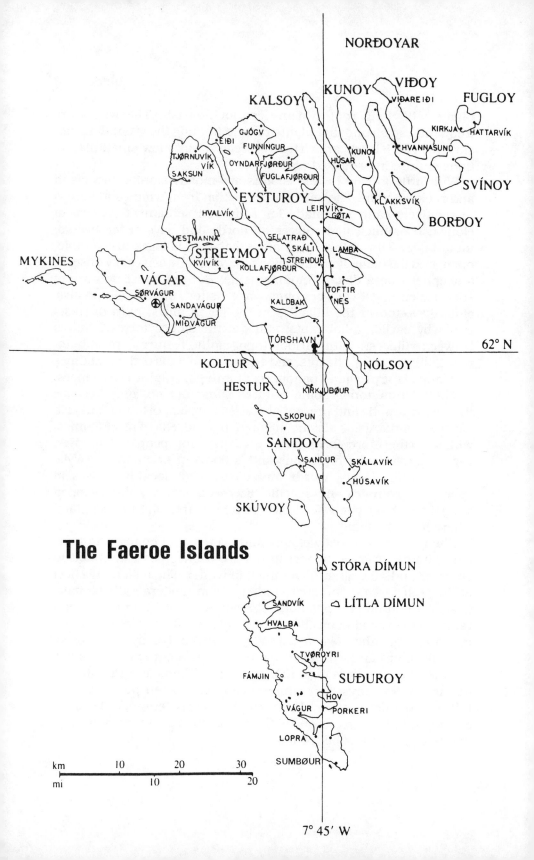

NORÐOYAR

KUNOY   VIÐOY   FUGLOY

KALSOY   VIÐAREIÐI

KIRKJA   HATTARVÍK

GJÓGV
EIÐI   FUNNINGUR   KUNOY   HVANNASUND
TJØRNUVÍK   OYNDARFJØRÐUR   HÚSAR   SVÍNOY
VÍK
SAKSUN   FUGLAFJØRÐUR

KLAKKSVÍK

EYSTUROY   LEIRVÍK   BORÐOY
GØTA
HVALVÍK

SELATRAÐ
VESTMANNA   SKÁLI   LAMBA
STREYMOY   STRENDUR
KVÍVÍK   KOLLAFJØRÐUR
VÁGAR   TOFTIR
SØRVÁGUR   KALDBAK   NES
SANDAVÁGUR

MYKINES   MIÐVÁGUR

TÓRSHAVN   62° N

KOLTUR   NÓLSOY

HESTUR   KIRKJUBØUR

SKOPUN

SANDOY
SKÁLAVÍK
SANDUR
HÚSAVÍK

SKÚVOY

The Faeroe Islands

STÓRA DÍMUN

LÍTLA DÍMUN
SANDVÍK

HVALBA

TVØROYRI
FÁMJIN   SUÐUROY
HOV
VÁGUR   PORKERI

LOPRA

SUMBØUR

km   10   20   30
mi   10   20

7° 45′ W

The stark, treeless landscape of the Faeroe Islands. Taken from atop a mountain, this view of northern Eysturoy ('East Island') shows the remoteness of many places, despite the islands' relatively small land mass of 540 square miles.

The overall effect of the weather is a heaviness of atmosphere that can dampen the spirit. One man said that maybe the cloudiness was one of the reasons for the unexcitable Faeroese temperament and that "if we had a few more sunny days, people would be more happy." But villagers, quite accustomed to the uniformly cloudy sky, are generally agreeable and take notice more of changing foreground activities than of the backdrop of the open, flat sky.

Ornithologists from distant countries occasionally visit the islands to observe and record birds, the islands being famous for their numerous seabirds. Among others there are puffins, kittiwakes, guillemots, gannets, shearwaters, fulmars, oystercatchers, and Faeroese eider ducks. The national bird is the oystercatcher (*tjaldur*), a noisy black and white bird with a long reddish bill, which drives away less desirable birds like ravens and crows. The species villagers now use most for food, at least in Sumbøur, is the gull-like fulmar (*havhestur* or *náti*), but the attractive, clown-faced puffin (*lundi*) remains a favorite delicacy. Inland, one often sees pipits, wagtails, whimbrels, plovers, skuas, and starlings.

Although it has long been spoken, written Faeroese is only about 140 years old. Before the Reformation of 1540 Norway owned the Faeroe Islands, and old West Scandinavian was spoken. Then Denmark took over. For seven hundred years both nations more or less administered the islands as a fiefdom. In 1948 Denmark granted the islands home rule. Since then the Faeroese have maintained their own parliament. Although foreign policy is officially the jurisdiction of the Danish government, the Faeroese government can and often does negotiate directly with other nations, especially in matters of fishing. Today the Faeroes (Føroyar in Faeroese) are a bilingual country with Faeroese as the common household and official language. Danish is a secondary language, mandatorily taught in school. It is primarily spoken with visiting Danes and by non-Faeroese officials. The islands are now a prosperous fishing nation of over forty-five thousand people. Unlike Denmark, the Faeroes have rejected membership in the European Economic Community (EEC).

The specific setting of this study is Sumbøur, an average-sized village of 350 persons on the island of Suðuroy. The high mountain that separates the village from other villages of the island has helped maintain the local independence of people there. It has also provided a reliable food source from seabirds that nest on the sheer cliffs. Most men work on small fishing boats that ply the local fishing grounds or on large Faeroese or Norwegian trawlers working more distant waters. Yet fowling, sheep-raising, whale hunting, and noncommercial fishing are still important. Financially and politically connected to faraway social democratic Denmark, the inhabitants of Sumbøur belong to families who generally live in the same size houses, own relatively equal plots of land, raise about the same number of sheep, and enjoy the same standard of living. Although they live in a recently modernized community, men still jump out of their cars into small boats in the bays to slaughter pilot whales (*Globicephala melaena*) or park their cars at the top of mountains to climb down ropes over cliffs to hunt birds, their lives a mix of modern and peasant activities. While it might be best to characterize the Faeroes as a postpeasant society, the inhabitants of Sumbøur have long been isolated and remain one of the last outposts of a peasantlike worldview and set of activities. Even villagers from other islands regard Sumbøur, now changing, as a stronghold of traditional Faeroese culture.

In Sumbøur, as elsewhere in the Faeroes, there are no trees, and houses line the sides of one main street at the base of sloping hillsides. Therefore almost all outdoor activities are public. As villagers are intricately intermarried, a strong familiarity with other persons complements the visibility of activity. Crimes common in other parts of the world (theft, vandalism, assault, and so on) are absent in the peaceful village. Local forms of nonconformity—excessive drinking, emotional dysfunction, physical disability, quarrelsomeness, or belief in a minority religion—usually do not directly threaten a household's physical or economic safety. Villagers leave their houses unlocked and unattended. Moreover, visiting etiquette lets people enter houses unannounced without knocking on doors. The proximity of others, the interconnectedness of kin and social ties, public scrutiny and comment, and a strong sense of belonging to the land and community maintain group order and survival.

The village of Sumbøur lies at the southern end of the southernmost island of Suðuroy.

One villager summarizes local living conditions and Faeroese endurance:

> Most persons here have got the ability to survive. It's proof I think that a person is not very disabled when he can survive here in the Faeroes. If you can see what kind of conditions we have lived under—very bad weather and extremely rough conditions also concerning your psychological health. You are put under extreme pressures during those rough and cold and windy nights and days, and you have to work outside. They are very bad conditions to live under. And it was much worse in the older days. They could not even get fish from the sea sometimes. . . . But the Faeroese people have always been said to be stubborn. Because if you want to survive here, you must be stubborn.

Capriciousness of seas, weather, animals, and humans figures in the man's general watchfulness. Here he compares sheep to humans:

> The most tame sheep are really the wildest. If you have wild sheep, you know exactly how they will react and how you can handle them. You can get them by rounding them up. But tame sheep you cannot catch by rounding them up. They will attack you and try to sneak around you, and they won't want to listen to you. Sometimes you try to push away a lamb that has been eating from your hand and you cannot get rid of it. But as soon as you want to catch that lamb, it is impossible. It will run away from you. Those who are most tame and know about you, they will try to get away . . . But the wild ones will be easy to catch. It is similar with men; the ones you know best can be very surprising.

Villagers clearly identify and maintain constant vigilance over their environs and their people.

In a discomfiting, parting moment with a middle-aged Faeroese friend at the end of my stay in Sumbøur, I said that maybe we would see each other again in America. He responded wisely: "Perhaps, for there is an old Faeroese proverb: 'One knows not in the morning what might happen in the evening.'" At the time I did not fully realize that his invocation of the basic uncertainty—and the myriad possibilities—of life was a hallmark of Faeroese culture. In a way, any culture is an attempt to come to terms with the whims and follies of fate. But in the rugged Faeroe Islands, accidents, fickle winds, and turbulent seas are ever present reminders of one's place within nature.

The Fieldwork: The Experience of Research

The only other ethnographies of the Faeroes are unpublished doctoral dissertations (Wylie 1974; Gaffin 1987). Articles on Faeroese culture are not common, and Scandinavian social scientists have not done extensive fieldwork on the islands. Most of the academic literature deals with fishing and whaling, though there are a few histories of the Faeroes in English, Danish, and Faeroese. Much of the scholarship is also archival and a result of collecting folklore and information about the past for the historical record. Jonathan Wylie's 1987 book itself straddles anthropology and history. My interest in doing research on the islands was sparked by their being a rather unknown and unstudied portion of the Western world.

Travel accounts about the islands and its people have depicted Faeroese as colorful, hardy Norsemen with quick wit, an economy of words, and a friendly, peaceful demeanor. It all seemed true in my experience, but Sumbøur is a closed community; my wife and I were the first outsiders other than close consanguines or new spouses ever to reside in the village for longer than a month. Like other villages and hamlets, it has no signs or printed maps with its commonly used place-names. Nor does it have a handy roster of people's customary names, which often incorporate names of houses, homesteads, hillsides, village sectors, and other features of the landscape. It took me several weeks to become familiar with the named spots villagers mention in ordinary talk about going to the store, walking to school, visiting relatives, rounding up sheep, and so forth.

In the small village, where almost everyone was either born or married into the village and where most occurrences are public and observable, each person and each place comes to be a "tradition" of the village. Places themselves have multiple meanings to the local inhabitants: they have associations of different persons and experiences of the past and present. Places are thus multi- and differentially symbolic to individuals and groups—"multilocal and multivocal" (Rodman 1992).

As an amateur naturalist and birdwatcher, I found an array of maritime flora, fauna, and experiences in the village environs. In frequent walks up and down mountain slopes—with camera, binoculars, and nature guides in hand—I learned about local seabirds, plants, and geography. Despite the seeming barrenness of the countryside, the subtly hued moorlands and fantastic cliffs provided endless adventure among divebombing Arctic skuas, chirping oystercatchers protecting their young, wandering multicolored sheep, and small waterfalls in ravines. I came to know the physical landscape and feel a part of it. In this way I obtained some privacy, fleeting moments of oceanic serenity, and overviews of where I was and what I was doing.

One of my first major data-gathering tasks was to systematically collect the place-names. Since names are short and my conversational skills were initially not good, place-names were concrete, uncontroversial subject matter around which to interview villagers, further study Faeroese, and begin to learn about social life. Checking back and forth with different villagers, I made several place-name maps of the village, fields, and nearby islets, including a map of the reputed haunts of *huldufólk*, supernatural "gray" people who live in hillside boulders.

Since many names are ancient and unrecorded, I initially talked mostly to older residents. They were more patient with my broken Faeroese than were younger persons, and they had more time to talk. The older people also appeared to take pleasure and pride in talking and reminiscing about people, places, and events. From them, via names, I learned about kinship, work patterns, and local history and legend. I came to comprehend local landmarks and named places as spatial records, partly as the Faeroese "spatial anchoring of myth" (Kahn 1990). As I learned more and more about the details of local uses of and interactions with the land and sea and the significance of places in villagers' own lives, I came to feel part of the social territory. Eventually, especially as I sometimes came to be known as Dennis eystan Á, (Dennis 'east of the Stream'), I came to believe that, in part, I had become a fixture of local space, that I too had taken on, and contributed to, the physical and social landscape.

Although names remained of interest throughout my stay and play a major role in understanding Faeroese culture, one of my major foci was on how villagers maintain conformity and how they talk about, label, and treat nonconformists. Thus private opinions and judgments of others were crucial to my study. Luckily I chose the right village in which to live. According to every Faeroese person with whom I have discussed the issue, *Suðuringar* ("natives of the southern island of Suðuroy") and particularly *Sumbingar* ("natives of the village of Sumbøur") are more open, verbal, and humorous than other islanders. I suspect that had my fieldsite been in the north, where people are reputedly less willing to volunteer information, I would have not penetrated as far into the dynamics of social life and would have glimpsed less the local ethos of landscape. My selection of Sumbøur therefore largely influenced the kind of information I would be able to evoke. This suggests that local levels of vocalness about place may vary considerably and that ethnography itself can be delicately dependent on characteristics of particular places.

I read English-language accounts of the Faeroes and English translations of Faeroese short stories, poetry, and literature. The effect of weather, geography, gossip, character, and folklore on Faeroese life were recurrent themes. Both in literature and in village conversation, the closely observed details of the physical landscape and of people's personalities seemed to balance the open countryside and ocean. Specific objects and individuals markedly contrasted with the environment and took on exaggerated, unique qualities. Human characters, literary or flesh and blood, became caricatures, images beyond precise description. I came to realize that even the most objective and empirical study, in addition to recording what is observably apparent in the environment and in behavior, must ultimately also try to take into account people's innermost thoughts and sensibilities and incorporate local cultural meaning.

I then began to read original Faeroese literature, legends, and short stories. I visited island court sessions, helped some villagers with haying and rounding up sheep, fished out on the open ocean, and participated in a pilot whale chase. I attended festivals, holiday church activities, parties, and dances. In these ways I was able to observe and participate in daily and seasonal economic rounds of activities as well as understand how villagers use their time and carry out secular and religious rituals. Drinking and dancing with villagers was fun. Some Sumbingar might still talk about the day I made some gathered shepherds laugh when I said, passing the liquor bottle to another, "Johan says 'Jesus Christ' when he gets the bottle, but he drinks it anyway!" or the night I stayed up until six in the morning ring-dancing and drinking with villagers.

After awhile I lost a sense of proportion, a sense of my own distinct historical identity from another country. I began to think that I was living in a well-scripted storybook, filled with vivid characters of a particular landscape. I, too, became a character and a caricature of myself. Patterns began to emerge. I was learning not only about subsistence practices and social behavior but about Faeroese ideas of history and legend, humor and peace, space and time. Phenomena as seemingly disparate as place-names, jokes, cartoons, greetings, proverbs, story subjects, body gestures, and tidily kept houses came to make sense in the context of their particular history, ecology, and worldview.

Although the Faeroese are not emotionally demonstrative, the day we left some villagers came to say good-bye and gave us presents. Even those with whom we were not close gave us small presents or money. And in a touching, silent moment, one man, Georg í Kjeri (Georg 'in the Hollow'), in a gesture of friendship, held my face, then my wife's face, gently in his hands. Another drove to the next village to watch us catch the local ferry to sail north to Tórshavn. Seeing the islands pass behind in the distance on the large ship heading south to Scotland, I once again thought about the dramatic interchange among the environment, the personalities, and the culture of the people. Living their own brand of maritime life, the Faeroese are a salty people, robust, pithy, cooperative, and colorful.

Chapter Two

History and Subsistence

History and Saga

Historians speculate that because the Faeroes lie in the middle of the North Atlantic, off the paths of ancient sea exploration, they remained unsettled until relatively recently. There are no prehistoric remains, and the early history of the islands is obscure. Many think that at the beginning of the ninth century Vikings were traveling around the general area by the Shetlands and into Ireland, but they did not settle in the Faeroes (see map). The Irish monk Dicuil mentioned the Faeroes in A.D. 825 and said that a colony of Irish anchorites had already been there for a hundred years. Recent archaeological discoveries at Tjørnuvik, on the northern tip of Streymoy Island, suggest that Irish monks may have settled Faeroe even earlier than that. Later, in the tenth century, the Vikings expelled the Irish monks. The Norse *Faeroese Saga* (Faeringasaga), written in Iceland during the thirteenth century, is one of the earliest accounts of Faeroe history. Other literary sources, including traditional Faeroese ballads, do describe permanent settlement as taking place around the year 1000, when Christianity arrived and Norwegian kings began the systematic collection of taxes.

As a faraway place in the midst of ocean, the Faeroes have always been almost mythical in character. Despite the archipelago's European location between such well-known spots as Iceland, Scotland, and Norway, the islands have escaped much attention in the world. Even though the Faeroese Saga speaks somewhat definitively about the Faeroes and their Viking discovery, other portions of the Western world had erroneously plotted their location and size. Moreover, the Faeroes were sometimes confused with other islands in the North Atlantic and were on explorers' and cartographers' maps that included imaginary islands. They were first mentioned on a map, the Hereford map, in the year A.D. 1280 and were called the *farei*. One influential map of 1558 by the Venetian voyagers Nicolo and Antonio Zeno calls the Faeroe Islands Frisland and places them in the North Atlantic along with the legendary islands of Estotiland, Drogio, and Icaria. The map also portrays the Faeroes as one large island nearly as big as Islanda (Iceland) and many times larger than Estland (Shetland). Even the legendary island continent of Atlantis, of which Plato wrote 2,300 years ago, and which most contemporary authorities consider as entirely fictional, also looms somewhere in the human imagination of nearby Atlantic landmasses.

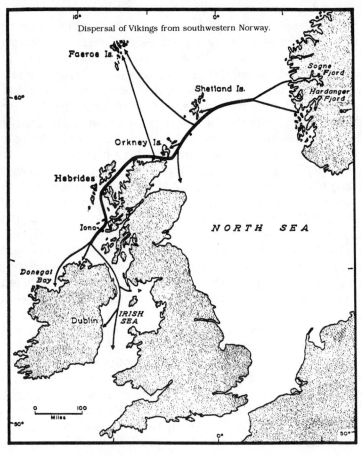

Geographic and descriptive information, whether scientifically true or not, often lingers, and little-known, distant places often come to take on traits and truths of their own. William Babcock (1922:143) discusses the effect of Nicolo Zeno's cartographic work:

> . . . his unscrupulous and misleading achievements in imaginary cartography remain as historic facts. For a century or more he supplied the maps of the world with several new great islands: he shifted others widely into new positions; he adorned other regions with new names that were loath to depart: and he presented a story of pre-Columbian discovery of America which was long accepted as true and is not wholly discarded even yet.

Thus even Europeans have long been unaware of the Faeroes or confused them with other lands.

There has been an explorers' tradition naming islands in this part of the world with the ending -land or -island in English. To designate "island" Scandinavian languages utilize an ending such as -*oe* in Danish or -*oy* and -*oyar* (plural) in Faeroese, as in Føroyar. Sometimes, when referring to such places in English, particularly in Britain, the "island" part is deleted so that we have Shetland, Orkney, Faeroe, and so on.

To confuse matters more, Faeroe, because it sounds in English like the pharaoh of old Egyptian times, is occasionally thought to be part of Egypt! And there has yet to come into English a definitive spelling of the islands, sometimes spelled Faeroe, as by the U.S. Post Office and National Geographic Society, while some scholars advocate the simpler Faroe spelling. Moreover, there are two theories about the etymology, the origin of the name, of Føroyar. Some say the islands' name derives from the ancient Scandinavian word *faar* for sheep, which have grazed on the islands for about a thousand years. Others say the name derives from the Gaelic *fear an* meaning "far islands." Despite their dramatic geography and unmistakably unique location at 62 degrees north latitude and 7 degrees 45 minutes west longitude (at Tórshavn), the islands long have had an aura of ambiguity about them. This theme will appear in various ways as we continue to explore the culture and ecology of the islands.

Parts of Scotland and other places in the Atlantic region have been heavily influenced and sometimes settled by Scandinavians. The former language of the Shetland Islands, Norn, spoken until about two hundred years ago, was a Norse language, like today's five Scandinavian languages—Faeroese, Danish, Norwegian, Swedish, and Icelandic. Similarities in place-names occur. Moreover, even the physical geography of many of these islands, as well as the western coast of much of continental Europe, is very similar, with high cliffs above the western shoreline.

Faeroese history is also a little murky. Most historians see the *Faeroese Saga* of the 1200s as more or less authoritative, despite its having been written more than two hundred years after events it recounts. Much of present-day Tórshavn, the capital city and largest town of the islands, is strewn with street names derived from the Norse characters of the *Faeroese Saga*. (Tórshavn is "Thor's harbor," Thor being the Viking god of thunder.) Most Faeroese first names are of Norse origin, and islanders still dance and sing medieval ballads recounting olden days. The islanders' northern heritage, uninterrupted since around the year 1000, is proclaimed at the very beginning of the *Faeroese Saga:*

> There was a man named Grim Kamban. He was the first to
> settle on the Faeroes in the days of Harald Fair Hair. At that
> time many fled the king's seeking of power. Many came to live
> in the Faeroes and built their homesteads there; some fared on

to other uninhabited islands. Aud the Deep-Minded, on his way
to Iceland, came to the Faeroes and married Aloef, daughter of
Thorstein the Red, and from her is descended the noblest
lineage of the Faeroes.

Contemporary Faeroese literature, oral storytelling, and every
day village life still seem similarly composed of nicknamed characters, simple but significant events, and terseness of phrase. Saga,
ballad, and folklore become part of history. The Faeroes, from their
very inception, have been a special sort of place where legend and
reality, the past and the future, merge.

Toward the end of the eleventh century, Norway made the Faeroes
a bishopric, a formal religious jurisdiction under the aegis of a
bishop. Both church and Norwegian administrators ruled the local
government assembly, the Løgting. It met on a jutty of land—Tinganes (*ting* "assembly" and *nes* "headland"), still part of the capital.
In those days the Faeroes were part of a network of Norwegian
possessions, which included the Hebrides, Shetland, Orkney,
Greenland, and Iceland.

Faeroese pride takes shape in a historical consciousness, particularly about the islanders' surviving myriad hardships over the
centuries. The Black Plague hit the Faeroes around 1349 and wiped
out whole villages. It still lives on in memory and legend in the story
"Sneppan í Hamrabyrgi." This now-written *søgn* ("legend"), only
three or four short paragraphs, takes place in the then-populous
village of Víkarbyrgi on the island of Suðuroy and relates how a
woman threw meat over the side of a tall bluff to people facing
starvation below. When I was in Víkarbyrgi, not far from Sumbøur,
villagers, telling the tale as if the events had only happened recently,
showed me the bluff from which Sneppan had reputedly thrown
the food.

In 1397 Norway was united with Sweden and Denmark, and
Norway's previous interests in the Faeroes (and Iceland) eventually
gave way to the less enlightened, less concerned rule of Denmark.
The Protestant Reformation reached the Faeroes around 1540.
That more or less established Denmark as the single colonial
power, although the Faeroes were ruled from Bergen until the
1620s. Denmark was the Faeroes' only major connection with the
continent and outside world for the next three centuries. Danish
became the official language. Although the governmental system
was little changed, the imposition of new officials speaking an alien

language must have strengthened daily use of the indigenous Faeroese language. Jonathan Wylie (1987) and Wylie and David Margolin (1981) also argue that because the economic system changed little, Faeroese survived. From either perspective, the Faeroese language, more closely akin to (West Scandinavian) Norwegian and Icelandic than to (East Scandinavian) Danish, developed separately and helped preserve village traditions.

Pirates invaded the islands around 1500. There were raids by English, Irish, and French pirates. Legendary reports say that pirates kidnapped some women, who were never heard from again. Another legend, "Turkar í Suðuroy" ("Turks in Suðuroy"), recounts the invasion of pirates around 1629. The story has it that men from two or three ships came onto land in Suðuroy, stole sheep, kidnapped thirty women and children, and killed six people. A later account of an invasion tells of Frisian pirates who landed at Akraberg, near Sumbøur. Islanders both in the south and the north explain that because of the attacks and raping of women, villagers from Sumbøur have darker hair and skin than other islanders, who are generally fair haired and fair skinned.

Economic History

Monopolies regulated trade to and from the islands for many years. Between 1655 and 1708 Frederick and Christoffer von Gabel harshly regulated imports and made living very difficult for the Faeroese. These days are infamous as Gablatíðin ("The Gabels' Time"). The corruption of the infamous Christopher von Gabel and his agents on the island brought especially hard times. Villagers still remark about the era when inhabitants had to eat seaweed to survive, around 1658 to 1673, when Denmark was at war with Sweden. For three centuries the Faeroese depended on single companies or merchants chosen by the Danish crown to regulate imports and exports. Faeroese self-reliance and confidence in their resourcefulness to live off the land and sea derives in great part from having overcome such hard times and having preserved them in memory and story.

From 1709 to 1856 the Danish crown's trade monopoly was less harsh, although it still chartered the islands' export economy and continental contact to individuals interested in making money and preserving power. Faeroese exports included handmade woolens and dried fish. The monopoly allowed few imported goods, and those were only sold or traded in the capital. No other stores or markets were permitted. As a result, Faeroese continued a subsistence economy based on sheepherding, fowling, and harvesting of the sea. Their enduring independence and perseverance made for a stoic, hard-working people.

This period of stringent political and economic isolation kept the islands mostly free of continental influences. Oral traditions became more and more central to local identity and helped to maintain cultural distinctiveness. These traditions included folktales (*aevintýr*), legends (*sagnir*), often-told stories of supernatural beings like the huldufólk, as well as everyday village talk. Wylie (1987) argues that such beings as the huldufólk were central to the survival of Faeroese culture in face of Danish colonial officials, institutions, and language.

Some economic reform began in the late 1700s but failed, in part because of local resistance. Small-scale commercial fishing began in the early 1800s. But it was not until after 1856, when the Danes abolished their trade monopoly, and into the 1880s when a commercial fishing industry rapidly developed.

Until the middle of the nineteenth century there were two or three "classes" of people, those with landholdings, large or small, and those without land. But the abolition of the trading monopoly and growing economic independence via commercial fishing of already-skilled small fishermen/farmers quickly shrank inequality in landholdings and supported marked population growth. Any social or economic differences in the increasingly egalitarian society revolved more and more around maritime pursuits such as large fishing boat ownership. For much of the feudal history of the Faeroes a man had to own a certain amount of property before he was allowed to marry. Faeroese maritime skills, long since proven in the harsh waters of the surrounding ocean in village-based fishing, whaling, fowling, and sealing, had always been important. But now once-poor peasant farmers and fishermen could acquire cultivable land for themselves from landholders and through enlargements of the infields (*bøar*) belonging to "freeholders."

Mortan from Sumbøur summarizes how, after the beginning of large-scale commercial fishing, significant socioeconomic differences dwindled:

Before the farmers owned the boats . . . and the fish they got. But then came *slupptíðini* ["the days of commercial smack fishery"]. Men went out to fish . . . Now the land in Sumbøur is sectioned off pretty much [equally]. In Sumbøur there are many *millumfólk* ["middle-class people"]—neither rich nor poor, that own a little, but not so much.

Now Faeroese use sophisticated modern fishing and processing equipment, both on ships and in factories on land.

Political and Cultural Developments

With the growth of the fishing industry in the second half of the nineteenth century, the capital Tórshavn developed into an urban center. Previously it was primarily a meeting place and center of official activity. Formally educated Faeroese professionals, artists, and intellectuals who went to school in Copenhagen began to populate the capital. In 1846 V. U. Hammershaimb published an orthography for Faeroese. His work did not immediately stimulate much writing, but its republication in 1881, and an accompanying Faeroese-Danish glossary by Jakob Jakobsen, led to a blossoming of literature and political writing. Jakobsen, a noted expert on Norn, the former Norse language of the Shetland Islands, also promoted the growth of literature with his 1898–1901 published collection of Faeroese folktales and legends.

In 1906 Faeroese formed two political parties, the Sambandsflokkur ("Unionist Party") and the Sjálvstýrisflokkur ("Self-Rule Party"). The former stressed strengthening ties with Denmark and the latter, working toward autonomy. For the next thirty-five years or so, despite individuals' differences about independence, the Faeroese economy flourished under Danish rule. During the Second World War, when Germany occupied Denmark, the islands were separated from Denmark. Britain then occupied the Faeroes. The Faeroese fishing fleet was very busy supplying fish to Allied forces, particularly English, and many fishing ships were sunk by German mines.

During the period of relative self-governance, the separatist movement grew and eventually won home rule in 1948. Faeroese are now autonomous in local affairs, self-ruling with their own legislature (Løgting). The Løgting and Denmark jointly govern some matters, while Denmark alone controls defense, foreign affairs, and the currency in Danish. Although Denmark belongs to the European Economic Community, the Faeroes do not. Today there are four political parties with roughly equal representation in the Løgting, plus two other parties.

The Faeroese national holiday is Ólavsøka, celebrated on July 29. Filled with contests, expositions, dances, and merriment, this grand social event of the year, primarily in the capital, has a long history. It attests to thousand-year-old connections with Norway, and celebrates King Ólav II Haraldsson's fight and death for the spread of Christianity. For a long time the festival was a feast-day in northern countries, but it has survived (in changed form) mainly in the Faeroes (see Wylie 1983).

The queen of Denmark is titular head of state, but the Faeroese elect representatives to the Løgting, which appoints five ministers. The five compose the Landsstýri ("local government"), its leader the *løgmaður* ("law man"). Both Danish and Faeroese officials sit on the highest legal court, conducted officially in Danish, although Faeroese is spoken by many who appear. Danish officials usually do not speak Faeroese but often understand it. Danish is mandatory subject matter in schools, yet Faeroese is the first language of schooling and the everyday language in the home. All Faeroese also know Danish, although in many of the villages there is infrequent direct contact with Danes. As the vernacular has been Faeroese, villagers' Danish sounds much different from Danes' Danish.

Up until quite recently Denmark had been giving about 600 million kroner (about US $60 million) yearly to the Faeroes for various purposes. Many natives cite this income as the reason that the full independence movement has not been as strong as it could be. Most Faeroese do not want to give up the benefits of association with Denmark and consider Denmark a benevolent parent rather than a colonial power. Indeed, the Faeroes had no unemployment until a few years ago and many Danes had come from the continent to Tórshavn to seek work. But the economy has long rested heavily on exporting fish to the United States, Europe, and South America. Now a large debt and unemployment have caused a fiscal crisis on the islands.

In Tórshavn and the second largest town, Klaksvík, there is a small, growing group of well-educated, more well-to-do people. They have either been owners of shipping or fishing industries or have been educated on the continent and become part of the professionalism and commercialism of the capital. Yet most Faeroese are villagers living in the eighty *bygdir* ("villages"), straddling traditional peasant subsistence patterns with modern lifestyles with cars, stereos, and television.

Despite relatively rapid modernization since World War II, many older folks can describe in detail the times when families used peat for fuel, when villagers walked over mountains, and when men used rowboats instead of motorboats for local fishing. Even twenty-five-year-olds are nostalgic about their younger days before television programs were introduced on videocassettes in 1982. And in the villages, geographically and politically distant from other parts of the world and from each other, economic differences between families are slight.

Thus, even with the rapid economic advancement, classic traits of Faeroese village society remain. Notable is the persistence of egalitarian values. Despite past economic divisions between the two or three strata of Faeroese society up to the late 1800s, local subsistence practices have always fostered village-level social egalitarianism. As in other Scandinavian countries with a feudal history, class distinctions were more salient in the past than now.

All Faeroese villagers, with sexual divisions of labor, have been raised to participate in the various aspects of fishing, fowling, hunting whales, raising sheep, harvesting wool, knitting, raising potatoes and hay, and other subsistence pursuits. (As fishing and farming have historically formed the bulk of their pursuits, they have often been termed fishermen/farmers, an "ecotype" (Löfgren 1976) with a dual set of subsistence ecological relationships.)

An egalitarian society is a "political system in which as many valued positions exist as there are persons capable of filling them" (Haviland 1981:269).

> They need considerable knowledge and skill but this is freely available to all who are of the appropriate sex and is not, in general, transmitted by formal (or even informal) instruction: rather it is learnt by participation and emulation. . . . More important still, any person—man, woman or child—who seeks to obtain his or her requirements either individually or in association with others can do so without entering into commitments to and dependencies on kin, affines or contractual partners. (Woodburn 1982:438)

Faeroese equality is both spatial and temporal. Every person seems to feel a recognized part of the past and the present, of the land and the sea, without deference to any wealthy class of owners of large parts of the landscape. History and space are properties of all. All Faeroese can locate themselves individually in a place of history or a history of place

A Place to Live

A Danish Department of the Ministry and Foreign Affairs tourist fact sheet about the archipelago proclaims "Faroe Islands are a world of their own." Moreover, within the islands there are settlements that were long quite isolated from one another. Sumbøur is one of them. It also has an unusual geographic location for a Faeroese community. Not only is it on one of the more remote islands, so that travel to the capital and other islands used to be particularly long and dangerous, but it lies directly on the open ocean, not on a fjord or bay like most settlements. Were it not for an islet that breaks the stormy waves a few hundred yards out from shore, settlers never would have located the village there. As it is, the shore erodes. Where houses stood several hundred years ago is now ocean. One man says that five hundred years ago (another man says two hundred years ago) it was possible to walk to the islet, now separated from shore by deep waters. Such a location on the open ocean is a *brimpláss* ("surf place"). In Sumbøur it means there is no natural harbor and fishermen can only fish off the village shore in summer. Even then they must approach the landing dock carefully. In the winter, Sumbingar store their boats up and away from the dock to prevent damage from the winter seas. In fact they take the boats away from the dock in late August: older villagers' lore has it that the weather can change rapidly after Ólavsøka. Even in the summer, if seas are too rough for local landing, a fisherman must travel two or three extra hours to arrive at another village's bay.

The settlement also lies near the foot of one of the highest mountains in the Faeroes. Prior to the introduction of the car, one hiked over the mountain to get in or out of the village environs. Or one rowed a boat around the tip of the island to visit another village or island. Now travel is mostly by car, but as recently as forty years ago people usually walked. Yet motoring can also be risky: high winds have blown vans off the edge of the narrow road leading over the mountain. One man recalled his understanding of the mountain's general effect: "I once said to the mayor of Sumbøur that it was like there was a Great Wall of China up on the mountain—so it was that Sumbingar were fully isolated."

Yet this mountain has provided Sumbingar with much food over the ages. A precipice that drops over 1,500 feet straight down to the sea, it annually attracts thousands of puffins, fulmars, and other seabirds that villagers catch and eat. Sumbingar climb up and down these cliffs and nearby free-standing pinnacles (stacks) to capture the birds.

Facing the south, Sumbøur is also a good *sólpláss* ("sun place"). This far north in the hemisphere the sun's declination is generally so low that it rarely shines on Faeroese villages on northern slopes. Additionally, the abundance of cloud cover and the paucity of sunshine everywhere in the islands makes significant the few more days of sunshine in Sumbøur. Hay (and previously barley) cultivation has been a little more productive here than other sites in the

Looking south from the village of Sumbøur to the open North Atlantic, the narrow islet Sumbiarhólmur sits off shore as a natural breakwater.

The surrounds of Sumbøur along the southeastern coast of the island of Suðuroy.

Faeroes. The village environs also has a large *markatal* ("surrounding land acreage/quality") with a higher percentage of freehold farmers (*oðalsbøndur*) than most other villages. Some people say that thirty-five years ago a hundred cows grazed around the village, although today there are only five or six. Sheep are ubiquitous, as elsewhere in the Faeroes, and nearly every man plants potatoes for household consumption.

Sumbøur is old. One legend mentioning Sumbingar dates to the Black Death of 1349. Some land records mention village holdings in 1584. But somehow, Berthel, in her seventies, is sure of the even greater antiquity of the village: "Sumbøur is one of the oldest villages in the Faeroes. It is certain. When Sigmundur, son of Brester, came to the Faeroes around 1000 [A.D.] Sumbøur had long been a village."

Legend has it that some farmer's sons started the village up on Hamragarður, on the slope of the hillside above what is now the main section of the village. According to one young man, "From there you could see out into the sea against the pirates and could escape easily into the mountains."

Recounting the village's past, villagers jump from one legendary event to another, often hundreds of years apart. After the Black Plague, events people like to talk about are the pirate raids. Berthel continues:

> In 1700 they [pirates] came to the land here. Here they [Sumbingar] had no weapons but *fjallstavar* ("mountain staffs"). The pirates had swords. One man with a sword came, but a Sumbøur man was so quick to smack the pirate on the arm. The pirate lost the sword, and then he was hit on the knee. They [the pirates] got nothing from here.
>
> One boat lay east by Hargabyrgi for several days. They tried to get ashore there. Nobody lived at Hargabyrgi then. When the pirates tried to come on land there, Sumbingar threw rocks down over the cliffs. The pirates got up the cliffs, however, and the Sumbingar went home to try to escape, there by Nási, coming east. There were two men that were hurt, Leif í Garðini and another man. The pirates came on land and took a lamb [from the fields] eastwards from the stream.
>
> They lowered themselves back into the boats. They sailed by the shore here, but then went away. So they just came near. But they got nothing from here in the village.

A similar story and three or four others mentioning Sumbingar appear in Jakobsen's (1898–1901) collection of Faeroese legends and folktales. Berthel's account here derives either from reading the written version or from hearing it from others. Recognizable places and names of individuals or families inevitably appear in such accounts, written or otherwise.

One local story points, like others, to the hard times of yesteryear:

> We have a story in Sumbøur of an old teacher. He was foreman in the *kommuna* ("village council"), and he was playing the organ in the church, and he was *degnur* ("deacon") and he was everything. And the biggest farmer in Sumbøur also. He was a rich man. So one day his brother was putting the potatoes in the earth to grow. But he had only one cow, and he needed some more cow shit to get the potatoes to grow. Eh? And so he goes to his brother and asks him if it was possible to get some *leypar* ("creelfuls") of cow shit. The man answered back with *Tøð eru ikki gávuvara* ("Cow shit is not something to give away").

In typical Faeroese fashion, the man laughed while reciting the anecdote's last line. He alludes, amusingly, to the difficulty in the past of getting by, even for the allegedly well-off.

Elsebeth Vestergaard (1975:9) begins her book of tales and recollections set on the southern half of Suðuroy with a description of some of Sumbøur's past:

> In the beginning of the 19th century Sumba was one of the oldest and biggest villages on Suðuroy, with several big farmers with a lot of land. The total area was from the south end of the island to the boundary between the parishes of Sumba and Vágur, between Onavík and Lopranseiði.
>
> For a long time the farmers had been trying to get shepherds for the most remote parts of their land, but this was not possible unless the shepherds could settle in their own houses there which could not easily be reached in the wintertime. The farmers offered the right man enough land so that he could be self-supporting. This was a good deal because the saying "Wool is Faeroese Gold" was true then because a man without land, by a law of 1777, was put under tutelage and had to work for a farmer all his life. Although it was a good offer men were still reluctant because of the poor connection between the villages. A man alone would be in great trouble if something happened to him, what with no telephone and no road. The only thing he could rely upon was a rowboat and his feet, but eventually three more settlements were built in the beginning of the 19th century. (Unpublished trans. by Jaspur Midjord)

Sumbingar, like Faeroese generally, take pride in their past and "serve up history like a myth" (Wylie 1987). And the history, the myth, is much about living prudently off the land and the sea.

Over the centuries, barley (now potatoes), fish, sheep, birds, seals, whales, and cows have provided Sumbingar, like other Faeroese, with food and clothing. Still many men split their time between fishing, farming, fowling, and whaling. But modernity has modified this diversified subsistence pattern. Since lack of a good harbor makes local commercial fishing impractical, the livelihood of Sumbingar derives from multiple pursuits. Some people work only around the village. Others work on small commercial fishing boats that dock at a nearby village or on large commercial Faeroese, Danish, or Norwegian trawlers that sail out to distant waters. Some men combine all these activities. Most women work in the home, but some women now earn a living in a nearby town's fish factory or doing elderly homecare in the village. Although some younger couples are still paying off their house mortgages, there is little differentiation in economic standing among people of the same age. As in other Faeroese villages, every house and car resembles others in size and quality, and no man or family stands out as wealthier or poorer than the next.

The Land of Maybe

> "Kanska" is the Faeroese word for "maybe"—it is the most used word on the islands. They are ruled under a despotism—the not so benevolent despotism of the weather. Five times as much rain as the wettest part of the British Isles—five hundred times as much wind as the windiest part. Maybe we'll go fishing tomorrow—maybe we'll try and do a bit of haymaking—maybe we'll get married. All and every one of these things is conditional—you see maybe it will be too wet to bother with the hay and a rough seas makes it alike impossible to go fishing or get married. —if the boat can't get in the priest won't be there so we'll get married another day. Did we say that if it's too rough maybe the sea dashing on the rocks will kill a lot of fish and tomorrow we can maybe have a colossal catch without the preliminary of baiting a hook or setting a net? (Norgate 1943:3)

The Land of Maybe is the name the Englishman Sydney Norgate gave to the Faeroes during the Second World War. Both outsiders and natives recurrently refer to the islands that way. Outcomes of fishing, fowling, and whaling are unpredictable and occasionally fishermen and fowlers themselves do not return from the perilous seas and cliffs. The tentativeness of daily harvests and events consequently affects the perspective of locals and visitors and adds a strong element of mystery to Faeroese affairs.

Fishing

Offshore fishing, even on propitious days, can be unproductive and dangerous. I have experienced it myself. One summer evening I made plans with a fisherman, formerly a sea captain. If the weather was "fine" the following morning, we would fish locally for the day in his small motorboat. The morning was calm and clear. We departed early and for an hour or two sailed out into the open ocean. We stopped to fish at four or five spots, with little luck. Then, as we moved further out to sea, the wind direction unexpectedly changed. That caused the ocean currents and winds to move in opposite directions. The sea (and my stomach) became turbulent with high-rolling waves that made even my seasoned fisherman friend a bit nervous. We estimated that our trip would take three times longer than originally expected, and we knew that fishing and sailing would be very difficult. As we headed for home, the boat stalled twice, and we drifted radically off course. After the skipper got the motor going and after two or three hours of rough sailing, we finally arrived near Sumbøur's dock. But the skipper was not sure whether to chance a landing because the choppy waves might crash us into neighboring rocks. For several minutes he considered heading for a safer harbor three hours away. Unsure whether we had enough gas for the long trip, he decided, finally, to land at Sumbøur. Fifteen minutes later we docked, without problem. The whole day was a dramatic lesson to me in the uncertainties of weather, seas, and fishing.

Coastal cliffs face the North Atlantic near the settlement of Sumbøur.

Even fishing on calm seas involves speculation and suspense. Fishermen combine their knowledge about weather and sea with superstitions and former luck at certain fishing sites to guess the best places to fish. And a fisherman may have his own secret method for choosing a very specific, secretly triangulated spot to fish. Thus, in fishing there is not only skill and science, but also art and omen.

If fish are plentiful, boats might stay at sea until brimful with their catch. If the catches are small, fishing trips might continue in vain for many days. Whether working on local fishing boats or large ocean-going trawlers, fishermen are not sure when, and with what, they will return to their village and families.

The North Atlantic is famous for its ferocity, and the tough Faeroese fisherman works right in the middle of it. Frequent fog lies low on the sea or land, and fishermen, in addition to their well-honed navigational skills, need a sixth sense in orientation. They are well informed about winds, tides, weather shifts, storms, and currents. Until the early 1940s knowledge of the sea and fishing locations and currents came only from firsthand experience in 6- or 8-man rowboats and open ocean sailing ships, without modern nautical instrumentation. Offshore fishermen, in their own boats, locate fishing spots (*mið*) by triangulating landmarks (*ýtir*). For example, when at sea, Hargamið ('Moundspot') is found when the landmarks Vestaraklettur ('West Rock') and Fossaberg ('Fall's Cliff') line up exactly. This practice contributes to the continuing use and importance of place-names.

Sometimes a village would collectively own boats, and the crews would share the catch with other villagers. With motorboats and economic advancement, collective ownership mostly gave way to persons individually or together owning boats for the use of one or two families. Such subsistence practices and ownership arrangements do affect social relations. One man talks about the effect of changes in Sumbøur in recent times:

> Twenty, twenty-five years ago, during the war and after the war, I would say that people needed each other more than they do today. Because when you live in such a place as this you couldn't go out fishing if there were not five or six men in a boat, because they were big. But today we have electricity and we have boats on wheels and two men can handle them. . . . But twenty years ago there had to be four or five men, not less than five men, to

handle a boat. . . . But today two or three work together.
Everybody needs each other, sometimes, but not so much as
before.

Social skills needed to work alongside one another in the dangerous seas are still crucial, particularly as crew membership often
varies. Men thus become adept at fishing, not through formal
education, but through working at different times with different
individuals. They learn to work and get along with any crew
member. This helps foster levelheadedness and an even temperament.

In older times some villages had their own full-time shipwrights
for making Faeroe Islanders' own style of rowboat to ply offshore
waters. Faeroese boats have a wide beam and an attractive curve
that moves upward to the high, pointed stem and stern. They have
a high, slender bow; a deep keel; and the oars are mostly the same
width over their length, without a very wide blade. Historically there
were six types of boats, made for two or three, four, six, eight, ten,
or twelve persons. They look, in smaller size, like the Viking boats
that crossed the open North Atlantic. Although most now have
motors attached or have been replaced by more modern motorboats, many traditional boats are still around. Ancient, sturdy
vehicles, they attest to the seafaring skills of past and present and
contribute to the near timelessness of the islands.

Offshore fishermen use handmade or commercial fishing poles
and lines. During summer day excursions they can sometimes
bring back a hefty catch of cod, plaice, sea salmon, and numerous
other kinds of fish. (Villagers dry some of the fish outside on lines:
this fish (*raestur fiskur*), when boiled, has a strong musky odor
and flavor.) Faeroese have long lived as subsistence offshore fishermen, but starting in the 1840s islanders started fishing more
distant waters and exported a good deal of dried fish, *klippfisk*.
The population of the islands until the late 1700s had never
reached more than 5,000, permitting local fishing as a major
component of subsistence. But the population rise in the 1800s
itself propelled islanders to look to the more distant, commercial
sea for a living. (Population size, available resources, and technology are central components to an ecological system, and changes
in one or more of these factors catalyzes changes in others.)

Larger locally owned commercial fishing boats that stay out over
nights usually utilize long-lines, hundreds of feet of rope with hooks

and bait attached every few feet. At sea the fishermen uncoil the baited line, prepared a day or two before in large buckets. The preparers are either the boat owners and/or local men and boys hired to do the baiting of the line. After throwing the line out to sea, the boat drags the line until after the many fish have been hooked, then the line is pulled back aboard as the fish are detached. Then the fish are brought to dock and sold to a fish factory and/or distributed among villagers. (Sumbøur has no harbor for small commercial boats, and some Sumbingar dock their commercial boats at a nearby larger town and travel to and from the village by car.) Earnings of individual crew members of commercial fishing boats depend upon the size of the catch, the predetermined percentage share of crew members, and the rank of the crew member.

(To earn money to continue my fieldwork, I sometimes worked in bait houses preparing fishing lines by placing bait onto the hooks and coiling the line round and round into a bucket. Standing all day in one spot, the other workers and I would put pieces of frozen squid onto the hooks. As a novice with fingers unused to rough work, often at the end of the day I would soak my fingers in salt water to treat the numerous pricks. After several days of such work, I came to be nearly as fast and efficient as several older boys doing the same work!)

The large commercial fishing companies, owned by either Faeroese or Norwegians, harvest fish from deeper, distant waters. They usually use trawlers. These boats let out huge nets —trawls—and employ strong motor-run winches to haul back the schools of netted fish. Then the fish—usually cod, haddock, halibut, saithe, herring, and mackerel—are partly processed, cut up aboard ship for later delivery to fish factories, or, in some cases, nearly fully processed for immediate freezing. Some fish is preserved as saltfish, other as fresh, frozen fish. "Product of the Faroe Islands" is not uncommonly found on packages of frozen cod in supermarkets in the United States, Europe, and South America. The Faeroes have been so successful in commercial fishing, as "farmers of the sea," that they often have had the highest per capita catch of any country in the world.

The islanders do live in the middle of plentiful fishing grounds. But since the Faeroese economy is heavily reliant on fish and fish exports for its stability, much fishing has also been done, at different times of the century, around Newfoundland, Greenland,

Villagemen still use small wooden boats to fish locally. Most of the year, however, to protect the boats from stormy seas, the fishermen keep the boats in boathouses like these on the island of Vágar.

This boat's name, 'Mounds Falls', derives from a place in Sumbøur where the owners live. The boat sits in front of the boathouses above the village dock.

Norway, and the North Sea. Indeed, now less than 25 percent of the catch is caught around the islands. Faeroese also fish for prawns near Greenland and Svalbard north of continental Norway. The Faeroese economy began to suffer a major decline in 1993 because of overdevelopment of fishing endeavors and, as mentioned above, the large debt to Denmark. (Unemployment has led some islanders to migrate to continental Scandinavia, particularly Copenhagen, where a fairly large Faeroese community has been growing over the years.)

Others (e.g., Joensen 1975, 1989; Wylie 1987) have written about the rise of the commercial fishing industry, particularly in the late 19th and early 20th centuries, when Faeroese used fishing sloops or "smacks," large sailboats. Faeroeman Jóan Pauli Joensen (1975) wrote *Faerøske sluppfiskere*, a notable history book (in Danish) about the days of the commercial smack fishery, slupptíðini, "the sloop times." Those days, like much of the past, are legendary to villagers, and old men still tell anecdotes and stories about them. Life aboard sloops was quite difficult. Engines were not fitted to all the sloops until the 1930s. Accounts of those days, as of earlier history, provide continuing material for a shared, common approach to and pride in the past.

The austere conditions were greatly overcome during the English occupation of World War II. Sea vessels became crucial for the harvesting and transport of fish from Faeroe and Iceland to Britain. The business was lucrative, but the cost in loss of Faeroese lives and boats was great: 131 men and 26 ships were bombed and mined. The people held on, though, and their tenaciousness ultimately aided in gaining home rule from Denmark.

The Faeroese are an independent people and, though technically part of the kingdom of Denmark, chose not to be part of the European Economic Community primarily because of fishing rights issues. In 1977 fishing limits were extended to two hundred miles offshore, as were other North Atlantic countries' limits. Fishing nations often regulate the mileage limits of their own fishing rights to hinder other nations from fishing within those waters. The fishing range, the type of fish, competition, the international pricing of fish, and political relations between nations are very significant in the ecology of modern, specialized economies like that of the Faeroes, so dependent upon commercial fishing. Regulated or unregulated practices regarding the permitted sizes of catches and/or the possible depletions of certain species of fish are also of the utmost importance. The high standard of living in the Faeroes is due to the historically profitable fishing industry and the Danish support of the islands. Now, lessened availability of loans and reduced fishing have caused some dramatic economic changes and led to a recession and a reduction in the fishing fleet. Fortunately, village subsistence still depends in part on local fishing, whaling, fowling, and sheepherding.

Fishing and Village Relationships

Large modern commercial fishing ships recruit crews before each departure, and although each crew has regular members, some changes in membership inevitably occur. Commercial captains receive respect and more money, but no captains live in Sumbøur. The added respect they receive reflects shipboard necessity rather than hierarchical sentiment. Additionally, earning a living from the sea tends to equalize village statuses. Depending on the season, the type of ship, the catch, and the company, commercial fishermen leave their village for periods of a few days to a few months. Many men's residence in the village is therefore discontinuous, and the duration of their presence or absence is often uncertain. This tends to prevent long-term social and political alliances and factions in the village.

Fishermen's long, irregular absences from the village also act to maintain equal status for women. Although men provide most of the earned money, women keep a constant presence in home, family, and village. Women need money to run the households, and with men away, women often have unchecked economic power. In addition, after sea voyages men seem eager to indulge their wives and children and to maintain harmony. Moreover, as women often learn about village affairs when men are absent, men often rely on much of the information women choose to share. Thus women can be equally as powerful as men. Once again we see the effects of work and subsistence practices on the dynamics of social life and order in the social ecology of Faeroese life.

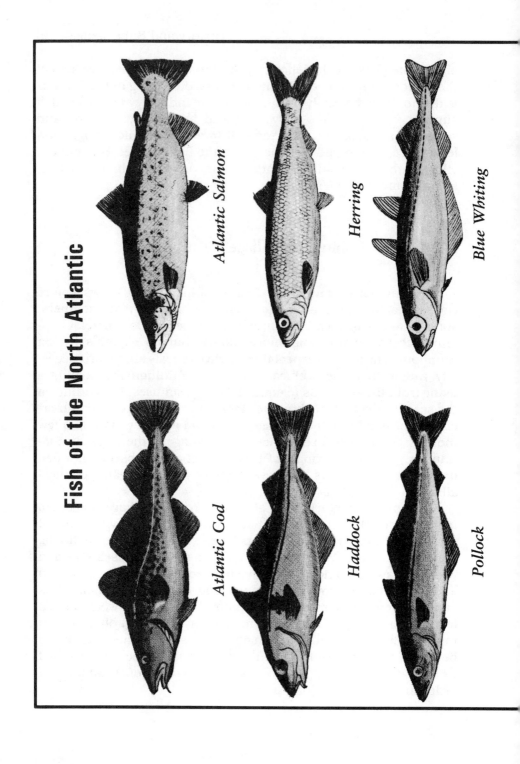

Fish of the North Atlantic

Atlantic Salmon

Herring

Blue Whiting

Atlantic Cod

Haddock

Pollock

Grenadier

Lemon Sole

Atlantic Halibut

Cusk

European Ling

Monkfish

Whaling

To most Scandinavians, particularly Danes, the Faeroes are a relatively known entity. They are known, among other things, as the home of one of the five Scandinavian languages and as a peasantlike, "primitive" throwback culture, a distant outpost of now mostly disappeared old-time society. Inhabitants of the British Isles know the Faeroes from frequent mentioning in North Atlantic weather forecasts on radio and television. To others in the world, including some Americans, the Faeroes have recently become known for their whaling practices. In fact, organizations such as Greenpeace have made the Faeroese infamous, although those groups' understanding of the economic, logistical, and cultural dimensions of Faeroese pilot whaling often lacks depth. A short ethnographic and ecological treatment of Faeroe Island whaling helps provide perspective.

At the end of the nineteenth century and into the 1920s and 1930s, the Faeroese, like many other North Atlantic societies, east and west, had somewhat regular commercial whaling stations in operation for the processing of large whales like the blue whale. After that period Faeroe commercial whaling of large whales only sporadically occurred, finally ceasing forever in 1966. (Seal hunting for local subsistence has also ended.) But the practice of hunting the small twenty- to twenty-five-foot pilot whale, also called the caaing whale or blackfish (*Globicepala melaena*), has long been a crucial subsistence and culturally meaningful practice for Faeroe Islanders.

For centuries, and still today, Faeroese have harvested pilot whale schools (pods), ranging in size from a few dozen to a thousand or more. These whales were historically the object of hunting in Newfoundland, Greenland, Orkney, and Shetland. Faeroese call the pilot whale *grind* and the call of a man spotting a group close to shore is *grindaboð*, "surely the most exciting word in Faroese" (Wylie and Margolin 1981:95). Written statistics of catches go back as far as 1584. Some historians believe that the practice dates back to Norse days more than a thousand years ago. Rules about the ownership of whales found close to land have existed since at least 1298, when the Norwegian "Sheep Letter" laws were written for application to the islands (see below). Whole schools are sighted offshore and then driven into bays by small fishing boats where men in boats and on shore proceed to sever the whales' spinal chords as quickly as possible.

A number of native and nonnative authors—anthropologists, historians, economists, businessmen, journalists, tourists, environmentalists, animal rights activists—have written about Faeroese whaling. Some of the writing links Faeroese whaling to the larger ecological and cultural context, some is quite impressionistic, (see, e.g., *Sierra*, April 1993). Anthropologists Wylie and Margolin (1981:95) describe the slaughter as composed of five stages, the sighting (grindaboð), the chase (*grindarakstur*), the slaughter (*grindadráp*) proper, the dance (*grindadansur*), and the whale divide, carving, and distribution (*grindabýti*). Kenneth Williamson (1970/1948:96), an Englishman who spent World War II on the islands, most lucidly describes pilot whaling and its meaning to the Faeroese:

This boat, like most, sports the name of the village (alternately spelled) where the owners live.

... a supremely well-organised affair in which most able-bodied men, whatever their vocation, cooperate. It relies for its success on the disciplined obedience of the participants to the orders and instructions of a chosen master of the game, and although disobedience is punishable by the law, the shame of it is feared more greatly than any fine. It is only natural that such a remarkable phenomenon as this should have made many ineradicable marks on the material culture of the Faeroese.

To the casual observer from abroad the *grindadráp* must seem to be one of the cruellest forms of hunting in existence. The Faeroese, who by natural temper are a kindly, hospitable and well-educated people, admit this much themselves. But the *grindadráp* is the only method by which these whales can be killed successfully, and the conditions of life among the islands are such that the *grind*, like the sea-fowl, remains a vital source of the country's meat supply.

... Knowing the conditions, it is easy, and only right, to condone the *grindadráp*. And to any one who is interested in ethnology, its picturesqueness as a form of hunting, its moral value as a skilful and exciting sport and excuse for social celebration, and its importance as an event upon which something of the economic structure of the Faeroe Islands rests, have great appeal. Should this very remarkable practice ever vanish from the Faeroe scene, then this small nation will have lost an integral part of its nationhood, and one of the most significant factors in the curious identity of its life.

Grind laws dating to 1709 mention equal distribution of spoils to participants. Today sheriffs still regulate communal pilot whale hunts, and written codes detail the exact division of spoils. Villagers designated by the sheriff first assess the size of the catch, scratch numbers on the skins to count, determine how much each person or family receives, and then cut and divide the meat. Although Faeroese men find the hunts and slaughters exciting, there is no obligation to participate, and even villagers who do not participate receive shares of meat (*tvøst*) and blubber (*spik*). Even my wife and I, as visiting residents of Sumbøur, were entitled to a portion of the catch. This Faeroese practice resembles that of other egalitarian peoples:

Anyone who is present may participate according to his or her sex role and is entitled to a proportion of the yield. There is no

> commitment to participate and no basis for exclusion from
> participation. Each hunt is complete in itself and participation
> today apparently carries no obligation to participate tomorrow.
> (Woodburn 1982:438)

Residents of Sumbøur, not situated on a bay suitable for whale slaughter, cannot easily participate in a grindadráp as fully as others. Sumbingar have to travel to slaughter sites from further away than other villagers and are sometimes late. Yet in the summer, when the schools usually come close to shore, Sumbingar, like other villagers, are constantly on the lookout, on land or at sea. In previous centuries a school might mean the difference between winter hunger and plentiful food supplies. Sometimes the schools are large, sometimes small. Sometimes they elude the islanders' efforts to surround and drive them ashore. Yet other times they beach themselves, as they not uncommonly do on the shores of Massachusetts, Newfoundland, and northern continental Europe. The vagaries and surprises of pilot whale behavior and the catch size contribute, like the weather and fishing generally, to the uncertain character of daily life.

The whales' arrival means rapid spread of the news and quick mustering of resources. In older days runners and fire signals were used to communicate. Today communication is by radio and telephone. Sumbøur is in the whaling district that includes half of Suðuroy, and "grindaboð!" propels villagers from all over the region to rush to boats to cooperate in driving the school from open ocean into a bay. Most all the available males in a whale district will participate. Although Faeroese are always ready for a grindadráp, the occasion arises only three or four times a year. If there is sufficient whale meat and blubber for locals, the sheriff of the district will prohibit any further hunting and killing of grind.

Faeroese rowboats, including those motorized, gather in a group offshore near the sighting. The foreman flies the Faeroe flag. Then, spacing themselves into a crescent shape behind the school, the boatmen drive it into a nearby bay, preferably one with a gentle underwater slope to shore. The participants drive by throwing stones or weights attached to lines into the water. They dearly want to avoid a panic in the whales, and the grind cannot be driven against the tide. Daylight is also important, of course, as well as the number of boats. Often a quite tricky affair, a hunt may go on for several days and nights, with many factors important in the drive.

Once the slaughter begins, when the foreman throws a spear into the whale's back, care and precision are taken in killing as fast and neatly as possible. Alertness minimizes pain and prevents too much chaos among the whales; thrashing could allow a group to escape back to open ocean. With special whale knives (*grindaknívar*), men skillfully sever the spinal cords of the now-confused whales. As the whales run aground or arrive in the shallows, men, whale knives in hand, leap from the boats or scurry into the water from shore.

The grindadráp begins a celebration of festivities, a holiday of sorts, in which relatives and friends from different villages socialize. After a day or more of excited, yet careful, cooperative hard work, the townspeople begin to drink and dance. Often the dancing continues until five or six in the morning in a town or village dancehouse. There Faeroese dance their own medieval ringdances, and unaccompanied by music, sing and chant traditional Faeroese and Danish ballads.

The divided fresh spoils, an important component of the subsistence economy, are delivered in regulated shares to all the inhabitants of the district. The fresh meat and blubber are often boiled for dinner, and some is kept fresh for a day or two. Today some is frozen. Most of it, however, is preserved in traditional fashion. The blubber, cut in chunks, is placed in salt, where it stays almost indefinitely. The meat is cut in large strips and salted or hung to dry in a small separate building outside almost every village family's home. This drying shed (*hjallur*) is a distinctively Faeroese part of the village landscape. It is made of upright laths spaced so as to allow the wind to blow through. Here hangs not only the Faeroese whale meat to cure in the salty air, but also the raw, wind-dried mutton (*skerpikjøt*). After several weeks the whale meat cures and is later boiled with the blubber or eaten uncooked alongside potatoes. The taste is distinctive and usually delicious! Faeroese always eat the blubber when they eat the meat, and it is considered a very healthy food. The oils and fats of the whale are not like those of beef, and, like fish oils generally, are quite nutritious. One aged Faeroeman swore that his longevity was due to the fact that he had whale blubber every morning.

Many Faeroese words and practices are connected to the pilot whale—special tools, foods, activities, regulations, songs, dances, and so on. Inedible parts of the whale carcass are used for various purposes: stomach skins for buoys, dried skin as thongs for boat oars, whalebone for carved brooches and other ornaments. The whale itself is a motif in artwork and symbols in Faeroese culture.

The word *grind*, like much in Faeroese vocabulary that makes reference to phenomena of nature, appears in the word *grindamjørki*, a murky fog (literally, "pilot whale fog"), which sometimes suddenly falls in late summer and often hides the pilot whale school from hunters. The crane fly is called *grindalokkur* because natives say it appears in summer just before the whales. This characteristic Faeroese practice of combining two words referring to nature or topography to make a third word in itself displays the Faeroese intimacy with and adaptation to nature.

Fowling and Birds

Visits by ornithologists are fairly common in the Faeroes, with their numerous seabird colonies. The Faeroes are in the flight path of migrating birds, and millions of seabirds nest around the islands. The national bird, the oystercatcher, is the namesake of the *Tjaldur*, the Faeroese coast guard rescue boat.

The house in the center of this photo is where the author and his wife lived. The smaller building in the right foreground is a hjallur, a wind-drying shed for hanging and curing sheep and whale meat.

Although Sumbøur is located near some of the most plentiful
bird cliffs in the Faeroes, not all villages are located so advanta-
geously for fowling. Consequently villagers from some places fowl
more than others. Also, rights to fowl for certain birds in certain
places are connected with private landownership. Since each village has a different amount of land within its control and a
different proportion of types of landownership, access to cliffs may
vary from village to village. Although in former times birding rights
were primarily held by the few large landowners, today sometimes
"ownership" of fowling rights simply means one needs to ask
permission to fowl in certain areas. (For a discussion of rights to
birds, see Norrevang [1979]).

Faeroese used to also collect birds' eggs for food, but it is now
prohibited. Birdhounds and the Manx shearwater dog were mentioned in the Hundabraev (Dog Letter) laws of the 1300s. These
now-extinct dog species were used for catching young Manx shearwater seabirds. Thus, bird catching has been a recognized seasonal
occupation since at least the fourteenth century.

Despite fishing, whaling, and farming, there have been periods
in Faeroe history, as mentioned above, when natives had to eat
various species of seaweed to survive. The latter half of the seventeenth century and around the turn of the nineteenth century, for
example, were times of much hunger in the Faeroes because very
little fish and few pilot whales were eaten. It was believed that the
Gulf Stream, which warms the waters around the islands, changed
its direction then and left the surrounding waters cold and unin-
habitable by many species. Climatologists recently have come to
think that the famine times were caused by a close polar front, now
distant from the islands, which made for an unusually cold sea
temperature. During these periods birds were especially essential
foodstuffs for the people. Their historical importance is reflected
in the islanders' catch in 1866 of an estimated 235,000 puffins and
55,000 guillemots and in 1939 (S. Patursson 1948) of 200,000
puffins and 140,000 guillemots and razorbills. Williamson (1948)
estimated that each year Faeroese captured 400,000 to 500,000
puffins!

Most of the fowling cliffs (fuglabjørg, "bird cliffs") are on the
western or northern coasts of the islands. The characteristic geo-
logical structure of the cliffs, with alternating strata of exposed lava
flows, tuff, and short, steep grassy slopes, are well suited to seabird

nesting. Also, fallen rocks and debris pile up at the bottom of some cliffs and provide shelter for other birds. The sheer, perpendicular cliffs near Sumbøur reach a height of about 1,500 feet. Today, in a seemingly anachronistic combining of peasant pursuits and modern technology, Sumbingar sometimes drive their cars on relatively recently constructed roads to get near the top of the mountain to go fowling. They will drive wooden stakes into earth at the top of a cliffside, attach a rope to the stake, and then climb down with a birding pole to get to an advantageous position to catch fulmars (náti), a seagull-like bird that flies and roosts near the top of the tall cliffs. On the precipitous cliff ledges the men will attract the curious birds by waving an object and, when they approach, use the net at the end of the pole to catch the bird. The fowler, wringing the neck to quickly kill the bird, will continue until satisfied with the quantity of his catch.

Other kinds of birds nest in colonies at different heights of the cliffs or on tops of sea stacks or in different areas on the islands. The largest seabird, the gannet, a beautiful white bird, only breeds around the island of Mykines. Guillemots and others are harvested near the islands of Litla Dímun, Stóra Dímun, and Skúvoy. When guillemots are young, fowlers net the birds from boats, a practice called *omanfleying*, literally "netting from above." To catch puffins, the colorful clownlike, penguinlike bird, for example, villagers will often take their boats in summer up to the base of a stack and then climb up to reach the puffin nests. Thus there are different methods to catch different birds, each with their own habits and behavior.

Fowling, like fishing, also involves shifting arrangements. Fowlers can use boats to capture fledglings on the water before they can fly, go in pairs down cliffs on fowling lines, or gather in groups to catch puffins nesting on nearby stacks, high rocks standing in the sea. Participation in fowling pursuits is partly a matter of individual or collective ownership or part ownership of bird cliffs or of rights to them. Fowling with one group during some summer expeditions does not necessarily entail participation in other hunts of the summer or following years. Each fowling group communally defeathers and cleans the birds and distributes the spoils among its members.

Puffins are considered a delicacy among islanders who usually eat two or three birds per person for a meal. Like other birds, they are often salted for winter storage. As in most seasonal activities of

Faeroese subsistence, puffin harvest begins on a certain, named day. Their harvest historically has begun on July 2, called Fyrsti-fleygidagur (First Netting Day). A large triangular net or *fleyg* is attached to the end of the netting pole (*fleygastong*). Faeroese do not kill the breeding puffin, the "herring-bearer" (*sildberi*) who brings fish back to its young in the nest. Like hunters and gatherers of many cultures, the Faeroese are cognizant of both the morality and the long-range ecological consequences of preserving mothers and young.

As with all activities, knowledge of the weather and behavior of animals plays an important role in both the safety and practicality of the seabird hunt. For example, Faeroese know that young puffins tend to go far out to sea during wet weather. Thus even the day after a big rain, there are few upon the cliffs. Familiarity with bird behavior comes second nature to a person and culture steeped in traditional practices and ecological awareness.

Sometimes, in Sumbøur, one can also see defeathered seabird carcasses, split-halved open, hanging on a line outside to dry; these cure before storing. The catch and preparation of a family's seabird harvest is, like other Faeroese subsistence pursuits, a source of pride and one of the many observable links to the land, sea, and air. One day I visited the small assembly-line processing of hundreds of birds in one of my neighbors' basements. They set up three or four long tables, end to end, and proceeded to butcher the birds, dunk them in hot water to loosen the feathers, and then pluck them before putting them into a freezer. Home preparation of such food makes the Faeroese village a wondrous natural and culinary experience.

Much folklore and nicknaming activity are also associated with Faeroese seabirds, as are descriptions and accounts of land- and shorebirds. Only an amateur ornithologist and naturalist, I spent untold hours identifying and observing the numerous birds. Perhaps one of the most interesting English-language books about the

This photo was taken at the top of the mountain above Sumbøur (looking northward along the west coast of Suðuroy). Villagers climb down some of these cliffs to capture fulmars; all of the coves, chasms, promontories, and so on, along the coast have proper names. ▶

Faeroes is W. B. Lockwood's (1961) *The Faroese Bird Names*. It
discusses the origins of and relationships between birds, bird
names, bird behavior, birdlore, and the Faeroese language. His
delineation of the Norse origins of many words and their similarities to Scottish English and Norn words helps to establish the
historical links between Faeroe and other parts of Scandinavia and
the British Isles. Moreover, he discusses local differences in bird
name usage, thus demonstrating the historical isolation of communities even within the Faeroes. In Sumbøur talk, for example,
many Faeroese words and expressions generally differ from
those used elsewhere in the islands. Although an Englishman,
Lockwood is similar to Scandinavians generally, who find much
importance and symbol in items of language, nature, and the past
(Wylie 1989). My work here, in great part also concerned with
these aspects of Faeroese culture, also falls within the Scandinavian tradition.

Faeroese familiarity with bird behavior often appears in names.
For example, the *kjógvi* ("thief") is the arctic skua (*Stercorarius
parasiticus*), an eerie, agile bird that circles and caws above the
moorlands, pursuing and diving at other birds, especially the
kittiwake. The arctic skua harasses other birds until they spit out
food intended for their own young. Then the arctic skua quickly
catches the foodscraps in the air and eats them! To the Faeroese
its "real" name, not even its nickname, is "thief."

Nicknames also reveal the habit of naming things by their behavior. The crow (*kráka*) in some places was called "midden" (*kostur*)
or "middenbird" (*kosturfuglur*). Another example is discussed by
Lockwood (1961:63). He describes an amusing term he discovered
for the heron (*hegri*), *pinnur í reyv*, which he, in civil fashion,
translates as "stick in the backside":

> It remains to be discovered whether this ever rose to become a
> respectable noa term or whether it remained on the level of
> facetious nickname only. But the imagery is clear. Standing as
> the heron often does, crouched forward on one leg, the "knee"
> joint invisible beneath the feathers, the bird's body may well
> appear to be supported only by a stick fixed into the rectum.

A noa term is a byname or an alternate name for something, often
used out of superstition. Faeroese fishermen and sailors, like other
cultural groups dependent on the whims and fortunes of nature,
utilize luck and superstition in their pursuits. They thus sometimes

use special words in their "sea language" (*sjómal*). For example, fishermen at sea are not known to mention the raven, generally thought to be a bearer of bad omens by its regular name *ravnur*. Instead a fisherman would call it "black one" (*svarti*). Even the uncertainty about whether a raven is possibly bad luck leads fishermen to behave so as not to possibly offend forces of nature.

Elisabeth Vestergaard (1989:36) generally discusses the use of noa terms in sjómal as a superstitious and cultural practice of men in areas where they are "exposed to the non-controllable in nature," which sometimes includes women. Some things with noa terms are "objects associated with land and classified as female, like women, cats, crows, fire and smoke."

Faeroese, like other peoples intimately connected to the earth, see even the characters of the natural world as composed of different temperaments and traits. They thus anthropomorphize aspects of nature and naturalize aspects of culture. Two or three famous traditional ballads of the islands are known as Fuglakvaeði, "The Ballad of the Birds." The first was written down in the 1780s and thought to have been in oral existence since around 1500. Another "Ballad of the Birds" was written by Páll Nolsoy, who tells of how the Faeroese struggled against the hardships of the Danish trading monopoly. The hero is the oystercatcher (tjaldur; really Páll himself), the noisy bird that scares off less desirable birds. Since that ballad was written the tjaldur came to be the national bird. Nearly every Faeroese person knows the ballad's refrain:

The bird by the shore	Fuglin í fjøruni
With his red bil	við sínum nevi reyða
Many a creature and fine bird	mangt eitt djór og høviskan fugl
Has he saved from death,	hevur hann greitt frá deyða
The bird by the shore	Fuglin í fjøruni

The interconnected forces, fates, and mysteries of nature—and of human relationships—are integral to Faeroese culture and ecology.

Shepherding

Nearly every villageman could be called a shepherd. Almost every family in a village like Sumbøur owns at least a few sheep. On cultivated "infields" (bøur, pl. bøar) Faeroese raise hay for about

The national bird, the oystercatcher (tjaldur), is a red-beaked bird commonly found on the islands.

seventy thousand sheep, almost double the human population. For grazing, men use the uncultivated "outfields" (*hagi*, pl. *hagar*), outside the village proper. Sheep graze and shepherds walk the environs, sometimes quite distantly from the village center.

In winter sheep clatter freely up and down Sumbøur's streets and paths and gather in groups in the lee of houses. During nonwinter months sheep are driven or taken out of the infields, where they scatter over the hillsides within village view or in distant grazing areas, some accessible only by boat. Some pastures naturally fertilized by bird droppings, guano, are especially prized for good grazing land. One such area is Feitilendir ('Fatlands'), a cliffside promontory on the other side of the mountain from Sumbøur, to which villagers bring sheep for the summer.

Sheep are raised primarily for food and wool, although several other facets of culture and ecology emanate from sheep raising. Such facets include communal sheep management, ritual slaughter days, local foodstuffs, and traditional recipes through which Faeroese activate their identity and pride.

Lamb and mutton, boiled, roasted, or wind-dried, are commonly eaten. Some villagers say the national food is the tasty wind-dried raw form, skerpikjøt, cured in the hjallur for about three months like the whale meat. Beef is now mostly imported but is often prepared like lamb or mutton. The only other land mammals are wild—hares, mice, and rats.

Sheep raising is partly communal. Each man owns certain sheep and feeds them near his own house in winter, although one man's sheep can, and often do, travel anywhere in the village during the winter. In summer sheep graze in jointly owned and demarcated sections of the hagi. The shepherds elect one person "sheepman" (seyðamaður), the primary caretaker of the sheep and of fencing for their area. But leadership rotates, in typically Faeroese unauthoritarian, egalitarian style. (One local form of wild vegetation [Cerastium vulgare] is called seyðamannagras ["sheepman's grass"].) There is also an annual public auction of summer grazing pastureland that belongs to the community as a whole. Any man can bid to receive summer use of these public lands. Also communal in organization, groups of men temporarily cooperate in rounding up the sheep each year at shearing time. Slaughtering, in the autumn, is usually left to the male head of the house, and he does everything from the killing to the hanging up of the raw meat in the hjallur to make skerpikjøt. Almost the entire anatomy of the sheep is used. Among other uses, Faeroese use the sheep's head for a meal, intestines for sausage casing, fat for fish cakes (knettir), horns for carvings, and the bladder as a Christmas ornament. Like other peoples who raise much of their own food, the Faeroese are not spendthrift with the spoils of nature.

The careful use of resources also manifests in the use of pastureland on Sumbiarhólmur ('Islet of Sumbøur'), the small island off the village coastline that breaks the open ocean waves before they hit Suðuroy. There, as in Feitilendir, because of seabird guano and because the pastures are not used but for a couple months in summer, the grass is fertile for grazing. Therefore, despite its offshore position, the islet becomes home for sheep in summer. The highest bidder at the communal land use auction transports his sheep via boat to the island and lets them wander unattended until he brings them back before autumn storms. Sumbiarhólmur itself has dozens of place-names on it, testifying to its constant usage over the centuries and the various experiences attached to it.

Thus despite possible differences in landholdings, size of sheep flocks, positions on fishing crews, and access to birding cliffs, various Faeroese communal subsistence practices help prevent the appearance of class distinctions. Group membership also shifts in the different activities and prevents cliques from forming. There is, however, a little competition for prestige within the predominantly egalitarian order.

Still today, on September 29, the traditional Faeroese sheep-slaughtering day, men go from house to house to see who butchered the heaviest ram. He receives no prize, but as one young villager put it, the winner "gets proud"; "the purpose of raising rams," he says, "is to get food and to be proud." Similarly, catching many fish

Knowledgeable in the ways of sheep and tradition, this Sumbingur proclaimed "what an enjoyable tour it is to go to the mountains after sheep."

or birds or slaughtering many pilot whales wins recognition, however unannounced. Yet such opportunities to have the largest harvest of a resource are open to any and every man. In small-scale egalitarian hunter-gatherer groups in many parts of the world, groups of men often gain some prestige by being good hunters and providing large amounts of food for families and the community (Harris 1993).

In some ways sheep are symbols of Faeroese culture. They roam almost everywhere one goes. Indeed, the name Føroyar itself may mean 'Sheep Islands.' Many activities revolve around shepherding, and there is the old popular saying "Wool is Faeroese gold," derived from its previous status as an important commodity. And speaking

After the summertime communal roundup, the sheep are penned before shearing.

from the heart and aesthetic of the culture, one old-time shepherd, with life's satisfaction in his voice, said "What an enjoyable tour it is to go to the mountains after sheep."

Prior to commercial fishing days of the twentieth century, sheep raising played a more crucial role in the subsistence of the people, including the exporting of sweaters and woolen goods to continental Europe. Sheep figure far back into Faerose history and provide a continuity of cultural meaning. Economic and legal order are nearly synonymous with rules and regulations concerning sheep management and the raising of hay for the sheep. In 1298 Duke Hakon and Bishop Erlendur of Norway published a code of laws covering sheep raising and agriculture, Seyðabraevi‚ the "Sheep Letter." The code regulated land use,

Some men work together on roundup and shearing day.

particularly the Faeroese system of land tenure and joint ownership of outfield sheep grazing areas. Even today, most of the provisions of the Sheep Letter remain in effect. They regulate such sheep-related activities as land rental, slaughtering unmarked sheep, sheep wandering into other men's pastures, the number of sheep permitted on pasture land, the maintenance of common sheep-folds, and dogs' molesting of sheep. (Denmark revised some outfield laws in 1866, and there have been some later versions as well.) Sheep Letter issues remain important foci of activity and concern. Once again, we have an example of how ecological relationships among and between Faeroese and nature, evident in the very name of the laws, are embedded in the very social order and orderliness of the society.

The Sheep Letter is a straightforward and uncomplicated set of laws: "It is not surprising that so much of it has remained unaltered for so long" (Young 1979:86). Here is a sample of Sheep Letter prose.

> 6. Now if men take dogs which are confirmed sheep worriers into pasture land and they attack the sheep, the owner is to be compensated with sheep as good as those he owned before; and if the dog attacks sheep again, the owner is to pay the same compensation he would pay if he had slaughtered them himself. But if the dogs which men have agreed are to be used in the pastures harm any sheep, then the man the dog follows is to compensate the owner with sheep as good as those he had before and so be warned to keep his dog under control. A dog is a sheep worrier if it harms sheep more than once or goes off into a pasture of its own accord to attack sheep. The number of sheep to be kept on an area of pasture shall be the same as it was in previous times, unless men see that it can accommodate more. In that case they are to have as many sheep as they agree on, and each man is to keep a flock proportionate to the size of his pasture. The same applies to other forms of livestock, cattle or horses. No-one is to keep a greater number than has previously been agreed upon by everyone. And no-one is to keep animals in any man's pasture but his own; but if he does, he is to answer for it as the law prescribes. (Ibid:143)

Some grievances about sheep, dogs, and land still occur, but the simplicity and long-standing tradition of the Sheep Letter may have helped to maintain a noncontentious and nonlitigious atmosphere in local affairs.

A villager picks his sheep out of the group corralled in a pen on the side of a mountain.

Faeroese Sheepear Markings

Faeroese sheep are of the Soay breed, similar to the ancient breeds found on the now depopulated Scottish island of St. Kilda. The sheep come in various colors and markings. I interviewed one old-timer shepherd for an hour or more about the traditional names for the various colors and color patterns. There are many. Basic sheep colors are solid white, light gray, middle gray, dark gray, black, moor red, dark moor red, or a mixture of white and some other color. Sheep color markings include such names as *eggsvart* ("black egg"), which refers to the dark circle of hair around the eyes of some white sheep. In typical transference of names and talk about animals to humans, and vice versa, Eggsvart, found in a satirical ballad, is also the nickname of a man with marks around his eyes.

With seventy thousand sheep roaming the archipelago, and hundreds in the vicinity of Sumbøur, means of identification for ownership becomes almost a necessity. Faeroese have an elaborate system of sheep markings made by docking differently shaped and sized parts of sheep ears. A book entitled *Seyðamarkini í Føroyum* (*Sheepmarkings in the Faeroe Islands*) details according to location on the islands the exact style of earmarkings.

Each sheep produces two kinds of wool, percentages of which are determined by the weather. Rainy and windy winter weather makes for a large percentage of long, hairy fibers in the wool; a mild winter makes for a fine underwool. *Broddur* is the former, coarse guard hairs about a foot long, and *rót* is the latter, fine hair. Broddur makes a strong knitting yarn.

Instead of shearing the wool, Faeroese sheep wool can sometimes be plucked, or roo'ed, as it is called in English. This possibility derives from the Soay breed and the weather. The two kinds of hair can be easily separated for different purposes. Wool that is taken during the midsummer roundup is *várull*, less shrinkable than the *skinnull* taken from the sheep slaughtered in the autumn. Different combinations of wool make for different textures, strengths, and durability and thus, different products.

Knitting

Sheep-connected activities continue in the hands of the women, who knit socks and sweaters and have done so for many years. Women have clubs that get together for social reasons and to knit.

One almost never finds a woman simply sitting around with a cup of tea or coffee by herself or even chatting with others without knitting needles and yarn in hand. Even girls walking to outlying pastures often knit while they walk.

Wool itself is a very efficient natural fiber, well suited to the Faeroese and North Atlantic climate. One does not have to kill a sheep to obtain the wool, and thus sheep continually provide wool for various kinds of clothing. If one does slaughter the sheep for meat, then the skin and wool together, the fleece, become useful as a lined leather for shoes, rugs, and other useful items. Woolen clothes are quite warm and are nearly waterproof, especially if felted (washed and shrunk). Fishermen have used wool gloves even in very wet conditions. In olden times Faeroese wore wool and sheepskin for every piece of clothing, from hat to shoes. It is the

Colorfully patterned sheep
are common on the islands.

natural oil, lanolin, in sheep wool that gives it its water-repellent quality. Moreover, wool can absorb up to about 40 percent of its weight in water without feeling damp, and thus even when wet, wool keeps a person warm.

Wool is washed and cleaned before it is carded, spun, and made into yarn. The varieties of wool and methods of preparing yarn and

A village woman, often called Marie í Kálgerði (Maria 'in the Cabbage Garden'), sits by the window knitting a sweater.

knitting and/or weaving yarn permit many different thicknesses, patterns, textures, and qualities for uses as various kinds of garments, rugs, or other textile goods. The Faeroese national folk costume also consists of special woven woolen garments, including women's colorful red and black skirts and the *húgva*, the man's tightly woven distinctive cap.

Even before the enactment of the Sheep Letter in 1298 the islands traded wool: the Faeroese Saga refers to the sale of wool in Norway. Initially wool was exported in raw form but, as records indicate, by 1361 the Faeroese were exporting homespun wool and heavy hand-knit stockings. In the 1600s knitting came to be of economic significance and by 1765, in addition to hand-knit sweaters, 100,000 pairs of stockings were exported. Woolen goods accounted for 92 percent of the exports around this time (West 1972:74). For the size of the population at the time, around 5,000, it was a very large amount of knitting, and it appears that it was during those days that the saying "Faeroese wool is Faeroese gold" became popular. Even into the 1840s more than half of the exports were in woolen goods. Though in olden days both Faeroese men and women knit, and males spun the wool, almost all knitting is now done by women. Faeroese weaving of cloth was not uncommon in the past, but now there are very few weavers. Knitting is often quite fast, partly depending upon the thickness (gauge) of the yarn. Madelynn Fatelewitz (1988:52) details the knitting practices of Faeroese women:

> I remember one night our next-door neighbor, a fisherman, called his wife from Norway to ask her to make three sweaters—one for a man, one for a woman, and one for a baby—for the next day, when he'd be returning home with a Norwegian friend to whom he wanted to give the sweaters. My neighbor lady called over her sister-in-law and mother-in-law, who sat up all night knitting with her. Had the sweaters been knit in the finer wool with a finer gauge, the deadline would never have been met.

Faeroese knitting patterns are distinctively their own and often are of long-standing tradition. Some patterns are even indigenous to particular villages. Sweater designs are generally made in horizontal bands, often separated by narrower bands. Hans Debes (1932) published a book of Faeroese sweater designs, *Føroysk Bindingarmynstur*, which one can find in almost every household.

Faeroese Knit Sweater Patterns

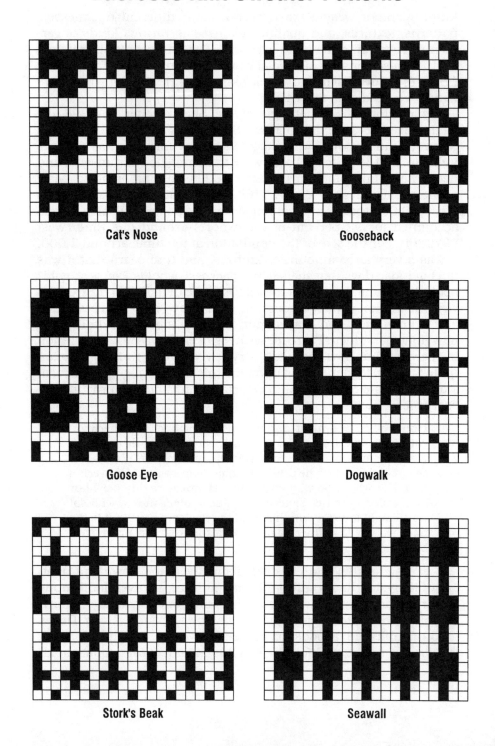

Cat's Nose

Gooseback

Goose Eye

Dogwalk

Stork's Beak

Seawall

Many of the pattern names derive from phenomena of nature and include Seawaves, Fleas, Sheeptracks, Hills and Dales, Day and Night, Stork Beak, Cat Nose, and Goosefootprints. Faeroese women also knit footlets for wearing in the house—like many Scandinavians, Faeroese take their shoes or shoecoverings off when they enter a house. Larger footlets are also used as overshoes for traction while walking on the occasionally icy surfaces. The Faeroese are also famous for their hand-knit shawls, becoming increasingly popular outside the Faeroes. (Fatelewitz [1988] gives instructions on knitting a Faeroese sweater, as does Olivia Joensen [1980] for Faeroese shawls.) The 'Sheep Islands' are certainly well named.

The Faeroese generally prefer to use naturally occurring wool colors for their hand-knit items, though in olden days there was more dyeing than today. Now only a few still use natural dyes to color the yarns before knitting. Natural dye sources are mainly lichens, found growing on the rocks and boulders of the seashore and mountainsides. One relatively common Faeroese dye lichen is *korki* (*Ochrolechia tartarea*), which is not prevalent in other parts of the world. It yields a pink-red color, unusual for natural dyestuffs. With this in mind, my wife, a weaver-dyer-knitter, and I spent an entire day scraping pieces of this lichen off boulders in Blaeing, a section of mountainous land east of Sumbøur.

Agriculture

As most of the archipelago is mountainous terrain, only about 4 percent of the Faeroese landscape is cultivable. Most places are rocky and steep, with very shallow soil. The hagar, partitioned and jointly owned, are not cultivated but are summer grazelands for sheep. The bøar are the cultivated parts, mostly hayfields, at lower elevations surrounding the villages and towns. Many families also grow potatoes. Potato garden plots are either next to houses or a short distance away on individual plots in the infield.

Introduced in the late eighteenth century, potatoes, which did not become widely grown until the early 1800s, replaced barley as a staple. The climate made raising barley difficult, and the grain had to be dried in kilns. Corn was also planted much more in the past than now, especially in northern Suðuroy. Sumbøur, the southernmost village of the islands, is known for having good soil. It thus had a reputation for being a good barley-growing area in days gone by. Mills for grinding grain and corn populated the Faeroes until recently.

Imported vegetables and fruits are only slowly becoming available in the villages: for hundreds of years the Faeroese lived with few fresh vegetables, getting their vitamin C from little plots of angelica (*hvønn, Archangelica officinalis*). One older house in Sumbøur still has such a garden. In typical separation of the local scene from the outside world, villagers generically call all imported food "Danish food," regardless of its origin. Many villagers pride themselves on buying little of it, although children gobble loads of imported (and some domestic) candy.

Farmers had long been of two types. Before the Protestant Reformation one set rented land from the Church. After the Danish crown took control of the church, these farmers rented land from the king and became *kongsbøndur* ("king's farmers"). These large landholders rented property on a yearly basis, but their holdings remained for life and were by law passed on intact to others, almost always to one of their sons. Other farmers were oðalsbøndur whose land was less secure in the long run because upon death their holdings were divided among their children, who sometimes sold them. Depending upon the size and location of infields, farmers had rights to have a certain number of sheep grazing in the outfields and have access to fowling on specific birding cliffs. The breakup of landholdings over the last hundred years often led to a family's ownership of widely scattered small plots of land. This made for difficult labor, going from one field to another to work them. However, in the 1940s and 1950s landowners' holdings were reapportioned so as to consolidate fields for more easy working of the land (see Jackson [1979]).

Fences do not frequently mark divisions between infields but especially in late summer, the patchwork landscape of fields in different shades of green is quite evident. Although manure is used today to fertilize the fields, sometimes seaweed is also used, as was commonly the case in earlier times. The plow is not used, and the common method of turning the ground is with the Faeroese flat spade (*haki*). Ditches are important features of the cultivated fields as they permit drainage for the abundant rain. The name for the special method of cultivation with ditches, *reinavelta*, is characteristic of the islands. Williamson (1948/1970:55) explains:

In spite of the rocky nature of the countryside and constant
weathering of the basalt by heavy rains and frost the Faeroese
keep their fields remarkably clean, sometimes gathering all
loose stones together in a corner . . . for removing them to the
shore.

The ditches are the most important feature of the fields. They
have an ancient history, and have determined not only the
curious topography, but also the high fertility of the shallow
soil. The heavy rainfall and impervious peaty subsoil lying on
a rocky bed make an efficient system of surface drainage
essential, for the little rills which are normally mere trickles
descending the slopes swell into angry spate after an hour of
heavy rain, and ground that has no channels to lead off the load
of water very quickly becomes a bog. The ditches are usually
parallel and run with the slope, if the slope is even, seldom
more than ten feet apart and often less; but where the surface

Stóra Á ('Big Stream') runs down the center of the valley into the village
settlement. On either side are cultivated hayfields, with their own
proper names, owned and worked by different residents. In the
foreground is an old stone hayhouse with a sod roof.

is undulating the ingenuity of the Faeroeman has often been
taxed in planning the most efficient course, and the fields often
appear to have been built in broken terraces or steps.

Faeroese harvest the hay in late summer and store the hay in
hayhouses standing in the fields or in barns behind their houses.
Formerly hayhouses were built of stone with turf roofs. A few still
remain.

For hundreds of years the Faeroese also worked the land in the
cutting of peat (turf) for heating fuel, as has been the case in other
parts of Scandinavia, Scotland, Ireland, the Isle of Man, and elsewhere in lands of the North Atlantic. Islanders also mined some
coal and gathered driftwood for fuel. Faeroese traditionally carried
peat and other items in creels. Peat has been replaced by heating
oil, although my wife and I burned coal mined in Suðuroy for the

This stone wall, Hamarsgarður ('Bluff's Wall'), separates the infields (on
the right), which are used for growing hay and winter pasturing of
sheep, from the uncultivated outfield (on the left), where sheep graze
during warmer months.

coal heat/cookstove in a house we rented in Sumbøur. (See Williamson [1948/1970] for discussion of traditional Faeroese methods of
agriculture and peat cutting.)

Agriculture is really part of the complex of sheep raising, as the
infields are primarily for the growing of hay. Even these fields have
proper place-names, which often go back centuries, earlier carefully husbanded also for now-rare cattle. Their importance goes
back to medieval Faeroese butter exports. Evidence of pigs and
horses in Viking times has been discovered from archaeological
excavations.

Homestead names and family genealogies reflect the importance
of the five or six large landholding families of earlier days in
Sumbøur. Some villagers even exhibit a little pride in their ances-
tral connections to larger landholders. But otherwise, past riches
do not affect contemporary social structure and the egalitarian
ethos of village life. As long as a person does not act today as if his
slightly larger holdings entitle him to more respect than others,
and, like other villagers, considers past inequalities as part of a
collective past, then little harm is done by tracing ties to "known
families." Villagers generally describe the past as a time of trial and
perseverance for all Faeroese.

Fields in different parts of the islands also produce wildflowers
such as white clover, sorrel, purple crane's bill, devil's bit scabious,
and northern eyebright. Jørgen Landt (1810) details some of the
many domestic uses of wild plants that the Faeroese used for many
generations. Some, like sorrel, were served as vegetables; others,
like bogbean leaves, were used as a tobacco substitute, some as
dyes and tannin, and many for medicinal purposes. *Hundaland*
(literally "dog's land") is the Faeroese name for a genus of mush-
room (*Agarius*) from which an antiseptic was produced. Although
some older persons are knowledgeable in these home arts and uses
of plants, modern times and products have replaced much of the
wild crafting of days gone by.

Faeroese plant names are interesting. Like much of Faeroese
language, plant names attest to plant traits and uses and the
merging of the characteristics of nature and human beings. For
example, according to folklore, hundaland gets its name from the
places where dogs urinate! R. Rasmussen's (1950) book details the
intricate origins of Faeroese plant names.

A Sumbingur carries harvested hay from his infield to the barn next to his house.

Ecology is at the very heart of Faeroese culture and penetrates deeply into various aspects of culture, from simple naming practices to complex social relationships. Ecology, increasingly throughout this book, is the study of relationships among and between nature, society, and cultural meaning. Thus subsistence practices, social order, values, and aesthetics comprise a system of interaction. Some ecologists conceptualize ecology as quantifiable or discrete behaviors and relationships within environment and culture. I advocate that cultural meaning is a priority in ecological equations and that it is crucial to comprehending worldviews and cultural difference. With cultural meaning as a primary factor in ecology, the study of place and landscape also becomes part of contemporary "cultural studies." Cultural studies is the recent multidisciplinary approach to the study of everyday culture in both the anthropological sense of culture and in the sense of fashion and fashions of behavior in popular culture and the so-called "high" culture of the well-educated and wealthy. A meaning-centered approach helps to see and understand the significance of the everyday cultural aesthetic of a people, such as the environmental sentiment of the Faeroese.

Chapter Three

A Landscape of Names

Proper names, of course, are human tags for places and people or whatever other items, earthly or unearthly, that are of special importance for a group. Different cultures demarcate their world, material and metaphysical (e.g., Gods, Holy days, etc.), with terms of reference that locate a group physically, aesthetically, and philosophically in its surroundings. Thus the study of the ways in which a group "places" itself is central to understanding local ecology and senses of place. This chapter details the variety of named locales, topographic features, and items of the natural and built landscape that frame the Faeroese experience. First a few words about culture and place.

Sheep graze and shepherds walk the environs sometimes quite distantly from villages. Fowling and fishing also take place away from a settlement and thus for the Faeroese, life is lived geographically more than just near the immediate village environment. Spatial awareness and ecological sensibilities, values and aesthetics incorporate expanses of land and sea all around. It would thus be artificial and inaccurate for this study to limit itself to the classic anthropological "village study."

In addition to the fact that the field of Faeroese activity is wide, the Scandinavian and Faeroese word *bygd*, often translated as "village," really means a farming community of farms sharing some common land (Wåhlin 1989), which could mean both infields and outfields in the Faeroese case. Thus the English word *village* misconstrues the spatial reference. I will often use it with the understanding that it includes not only an arrangement of buildings and social life, but also a more extensive ecological niche.

For hundreds of years Faeroese work has been in harvesting local resources of land, sea, and air. A self-contained inside world long flourished. With the rise in commercial fishing, men began to travel long distances on sea and experienced some of the outside world. Yet the Faeroese work on distant waters still fits into their classic separation between the outside and inside, the formal and the informal. Fishermen who earn their living far out at sea on huge modern trawlers do not talk a lot in the village about life in the distant waters. Local commercial and noncommercial fishermen do talk a lot about offshore fishing, as it fits more into the local sense of space.

Thus, much of this book is about local life, especially on land, and how the village community is the center of the world. Being a Sumbingur, or a Faeroese, *means* being local, rather than cosmopolitan or focused on the external. In keeping with the village culture's own main focus, this work will concentrate on Faeroese culture more or less independent of Danish or European elements.

Sumbøur is literally the name of a village, but the geographic area of importance to subsistence and experience for the villagers really coincides more or less with the political division of Sumbiarkommuna (the commune of Sumbøur) that encompasses the southern portion of the island of Suðuroy. It includes the village and its buildings, the cultivated infields, the outfields, the islet Sumbiarhólmur, coastal areas including coves, caves, stacks, and two small hamlets. Sumbiarkommuna is also the voting district and region of jurisdiction for the town council. Thus it is both a regional and political subdivision of the islands.(The spelling of the village's name varies on different maps. It is sometimes spelled Sumbøur, Sunnbøur, Sumba, or Sunnba, depending on the age and language of the map (Faerose or Danish or English) and on the custom of people from different parts of the islands.)

For the Faeroese the spatial order of things provides also a social order of things. By *social* I mean relationship to other humans as well as relationship to the surroundings. They are inseparable. When a Faeroese person looks around or describes his or her local world, he/she embeds in the landscape through numerous economic, social, and cultural activities of the past and present. Each person can say many things like "That's where to catch good fish." "That's where I net birds." "That's the sheepfold where we round up sheep." "That's where I plant potatoes." "That's where my brother lives." "That's where I pick up my mail." "That's where we dance." "That's where Maria drowned." "That's the house where I grew up." "That's where Hjartvar fell and broke his arm." "That's where the huldufólk lived." These are all the *right* places for activities.

The mountains and ocean bays have long dictated the nucleated settlement pattern and the arrangement of infields and outfields. Fowling, fishing, whaling, and other activities demand people's cooperation and joint attachment to places. With no trees on the sloping hillsides, almost all contacts are visible outside the home, and thus the topography itself channels much social activity as well.

Wind Directions

The North Atlantic is often windy and violent. The fisherman and fowler are especially dependent upon wind direction for safety and transportation. Navigation of the sea, climbing birdcliffs, and netting birds demand close attention to the winds. It is therefore not surprising that the Faeroese, like other maritime peoples, have a refined vocabulary for wind direction. Each year the Faeroese almanac prints a chart of the thirty-two winds and their compass points. Faeroese have their own specific names, such as *landnýrðingur* for northeast. (In Faeroese north is *norður* and east is *eystur*.) Compass terms have also been used to describe the time of day by referring to the position of the sun. For example, to say the time "is half-west" is to mean that it is 4:30 in the afternoon.

In addition to their own names for wind directions and the use of the compass to refer to times of day, the Faeroese also have their own system of compass use. Williamson (1948/1970:85) postulates that the system must be very ancient. The four main points of the compass landnýrðingur (NE), landsynningur (SE), útsynningur (SW), and útnyrðingur (NW) represent the four prevalent winds, and "there can be no question but that the same notation was used by the Vikings a thousand years ago." The term *landnýrðingur* suggests a wind from the north with the land and the term *landsynningur* suggests a wind from the south out of the land, toward the Norwegian coast, a northeast to southwest direction. Thus in the Faeroe system northeast replaces north as the orienting compass point normally used by other peoples. Faeroese boys grow up knowing both systems.

For some western wind and compass directions the Faeroese prefix is *út*, meaning "out," and for some eastern directions the Faeroese prefix is *land* ("land"). These two terms, in addition to their being part of the compass, derive from the Faeroe Islands' own location in the ocean rather than any general, worldwide nautical or wind principle. Thus some Faeroese words for location are unique to their own location. This is just one small example of a local vocabulary for orientation. The uniqueness of Faeroese vocabularies of direction at times becomes so localized that, depending upon one's exact location, even within a certain village, the words used to describe how to get somewhere are different.

Jonathan Wylie, in his book with David Margolin (1981:15), describes his own experience in coming to learn the "idioms of orientation" and the importance of local place to Faeroese.

> I . . . began to be able to orient myself in the native idiom. I began to realize, however, that as surely as speaking with a village accent, the unthinking mastery of such usages establishes one's place in the Faroese world. Throughout the Faroes, the same terms are used according to the same general principles; each district, village, neighborhood, and even household customarily uses them a little differently. People from other villages reassured me that they sometimes had as much trouble as I did in getting the hang of local usages, and when, on a trip round the islands a few years later, I began collecting idioms of orientation systematically, I quickly found that it was necessary to get them from "native speakers." Sometimes a woman who had lived for decades in her husband's village would be listening as eagerly as I was, and would put in from time to time, "Oh, is *that* how you say it; I never knew."

Idioms of Orientation

The archipelago is geographically intricate, with waterways and mountains, isthmuses and bays, cliffs and plains cutting across the islands. Fjords (firths) are passages of water that generally run east and west between islands, and sounds are waterways that generally run north and south. These geographic features and the rough ocean curtailed frequent contact between settlements over the centuries, and thus each settlement became almost a world unto its own, complete with its own dialect or subdialect of Faeroese. Expressions of direction and orientation became important for what transportation and contact there was, as well as for villagers' own need for precise description in their own subsistence practices.

Wylie and Margolin (1981) devote an entire chapter of their book to what they have called "idioms of orientation." Many idioms are culture specific to Scandinavia, the Faeroes, particular islands of the archipelago, sections of islands, particular villages, and where a speaker is specifically located at a moment in time. The system is quite complex. I will provide only a few examples.

Faeroese make adverbs of place by adding a suffix, *i*, to directions. Thus *eystur* is the direction east, but *eysturi* is a place in the east. They also add the suffix *an* to the root direction to denote "from a place." Thus *suðuran* means "from the south." Even more specific, the word *heim* literally means "home," the place of reference for the family, but with respect to directions, to the individual as a member of a village and its environs, it means "from a central place," usually the village church. This is the case even if one's own house lies in the opposite direction from the church.

People also use direction words to refer to places within their own houses or buildings, and it is not uncommon in Scandinavia to find the use of compass terms to denote place within a room. Faeroese also have special words like *niðan* ("from below"), which generally describes movement up a not-so-steep slope, and *oman* ("from above"), down the slope, although in some villages they are used specifically to refer to going to certain named places. Faeroese has numerous prepositions and combinations of prepositions for direction. One specific idiom is the use of *niður* ("down") to refer to Denmark. Often when referring to Denmark people simply say *har niðri* ("down there").

The idioms of orientation generally are in the form of "south to a place." The first word is an adverb of place or direction (north, east, out, over, etc.). The second is usually a preposition (to, from, in, etc.), and the third word is a place-name or geographical feature (Sumbøur, bluff, mountain peak, etc.). The prepositions also vary depending upon the name, that is, according to rules of grammar. In general, directions like "out" and "over" generally refer to movement within bounded spaces and directions like "east" and "south" refer to ongoing movement in a direction determined by the sun or stars. Faeroese conversation is full of prepositions, adverbs, and place-names. Even proper place-names incorporate many idioms of direction.

For an outsider, and even sometimes for natives from different parts of the country, understanding precisely how to get somewhere or correctly say how to go there can be tricky. Yet Faeroese are generally very well versed and grounded in their own spatial orderings, with an intricate grid for attaching themselves to and moving about within the local geography.

Divisions of the Landscape and Seascape

Although there are no trees to punctuate and divide fields or visual horizons, Faeroese geography has a bounty of topographic features from which to draw for boundaries of various kinds. And, like other peoples, Faeroese have their culture and imagination to create other kinds of divisions of the physical world. Thus, although nature has some clearly delimiting features, like shorelines, cliffsides, and mountain ridge lines, that channel how humans utilize the environment, it is people who ultimately make sense out of the environment visually, linguistically, and culturally. People make spaces into places. And the Faeroese are master place makers.

While the modern economy of the Faeroes rests in great part upon commercial fishing and the harvesting of the sea, as I described earlier, for hundreds of years Faeroese lived mainly off the land itself and fished for subsistence rather than for profit. Despite many men "going to ships," as the Faeroese expression has it for fishermen leaving for a fishing trip, the dominant frame of Faeroese reference in the environment has always been the land as opposed to the sea. Attitudes toward land have changed little. With the eventual equalizing of landholdings through the last two centuries, almost everyone came to have a piece of ground with which to identify and refer to with a name. In earlier days, more prestige was accorded to foodstuffs and activities garnered from the land rather than from fish. Moreover, methods of raising sheep and crops have not changed much in comparison with the technological changes in fishing and in the preparation of fish for export. Thus, while the sea is certainly an important component of local ecology, general orientation, personal and cultural identity, and history itself primarily center around the landscape as opposed to the seascape.

Faeroese also use the landscape to delineate the seascape. They use fixed-sight navigation markers (ýtir) to triangulate positions on the open, offshore sea for navigational and fishing purposes. Although nowadays large commercial fishing vessels out at deep sea locate themselves and schools of fish with modern instrumentation, local fishermen still use the numerous place-names of landmarks visible from sea to situate themselves on waters within sight of the islands' seacoasts. In motor and rowboats, as well as on small commercial boats, fishermen combine their knowledge of tides, winds, former luck, and superstition with their familiarity with the islands' landscape to triangulate. Fishermen use named streams, waterfalls, mountain peaks, rock formations, village buildings, and the like to determine fishing spots (mið). A fisherman wanting to remember exactly where he had a good midsummer cod catch, for example, might mark the location by saying to himself, "This is where I can see the tip of 'Noisy Mountain' lined up exactly with the big boulder 'Blue Stone'." Then he would give that triangulated open ocean location a proper name, like 'Shag Bank' or 'Aksal's Spot'. In this way knowledge of land helps one demarcate and know about the sea. One experienced angler with whom I went fishing let me copy his closely guarded list of thirty-eight mið, although he made me promise that I would not tell anyone about them.

Just as land directs some activities at sea, so the nature of the sea dictates some activities on land. Tides and stormy or calm ocean waters make the seashore or coastline more fluid than one might initially think. Some human activities, including some types of fowling and fishing, boating, sealing (in former days), and visiting areas on shore and cliffs are only possible during a few very calm summer days. Sumbingar can can only have their fishing boats tied at the village dock during summer because in other seasons the boats would be destroyed by a storm's violent waves. Although all villages have boathouses for storing boats away from the water's edge, in Sumbøur, with its nearly open ocean location, special care is necessary for docking and storing boats. On very stormy days the islet Sumbiarhólmur is virtually covered with water.

There are fjords and sounds between many of the islands, and some islands also have small lakes. Bays indent the coastline, and, as elsewhere in the world, these bodies of water have proper names. Faeroese unity with features of the sea and land is so fundamental that many proper, capitalized names for natural features of the seascape and landscape and for the built environment have simple, straightforward maritime names like 'Bay' (Vágur) (a town), 'Isthmus' (*Eiði*) (a village), and 'Shore' (Strendur) (a village); many fjords and sounds are named after the islands or villages by which they flow, e.g., 'South Island Fjord', 'Bird Island Fjord', and 'Westman's [a town] Sound'. Names such as these suggest to the outsider an almost fairytale character to the islands.

In addition to streams, slopes, valleys, ridges, mountain peaks, and typical topographic features found elsewhere, there are other archipelagic and geographic features especially characteristic of the Faeroes, as well as of some other islands of the North Atlantic. These include cliffs, cliff ledges, coves, capes, stacks (free-standing rock columns offshore), reefs, hammars (bluffs), promontories, spits of land, rocky mounds, chasms, sea caves, islets, skerries (rocks just at the surface of the ocean), harbors, and flat seashore rocks. These naturally occurring physical geographic features are incorporated into numerous place-names.

Faeroese geographic features and their generic names and place-names are especially similar in Shetland and Orkney. Since Shetland's now-extinct language, Norn, and Faeroese both derive from the same Norse origins, parallels are striking. In Shetland, place-names commonly contain the (dialect) words *ness, wick, holm*, and *burgh*, as in, for example, Fish Holm and Otter Wick. Faeroese uses *nes* ("cape"), Shetland uses *ness*; Faeroese has *hólmur* ("islet"), Shetland has *holm*. *Vík* and *vág* are "bay" in Faeroese, while they are *wick* and *voe* in Shetland. Indeed, Sumbøur ('South Field'), the southernmost village of the Faeroes, is almost identical in spelling and pronunciation to Sumburgh, the southernmost spot in Shetland.

As with all permanently settled peoples, the Faeroese have shaped the natural landscape with human modifications and constructions. Geography and subsistence practices dictate much of the methods and materials for cultural changes to the environment. In addition to styles of houses, stores, and churches found in other parts of Europe and Scandinavia, characteristically Faeroese constructions in the landscape include stone walls, sheepfolds, fenced cowpaths, cairns, hay houses, hjallar, boat docks, boat ramps, boathouses, and dance houses. The visible modifications and partitions of the landscape also include homesteads, farmsteads, and the infields, outfields, and gardens.

Less visible are the political, legal, historical, and symbolic divisions that people have made over the centuries. Some coincide with obvious physical features, such as islands. Faeroese generally refer to the two groups of islands as the Norðuroyar ('Northern Islands'), which include Fugloy, Svínoy, Viðoy, Borðoy, Kunoy, and Kalsoy and the Suðuroyar ('Southern Islands'), which include Suðuroy, Lítla Dímun, Stóra Dímun, Skúvoy, Sandoy, and Trøll-høvdi (uninhabited). Although people on Suðuroy could say that the other islands are central or west, north and south are the only general categories of islands. Thus Sumbingar generally refer to islands by their individual names, such as Eysturoy and Streymoy, the two largest and most central islands, or Vágar and Mykines in the west. All the islands comprise parts of different man-made whale districts and sheriffs' (law) districts.

Formal, political districts of the islands are of two kinds, one for juridical/legal purposes and one for whaling. Long ago, during the eleventh and twelfth centuries, the Norwegian crown established six official districts (sýslur), each of which had a sheriff. These districts, still in use, made easier the administration of legal matters, such as court sessions. These legal districts, segmented into individual islands or island groups, are those of Streymoy, Sandoy, Eysturoy, Vágar, Suðuroy, and the 'Northern Islands'. Although today Sumbingar, like other villagers, occasionally participate in formal legal sessions of a district, they tend to avoid outright conflict and eschew formal legal forums. Thus unofficial divisions of space discussed below play a much more daily role in the Faeroese worldview.

Whale districts were set up to help ensure regular and equitable divisions of whale meat and blubber for all the inhabitants of the islands. Some villages, depending upon their location, receive full or half-parts of the spoils. Over the years there have been some changes, but the Law of 1909 set up nine districts. In light of the economic and cultural importance of the grindadráp these districts are significant for Faeroese subsistence and for social gatherings connected with the harvesting of pilot whales.

Wylie (1987), in tracing the history of the Faeroes, also sees geography and spatial order as a dominant aspect of Faeroese culture. He points out that there are three main areas "outside the wall" (uttangarðs), as the Faeroese call the area outside the in-field/outfield fence or village "walls." The three areas are the outfields, the cliffs, and the sea. He suggests parallels between these areas of geography and economic use of animals within them and the officials, institutions, and levels of political organization:

> Faroese legal and political institutions also have geographical connotations, and to some extent seasonal ones. In the spring, at lambing time, local courts for each district (*sýsla*) met in the outfield; the Løgting for all the Faroes met in Tórshavn in summer on a rocky spit of land called the Tinganes; the royal court met "down there" (as people say), in Copenhagen. All of these places were peripheral to village-centered society although, paradoxically, they were politically central. Faroese did not live there, but only visited them. The spring courts met in bowls in the hills, attended by each district's sheriff and *løgraettumenn*, by the *løgmaður* (later the *sorinskrivari*), and by other interested parties from the district's scattered villages. The Tinganes, the political equivalent of a cliff or seaside, was the realm of the *løgmaður* and the bailiff, and in ecclesiastical affairs, of the dean. It was also the site of the company store and warehouses . . .
>
> The outfields, where sheep live, are the level of the Faroes' several districts and their officials and institutions, the cliffs are the level of bird life, of the Faroes as a whole, and of Tórshavn and its intermediary officials and institutions, which were increasingly Danish; the sea is the level of fish, of Denmark, and of foreign officialdom. (Ibid:55)

Table 1   The Faroes "outside the wall" (*uttangarðs*)

Geography	Animals	Areas	Courts	Sites	Political Officials	Ecclesiastical Officials	Trade
sea	fish	Denmark	royal court	Copenhagen	king, etc.	king, bishop, etc.	Iceland Co., Gabels', etc.
cliffs	birds	Faroes	Løgting	Tinganes (Tórshavn)	*Løgmaður*	bailiff	dean
outfield	sheep	districts (*sýslur*)	spring parliaments	traditional sites	*løgroettumenn*, sheriff	priest	
(stone wall).							

Place-Names and the Distribution of Space and Place

Informally and locally, the population centers—the towns, villages, and hamlets—are of perhaps most significance as partitions of the social landscape. Borne out of the need for the inhabitants to nestle away from the open ocean on bays and to cooperate economically with one another, nucleated settlement patterns dominate. Thus Faeroese primarily know each other as natives and residents of one village or another. Additionally many villages are comprised almost entirely of residents who were either born in the village or who married into it. This derives from the historically nearly self-contained economic world of each village and the patrilocal residence pattern, in which wives generally move to the village of their husbands. Anthropologists sometimes call these little societies closed communities because of their very tight and closely woven social character. Every male Sumbingur was either born in the village, or, in two or three exceptional cases, came to live with a marital or blood relation. Every woman was either born in the village or married a man who was born in the village. This is a strongly interlocked community, and thus because of the islands' geography, subsistence patterns, and social ties, villages and their surrounds become the primary intraislands spatial and cultural identifier for natives.

There are many further refinements and delineations of local space according to geography. Villages have their own "neighborhoods," which are defined geographically, not by social composition. In Sumbøur, for example, there are several informal but properly named sections such as 'under the Bluff' (undir Hamri), 'in the Rocky Mound' (í Hørg), and 'east of the Stream' (eystan Á). The multitude of these informal names kept me guessing for a long time about how to refer to where I was, where I was going, and with whom I was speaking.

I neither planned to study place-names nor anticipated that I would wind up with many hours of interviews and tape recordings about them and their locations, meanings, and histories. Nor did I suspect that the task of compilation would be virtually endless. I have nonexhaustive lists of 276 place-names within the general twenty-square-kilometer village vicinity, 113 place-names along twenty kilometers of nearby coastline, and 35 place-names on Sumbiarhólmur. Only after three or four months did I realize that the study of naming, like the study of a dominant pattern in any society, was a key to penetrating into Faeroese culture.

Just as for other peoples directly dependent on land or sea, place-names function in subsistence practices. We have already discussed the use of landmarks for marking fishing banks and for navigation. For the Faeroese, place-names also help to locate lost sheep and delineate the footholds on birding cliffs and stacks. Students of folklore and the European scene also point to the etiological functions of place-names. Stories about the origins of place-names and persons' names often help to order the universe of a community. They give explanations for unusual, obvious, and nonproductive portions of the landscape (Blum 1982). Yet, in the Faeroe Islands place-names not only demarcate unique features of the archipelagic geography but also nominalize everyday, seemingly mundane spaces: 'The Swing at Cowpath Slope' is the name of the turn in the road into Sumbøur.

More Place-Named Divisions:
The Developed Landscape

Faeroese delineations of space become especially evident in the prolific naming of the countryside. Even homesteads (farmsteads) and houses themselves have proper place-names. Such places as 'in the High Cowpath', 'in the Cabbage Garden', and 'on the Plain' describe particular family-based village areas with a house, a hjallur, a barn, a garden, and perhaps contiguous infields. Houses and buildings alone have proper names like 'The House of Jacob' (hjá Jacobi), still called by its deceased owner's name, 'Stonehouse' (Steinhús), and even 'Dancehouse'.

House names exist in other parts of the world, even in parts of nearby Britain. Yet there, it is most often the well-to-do that use such names as Penwick, Dunbar, and Highgrove for their large homes, estates, or castles. Unlike class-based, hierarchical society, in which usually only the rich have such cultural options to call their possessions by name, all Faeroese have named houses and homesteads. And all Faeroese have the opportunity to give names to the landscape. (Although almost every place and place-name

This farmstead, við Kvíggja ('by the Calves' Fold'), with house, barn, and hjallur, lies at the edge of the inhabited parts of Sumbøur.

mentioned in this book is real, persons' names and nicknames are pseudonyms or altered.)

Nearly every nook and cranny of Faeroese space seems to be named. More intricate connections to the land are small infields that have proper names, capitalized when written, like any other proper noun or place-name. Thus 'Blackfield','Cliffland', 'Crossland', and 'Haldan's Wife's Field' are small cultivated fields. Also, the expanses of sheep pasture, the outfields, are divided up into sections like 'Rock Outfield' and 'Pigeon Shelter'.

Place-names have been eminently practical reference points in shepherding and agricultural pursuits. Animals roam the slopes and sometimes get away from the areas where they are supposed to pasture. I heard one villager say to another, "I saw your black and white ram in the east section of 'Middle Outfield' near 'Creek's Edge', just west of 'Whimbrel Rock'." The names of the cultivated infields also help to differentiate landholdings.

Other places in the village and its surrounds are named. 'Milkmaid's Gate' is the entranceway to the area where young women went out to pasture to milk cows. 'Cow Land Slope', a walking path now used by everyone, also describes the land where men pre-

This sheepfold lies in the outfield far from human habitation. Like many of the man-made constructions, it seems to merge with the stony terrain.

viously led their cows to grazing areas and also gathered in the evenings to exchange news. Historical uses also carry on in contemporary dialogue. 'Angelica Garden' is where a garden of angelica once grew, and 'Sitting Room Rock' is where an old house—and its sitting room—once stood. Whether parts of the agricultural/shepherding landscape are groomed by people, resulting in infields, stone walls, paths, and so on, or by nature in outfields, chasms, coves, etc., islanders have long put colorful appellations upon them.

More Place-Named Divisions: The Natural Landscape

I have separated this section about natural divisions from the previous one about the developed landscape to emphasize that Faeroese not only divide up their world and name it by placing a human grid of activity upon the land and sea, but also incorporate naturally occurring items and characteristics of nature into their world. Although Elsebeth Vestergaard (1989) neatly divides Faeroese spatial organization by sex into "inside" versus "outside," paralleling men's work in public and women's work in private, merging of the natural and the humanly modified landscape seems in general at the heart of the Faeroese experience. Cairns, piles of rocks villagers make to mark the pathways between villages, are constructed simply by moving several rocks naturally strewn about. Stone walls are made by rearranging the stones already on the ground. Sheepfolds, corralling sheep at round-up times, are circular stone walls that seem to blend with the rocky mountain-sides. Thus the natural landscape unites with the humanly created one. Single place-names, like 'Sitting Room Flat', a large, flat coastal rock near an old house, also combine words describing human creations with natural ones. Others give human proper names to natural features, as in 'Gormund's Chasm'.

As with many cultures' place-names, Faeroese use descriptive, often anthropomorphic terms to describe natural features and shapes. They "place" cultural conceptions onto the landscape. On the island of Suðuroy, for example, the names of the promontory 'Knuckle' and the twin peaks 'The Teats' more or less describe themselves. Some other shapes and formations are less apparent, such as the small islet 'Dog's Tongue'. There is also 'The Beak', the mountain ridge that slopes down to the sea in a form resembling that part of a bird. Other places such as 'Big Point', 'Bulge Skerry', and 'Creek Boulder', combine together the names of shapes and/or natural phenomena.

The abundance of birds and the practice of fowling provide other examples of how Faeroese nature, subsistence, and toponymy merge. Gulls, fulmars, kittiwakes, puffins, guillemots, skuas, terns, shags, and countless other sea and land birds are plentiful almost everywhere—offshore, on hillsides, and on the fantastic cliffs. Birds appear in hamlet names like 'Kittiwake Bay', 'Goose Valley', 'Eider Bay', and 'Shag Headland'. Also there are 'Bird Island' and 'Great Skua Island', two of the seventeen inhabited islands of the Faeroes. Less accessible places include 'Pigeon Stack', 'Crow Rock Cave', 'Fulmar Gulley', 'Shag Pond', 'Eider Ridge', 'Black Guillemot Head', 'Pipit Knoll', and the twin rock pinnacles 'The Red-Throated Divers', to name only some.

Fowlers also depend upon knowledge and naming of the foot-holds of birding cliffs. 'The Long Shelf', 'Big Ledge', and 'Ganne

These twin peaks lie along the western coast of Suðuroy, not far from
Sumbøur. They are named after a kind of seabird, Lómirnar ('The Red-
Throated Divers'). This view is possible only on a few, rare, calm
summer days. Ordinarily, trubulent waves crash along the shore.

Rock' name small ledges of mountain cliffs, the anchorages from
which the fowlers gathered eggs or use birding poles to net the
seabirds. Students from Denmark and the Faeroese Academy
(Fróðskaparsetur Føroya) have recorded an amazing number of
over 300 names on the 1,500-foot-high fowling cliff near Sumbøur.
    Many sheep and an occasional person have tumbled to their
deaths at the bottom of seaside cliffs, and fishermen occasionally
perish on the perilous seas. Thus the need to refer to the nuances
of topography has been paramount for Faeroese fishermen/farm-
ers. Care and precision in spatial orientation have always been
crucial for safe transportation and communication. Such refined
perceptual and spatial skills are a product of survival needs and
self-reliance in nature (see also Tuan 1977:79). Thus the Faeroese
have come to be master delineators and namers of a complex
subsistence landscape and have come to incorporate geography
into their personhood and aesthetic.

More Place-Named Divisions:
The "Unnatural" Landscape

Figures of Faeroese geography are not limited to humans, birds,
mammals, fish, and the like. In addition to Christian supernatural
religious figures such as Jesus Christ, the Virgin Mary, and God,
many Faeroese have also long believed in other supernatural entities, such as elves, brownies, dwarfs, trolls, water kelpies, witches,
and ghosts. The traditional Christian religious figures fundamental
to the dominant Lutheran sects of the islands are invoked, but not
actually observed, in church or anywhere one prays or seeks their
presence. (The names of such deities do not appear in place-
names.) On the other hand, for many, huldufólk literally inhabit
the countryside, making themselves invisible as they disappear into
their living quarters inside mountainside boulders. Sometimes

huldufólk are called elves (*álvar*), especially in references to the mounds where they live(d). Such a mound is called an elf's howe (*álvheyggjur*).

While modern days have eroded some natives' beliefs in huldufólk, I witnessed a discussion between a forty-five-year-old man who swore that he saw several huldufólk and two younger men who thought the man could not have seen such things. One Sumbingur told me that with the introduction of electricity the huldufólk left the surrounds of Sumbøur. Younger people tend not to have had the experiences with such supernatural beings, although huldufólk are the subjects of numerous local and national stories, written and oral, not infrequently recounted by villagers (see Jakobsen [1898–1901] and West [1980]).

Some place-names either explicitly mark the habitats or adventures of nonhuman creatures or indirectly conjure up their presence in associations of place. Many place-names locate the haunts of dwarfs (*dvørgar*), trolls (*trøll*), and huldufólk. 'Dwarf's Stone' (Dvørgasteinur), just outside of Sumbøur, is where dwarfs had their home, while 'The Peak', 'The Cliff of Akrar', and 'Outer Mountain' are where trolls were known to have lived. 'Troll's Headland' (Trøllhøvdi), uninhabited by humans, is an islet off Sandoy, and 'Troll's Promontory' (Trøllanes), is a settlement on Kalsoy. 'Whispering Rock', 'Klummar's Bluff', and 'Kuran's Flatland', in the vicinity of Sumbøur, are said to be the places where huldufólk lived. One day, supervised by a knowledgeable elder of Sumbøur, I made a detailed map of nearby places with supernatural names and associations.

Place-names are also living "texts" about unique villagers who possess(ed) supernatural qualities. The legendary witch Barbara við Kvíggja of Sumbøur is still associated with the current 'By the Calves' Fold' (við Kvíggja) homestead. She had mystical powers of black magic, and you can still see 'Black Magic Rock' (Gandasteinur), the large boulder that only she had the ability to move. And even today villagers treat with caution Eyðtor, a man noted for his belief in black magic. The name of his house and section of the village often cause villagers to smirk. Some old folks, and some young ones who have heard tales, are uncertain yet wary of black magic and therefore maintain respectful distance from his house. Beings and legends inhere in the very rocks, crevices, and structures

This gulley was known as a place where huldufólk lived.

of the Faeroese landscape. Geographical names can give metaphysical dimensions to the land.

Some specific plots of land also have their characteristic background, sometimes supernatural. Here one villager tells me about the background of a family and the particular piece of property they own:

> There is a family in Skálabøur, as it is told, that one hundred years ago began to have bad luck. A farmer there had been

clearing his field of rocks so as to make it suitable for cultivation. He dreamt that if he moved and broke a certain boulder where "pixies" [*vaettrar*] lived, he would suffer one hundred years of bad luck and disasters. Nevertheless, the man broke the boulder into pieces to clear the land. And this family and its contemporary descendents, it is said, truly have had bad luck for all these years. Their house has been hurt several times by natural disasters and children of the family have been physically deformed and handicapped in various ways.

In the Faeroes it helps to know the origins of place-names and the characteristics of named spaces, even where supernatural beings have been.

A System of Understanding Space

Wylie's (1987) own discussion of spatial divisions incorporates huldufólk and other supernatural entities. In his interpretation of Faeroese history and legends, each kind of supernatural being is associated with a specific part of the local landscape. Near and in people's homes, for example, is where pixies thrive. He summarizes the literary history of Faeroese spatial order:

> The Faroese did in some measure control the borders of their world . . . through literature. Legends, ballads, and folktales were, after all, where everything was put in its proper place: Vikings in the past, Danes across the sea or in Tórshavn, trolls in the mountains, *huldufólk* in the outfields, the village in the middle. (Ibid:62)

Whether Faeroese are as deliberate as Wylie suggests may be beside the point, geography and spatial ordering are fundamental to the culture.

It is also instructive to link the Faeroese culture's prolific place-naming and geographic aesthetic to modern sociological thought. The noted French sociologist Pierre Bourdieu, like myself and many others, is also interested in social space, in how humans interact with space. He (1984) investigates how social relations within and between groups are connected to their movements through, and appreciation of, spaces. He notes how social groups are distributed geographically in certain ways and that that distribution is never "socially neutral," by which he means that people's location in space (e.g., suburbanites versus ghetto dwellers, those with master bedrooms versus housemaids' quarters, etc.) is part

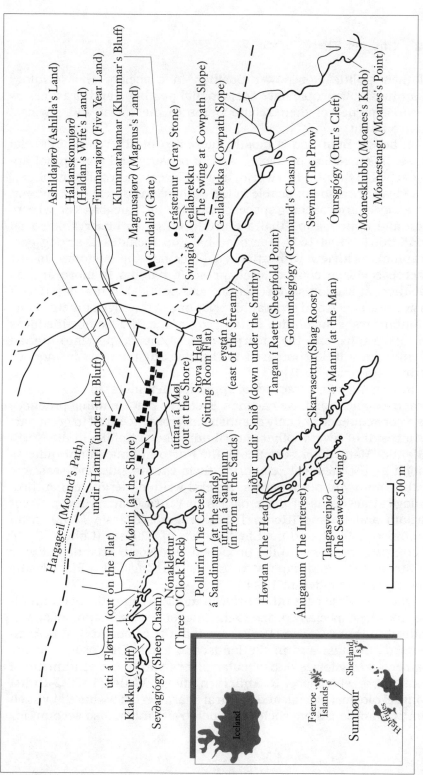

Place-Names Around Sumbøur

Ashildajörð (Ashilda's Land)
Háldanskonujörð (Haldan's Wife's Land)
Fimmrajörð (Five Year Land)
Klummarahamar (Klummar's Bluff)
Magnusajörð (Magnus's Land)
Grindalið (Gate)
Grásteinur (Gray Stone)
Svingið á Geilabrekku (The Swing at Cowpath Slope)
Geilabrekka (Cowpath Slope)
Stevnin (The Prow)
Ótursgjógy (Otur's Cleft)
Móanesklubbi (Moanes's Knob)
Móanestangi (Moanes's Point)

Hargageil (Mound's Path)
undir Hamri (under the Bluff)
á Mølini (at the Shore)
úttara á Møl (out at the Shore)
Stova Hella (Sitting Room Flat)
eystán Á (east of the Stream)
niður undir Smið (down under the Smithy)
Tangan í Raett (Sheepfold Point)
Gormundsgjógy (Gormund's Chasm)
á Manni (at the Man)

úti á Fløtum (out on the Flat)
Klakkur (Cliff)
Seyðagjógy (Sheep Chasm)
Nónaklettur (Three O'Clock Rock)
Pollurin (The Creek)
á Sandinum (at the sands)
úrinn á Sandinum (in from at the Sands)
Hovdan (The Head)
Skarvasettur (Shag Roost)
Áhuganum (The Interest)
Tangasveipið (The Seaweed Swing)

500 m

Iceland
Faeroe Islands
Sumbøur
Shetland Is.
Hebrides

I. Moriarty   Source: Gaffin

of their political or power position in a society. His sociology examines how people have sociospatial positions and practices as a consequence of their relationships to the social and physical environment.

Although Bourdieu is mostly interested in differences in social class, in questions of "taste," and in sensory and conceptual approaches to the physical world, in what he calls a group's "habitus," his ideas are also applicable in the egalitarian context of Sumbøur. As a way of approaching space, channeled by "categories of perception and appreciation that are produced by an observable social condition" (1984:101), Faeroese habitus includes a strong geographic worldview with attached place-naming customs. In the Faeroese village context, each person's habitus is more or less identical at least in socioeconomic and political terms, based as it is in equal social and geographic relations to the environment. Thus Sumbingars' sensibilities to the geographic, their embeddedness in topography, and the incorporation of topography into human identity vary little compared to the class distinctions in modern stratified French society.

In keeping with a traditional approach in understanding cultural practices and belief, we can view Faeroese place-naming practices as a consequence not only of subsistence practices but in great part as a result of several other contributing factors of life in the North Atlantic. Many other societies of the North Atlantic, if not quite as much as the Faeroese, elaborate their countryside and seascape with a bounty of place-names. Several written literary and anthropological accounts of place-names in Wales (Davies, n.d.), Great Britain and Ireland (Room 1983), Ireland (Glassie 1982), Aran (Robinson 1986), and the Shetland Isle of Whalsay (Cohen 1987), among others, attest to the propensity for North Atlantic cultures to strew their landscape with names. (In England a Place-Name Society was founded in 1924.)

North Atlantic peasant or fisherman/farmer maritime communities may be especially prone to the intensive demarcation of space. Indeed Anthony Cohen (1987) says that the Shetland past is "condensed" through and in the landscape itself. This occurs in the names and histories of particular places and in the sentiments of rootedness with place. R. Andersen and C. Wadel (1972:2–3) list some ecological, social, and cultural characteristics shared by such North Atlantic fishing societies. Such traits might also account for some of the Faeroese and North Atlantic emphasis on geography and, I suggest, might well encourage the proliferation of place-names. Such characteristics include (1) relatively small coastal settlements often accessible only by sea, (2) no roadways linking settlements, (3) surrounding land commonly unarable, (4) settlements with poor communication links with the outside, and (5) self-sufficiency and adaptability in a seasonally pluralistic economy. These factors certainly apply historically and today to the Faeroes.

Chapter Four
A Landscape of People

Language has the power to help people conceptualize. Thus words and phrases have the power to make something "real." With spatial orderings so crucial to Faeroese visual, economic, and aesthetic life, it is not surprising to think that other aspects of their social and cultural lives are demonstrably, dramatically, attached to place. In fact, in the various methods for the geographic naming of persons, and in the mutually influencing characteristics of place and people, place becomes central to Faeroese social life and identity at various levels of inclusion. Place is thus crucial to the social order of the society, the way people understand and trace their relationships to history and to each other.

Geographic Names for Persons

Faeroese name themselves using place, geography, and named features of the landscape. People use four general kinds of names for each other: patronymics, homestead names, nicknames, and surnames. All the types refer to physical spaces or structures.

Patronymics is a method of naming used in many parts of the world. In it a person receives a name derived from one's father or male ancestor. It shows a relationship of descent. It can take different language forms such as the addition of a suffix or prefix, for example, as in Stevenson, the son of Steven, or O'Brian, the descendant of Brian. The Faeroese have their own spatial twist on this kind of naming.

Faeroese patronymically designate persons such as Karl and Lina Vestergaard as Karl hjá Edvard, Karl (son) "of" Edvard, and Lina (daughter) "of" Edvard. A female can be "of" her father but after marriage usually becomes "of" her husband. But, blending place and person together, *hjá* in Faeroese also means "at the house of" or "the house of." Thus Alma hjá Eli signifies Eli's Alma and/or

95

"Alma from the house of Eli." They also generalize this naming practice to the proper names of houses and homesteads. A house, in addition to or instead of having its own name, such as Stonehouse, could be properly known as The House of Edvard. For six months my wife and I lived at hjá Jacobi, The House of Jacob, the then empty, former house of then deceased Jacob.

Patronyms also differentiate two people with the same first name, for example, Jon hjá Herluf from Jon hjá Tummas. Sumbingar might also differentiate two Jon's by using a patronym for one and a nickname for the other Jon, e.g., Jon hjá Herluf versus Stóra (Big) Jon. Faeroese patronyms usually last only one or two generations. Those for women that identify females as "belonging" to their husband or husband's house rather than to their father's might best be called *virinyms* (Gaffin 1987). Although patronyms and virinyms embody formal relationships insofar as they refer to links of blood, marriage, or residence, they use only individual, informal first names. Villagers use patronyms in conversation without using surnames. This is one way they avoid reference to larger kinship groupings. This practice also reflects the general lack of strong kin ties outside the nuclear family.

Knowledge about villagers, their kin, and social relations is necessary for understanding in context these kinds of names. One must know a woman's marital status and where she lives, for example, to distinguish whether one is talking about a woman's father or husband when saying Alma hjá Eli. Proper usage of patronyms and virinyms, like most Faeroese names, requires familiarity with people, their histories, and their spatial arrangements. Such naming reflects individualization in village life. The notion of belonging to a person or family *and* a house via name is crucial to Faeroese identity.

Everyday names of individuals often incorporate names for pieces of property, usually *homestead names*. Such nicknames are also used to trace descent. Families form what Sumbingar call a *slekt* (pl. *slektir*) and Faerose generally call an *aet*, which might best be translated as "lineage" or "patrilineage." The adverbial form is *slektaður*, used generally and loosely in tracing relationships "from" or "descended from." Again, in typical Faeroese identification with place, one is usually "descended from" a homestead or farmstead. Here the man commonly known as Albert í Høgeil (Albert in the High Cowpath) recounts some of Sumbøur's history:

Different slektir could quarrel with each other. There weren't so many slektir in Sumbøur. There was Laðangarði ['Pathway Farm'], the biggest, and við Kvíggja ['By the Calves' Fold'] and í Hørg ['in the Mound']. There was Hargastovu ['Mound Room'] and Abrahamstovu ['Abraham's Room']. They were slektir of seamen—they owned the most property before. And there was Kalgarði ['Cabbage Garden'], that was the slekt we are descended from.

Albert uses the names of the farms, without reference to formal last names of people, as the identifiers of groups, of lineages. Lineages—families in time—are directly associated with the land they own(ed) or the land their ancestors came from. Thus as well as a metaphorical kinship between people and place, there is a literal kinship.

Another man, using similar terminology, describes balladry of Sumbøur natives in earlier days.

Then [the people] always had *kvaeðir* [ballads] for themselves. Each had a ballad to chant. These *houses* in [the village sections of] í Keri ['in the Hollow'], undir Hamri ['under the Bluff'], perhaps í Hørg ['in the Mound'] and Høgeil ['High Cowpath']. And down there, there was niðri á Garðun ['down by the Field']. Each *family* had, perhaps, its own ballad. (Emphasis mine)

Family becomes almost interchangeable or synonymous with place. Individuals' and families' connections to pieces of land and to sectors of the village are central to local identity.

Homestead names have long been a Faeroese practice. Many homestead names date, like Danish surnames, to 1584 land records. Although the records themselves are in Danish, they cite Faeroese place-names and homestead names for people. Sofus 'in the High Cowpath', a typical, contemporary name refers to a long-standing village homestead, even if the homestead is not the same size as in earlier times. 'High Cowpath', an area of infield named long ago, was once probably a parcel of land owned by a certain family. Sofus owns part of that area; perhaps his ancestors have owned it for many generations. Yet villagers do not usually attach homestead names to nonresident descendants of former owners, unless the homestead no longer functions as a social and economic unit. Thus Sofus's son, Róland, who moved to another house in another homestead, is not called Róland 'in the High Cowpath'.

People say he is "from" 'High Cowpath', but his current name(s) of place, such as locational nicknames, would refer to where he lives now. The same is true of house-based names.

The most frequent names of village conversation are what I call *locational nicknames*, although the word *nickname* does not fully convey their predominance. While the attachment of homestead names to people just discussed could be termed locational nick-names because of their informality, I reserve the present discussion for villagers' geographic names that do not utilize homesteads. Since the breakup of many of the original homesteads into smaller parcels, many additional locational names have come into use. Such locational names, like other kinds of nicknames, are not used in direct address.

Villagers generally add place-names to individuals' first names, as in Hilmar 'under the Ledge' and Leif 'Post Office'. Such nick-names usually utilize names for village sectors, topographic features, and physical structures. Leif and Frida 'Post Office' (Posthús) work in the village's post office and live in the house above it. Those are the everyday names people use to identify those two people and a daughter who grew up there. I never did know what their "real" last name was. Similarly, Sigvarð 'Stonehouse' (Steinhús), formally known as Sigvarð Johanneson, lives in a house long called 'Stone-house'. The 'Stonehouse' family today includes Sigvarð, Jacobina 'Stonehouse', Eyðtor 'Stonehouse', and Egil 'Stonehouse'. Egil Vestergaard is commonly referred to as Egil 'under the Bluff', marking his village sector. Sectors, regions, and landmarks of the environs are also "families" to which individuals belong.

Attachment of place-names to first names also distinguishes individuals with the same first name or surname and/or tags one's place of residence. Two Pouls living in Sumbøur are known as 'Creek Poul' (Poul í Pollurin) and 'Bluff's Falls Poul' (Poul við Hamarfoss). Each villager is possibly known by a variety of locational names depending upon what level of spatial differentiation or geographic membership a speaker wants to invoke. People with homestead names attached to their first names can also be called by their patronym, house name, village sector, or other informal name. Within village sectors and within the village as a whole, individuals usually come to be called most frequently one particular locational name. Faeroese individualize each other with place-names even when other names could do.

Thus, each Faeroese community maps its natural and built environment onto people. In describing a similar phenomenon in the Shetland Isle of Whalsay, Cohen (1987:108–109) writes

> Whalsay families show a remarkable stability in their domicili-
> ary histories. For many people "home" is not just where one
> resides at present, nor even where one was born: it is "lineage"
> territory, the tiny, finite space in which much of one's history
> is located. As such it [the Scottish croft] is a fundamental
> referent of personal identity. *Through nicknaming it often
> becomes a referent of social identity.* (Emphasis mine)

The croft qua place in Whalsay, like the locational names of person in the Faeroes, are fundamental to social association. Such local-izing of person onto geography makes geography a dominant so-ciological frame of reference for individuals. For Faeroese, personal names that emanate from geographic names are fundamental badges of belonging not just somewhere, but in very particular places.

The types of persons' names discussed so far in this chapter are used in everyday dialogue. Despite their preponderance, they are informal names, and there appears no written list of them any-where. As mentioned, nowadays there are more formal last names, surnames. As if the identity with place via informal names was not enough, Faeroese, as we see below, even in the use of formal, written surnames, also use place-names.

Villagers' first names are usually biblical, as in Páll (Paul) and Maria (Mary); from Northern sagas, as in Sigmund or Turið; or old Norse names like Sverri, Egil, and Finn. Their *surnames* (*stam-nøvn*) are mostly Danish or Danicized names used with Christian names for official purposes such as voting, bank accounts, and birth certificates. Official Sumbøur land records, kept by Danes and Faeroese district officers for the benefit of taxes, indicate that, like homestead names, current Danish and Danicized last names go at least as far back as 1584. Last names ending in the Danish -*son* are often versions of the Faeroese patronymic -*sen*. As men-tioned, villagers rarely use last names in speech, and consequently they downplay formality and external Danish influence. Another reason that surnames often do not appear in ordinary conversation or in place-names is that the small population and intravillage marriages have led, over the years, to many families' sharing the same last names. In Sumbøur in 1984 seven surnames—Poulsen, Kjaerbo, Thomsen, Vestergaard, Jacobsen, Joensen, and Midjord—belonged to 157 villagers, nearly half the population. Almost all native villagers can trace their ancestry to fewer than twenty families.

In 1852 a Danish ordinance applied to the Faeroes required that at christening a child had to receive a family or surname. Formally, patronymics and other informal last naming were to be replaced, but informally Faeroese very much continued the use of the patronymic *hjá* and the use of locational nicknames. Since indigenous naming custom had always incorporated place-names, some Faeroese made it known that their official last names were to be partly or entirely Faeroese. Regin í Lið, (Regin 'in Gate'), (1871–1962) for example, wrote the first Faeroese novel, *Babelstornið (The Tower of Babel)*, and Mikkjal Danjalsson á Ryggi ('on Ridge'; 1879–1956) was a well-respected poet.

Moreover, some nationalist-minded Faeroese have begun to officially change their written Danish or Danish-style last names partly or entirely to Faeroese surnames, although surnames themselves are really Danish phenomena. These surnames use place-names and epitomize the cultural focus on placedness. Some such names in Sumbøur like Jon Kjaerbo sunnan Á (Jon Kjaerbo 'south of the Stream') combine a Danish last name (Kjaerbo) with a Faeroese place-name (sunnan Á), specifically from Sumbøur. Other last names use only Faeroese words. One family officially changed (*keypt*—literally "bought") its last name from Poulsen to Nónaklettur, Faeroese for 'Three O'Clock Rock', a large skerry off the village coastline. (The name 'Three O'Clock Rock' derives, one Sumbingur stated, from practices of the old days when milkmaids would parade to outlying pastures to milk the cows "when the sun was lined up with a big rock, about three o'clock in the afternoon.")

Other Faeroese surnames include Nólsoy and Hamrabrekka—Nólsoy refers to the island Nólsoy, and Hamrabrekka ('Bluff Slope') refers to a part of the village named for those features. The hundreds of place-names make the number of possible Faeroese surnames almost limitless. Now official, these names proudly invoke a local naming system. They point to an attitude of some that locational names for person, in addition to being informal and in contrast to Danish and continental officiality, *ought* to be officially Faeroese. Standing up for being Faeroese can entail formally recognizing and stating one's connection to the land. Such a geographic ethos is at the heart of the culture.

Names, Kinship, Social and Political Relations

Names are helpful in understanding Faeroese identity and relationships, internal and external, formal and informal. The prolific use of spatial names over kin names aligns with the probably greater importance of spatial alliances rather than kinship alliances outside the nuclear family. Despite the densely interlocking kinship system, or perhaps because of it, villagers do not necessarily feel strong obligations to their siblings once they grow up.

Although a person traces kinship bilaterally, patrilineal descent assigns people to a patrilineage associated with an ancestor and his property, his homestead. Terms sometimes used for the lineage include *fólk* or the Danicism *familjia*, attached to the formal last names. For example, a person is part of the Poulsenfólk or familjia Poulsen. I found the use of such terms rare (but see Wylie 1974:262–63). Neolocal residence, however, in which a newly married couple moves into a house of their own, weakens multigenerational patrilineality as did the breakup of landholding in the nineteenth and twentieth centuries.

Danish-style surnames connect people with extravillage economic and political institutions, and their very existence points to the historical (colonial) links with Denmark. Danish related names and Danish rule undercut individuality and local control over village life by working against the informality and familiarity so characteristic of village life. Thus, the Faeroese generally eschew formality and officialdom. Having been more or less isolated and self-sufficient for hundreds of years, villagers have a distaste for colonial or arrogant behavior, although most Faeroese are not bitter about their belonging to Denmark after the abolishment of the trading monopoly in 1856.

Other, less formal naming methods separate villagers from Danish and Faeroese officials and the written formality of the external world. Until about 125 years ago, Faeroese was primarily an oral language. Historically, informal methods of naming and communication tend to disregard any class or social status distinctions or differences between everyday and the "high," literate culture of formally well educated Danes or others. Thus, in contemporary cultural studies terms, the Faeroese vernacular forms of naming comprise "popular culture."

Nowadays lineages are not corporate groups, however. A lineage acts as a historical framework and a source of collective reputations, but little more. Large extended families or social and economic alliances that might otherwise be formed on the basis of common ancestors are absent because of neolocality, the interlocking cognatic relations, and the multiple naming systems. Migration of newlywed women into villages cross-links families and villages. In the tight settlement pattern with little privacy, the lack of strong kinship ties outside immediate families permits freedom of movement and flexibility in gossip.

Not even adult brothers, sisters, or first cousins are necessarily close. One man said he had as little as possible to do with one of his brothers and that brother's wife. Another said that he visited his brother a few houses away only once or twice a year and that occasional unplanned street encounters were enough. J. D. Freeman (1961) and C. N. Appell (1967) point out that bilateral kin reckoning provides people with a set of relationships that they can, but need not, exploit. By themselves, bilateral kin ties do not set up systems of obligation. Freeman (210) concludes:

> An even more important feature [than the gradation of obligations] of the kindred in bilateral societies is that it presents an individual with a wide range of optative relationships—relationships which, in the absence of any binding descent principle, it is possible for him to accentuate as he pleases or as suits his special interests. Thus . . . a man's kindred represents a field in which he is able to move largely at will.

While Faeroese kinship does channel some social contact and exchange of help, especially within a household, choice of social interchange is the rule. Among other reasons discussed above, it is in part because of the nonrestrictive blood and marital ties, I suggest, that attachment to space and spatial history is of great importance to the Faeroese. The looseness of social bonds goes hand in hand with cardinal features of Faeroese culture—individualism, egalitarianism, and spatial attachment and identity. (For more discussion of the Faeroese kinship system see Blehr 1963, Wylie 1974, Gaffin 1987.)

Thus, in the Faeroes, geography reveals itself as the metaphor of membership in communities. Even if there is no explicit place-names identifier in a person's commonly used name, as in some nicknames that do not refer to place, there are always associations between a person and particular places. A person potentially has several locational nicknames, whether frequently used or not. The man commonly called Andrew is from 'on the Rock'; lives at 'the House of Jaspur', in the sector 'Cowpath Flat'; and is a Sumbingur and a Suðuringur. House, homestead, village part, village, and island are immediately and necessarily parts of his (named) social identity. Thus Faeroese belong to their environment and their society at various levels of inclusion/exclusion, depending upon whom one is speaking to. Spatial association orders social identity.

Villagers' use of names not only reflects individuals' membership/participation in the community, but also sociopolitical relations. That is, Faeroese naming practices express and support social equality. Each person enjoys equal access to the public, orally transmitted knowledge of the origins and tales of place- and person names and the information encoded in names. Each person has access to the places people are named after. Each person equally has available a wealth of geographic, house, homestead, village sector, and other place-based names to identify others as he/she chooses.

This parity of naming differs strikingly from hierarchical and class-based communities where first names and surnames, titles, (e.g., Sir, Mr., Mrs.) and ranks (e.g., Supervisor Jones) are used in everyday social situations to indicate status differences. Also, vast differences in sizes of landholdings in less egalitarian contexts outside the archipelago let landholders keep large areas of (named) land private. Such conditions prohibit common access to and knowledge of the landscape.

The Faeroese landscape is public and portioned into more or less equal landholdings. Although much land in the Faeroes is privately owned, there are no keep-out signs and no class markers denying or permitting access to certain locations. (Even the open views and lack of trees contribute to the publicness of land.) Each person's land is worthy of a name, and each person potentially also has the power to invent and to place names on the landscape, to participate in the experience of naming places. Place-names comprise a nomenclature of egalitarianism, a simultaneous spatial and social order.

The long history and continuing use of locational names, alongside the less-used but nonetheless officially important surnames, illustrate the nature of Faeroese relationships to Denmark and the outside world. Denmark represents the formal, external world. Although Danish surnames, Danish priests, Danish laws, Danish food, Danish economic assistance, and so on have been around for a long time, as especially evident in the capital, villagers' daily lives seem mostly independent and informal. But they are not completely separate. Although village ethos, feeling, and most customs are clearly indigenous to the Faeroes, one should not forget official and financial ties to Denmark.

Faeroese society has historically been a peasant/fisherman one with many aspects of that way of life and thinking still extant in village life. A peasant community, however, is also a "part community" (Redfield 1960). By that he means that it is connected to an external system of economics and politics. Outside authorities determine the prices of items produced as well as lay down laws and appoint officials for their application. This, as we already know, is well the case of the Faeroes, despite their nearly complete self-reliance in previous centuries. Any rural people, as we might want to call Faeroese village society, exists in relation to urban and international forces and figures. Most Sumbingar do keep one ear and eye open to the outside world. Although certainly connected to external forces especially through many fishermen's employment on Norwegian and Faeroese commercial vessels, Sumbingar nevertheless, perhaps more than other villagers living closer to the capital, conceptualize their world as a quite local one. Most of the time Sumbingar are distant from the class-based differences of continental urban living. The primarily inward, local purview thus reinforces the longtime individuality and individualism of Faeroese culture and manifests itself in great part in use of informal locational names. Since villagers tend not to emphasize even extrafamilial social groupings, people mark each other namewise without respect to social, political, or economic affiliation. This contrasts with affiliation and names of clan, totem, club, occupation, class, caste, and the like in other cultures. In this way Faeroese individuals maintain their importance as the primary units of the egalitarian system. Locational names avoid focus on social or political groups that potentially might compete for attention or status and thus undercut social equality.

The environs of Sumbøur, therefore, become a world of individuals, a world of places, a world of events that continue to vibrate for its inhabitants. Local places and the people of those places take on extreme significance. It is the world that one belongs to and sees every day and hears about and creates. It animates not simply with activities of subsistence but with names, events, experiences, and personality traits.

Characters and Characteristics of Place

So far I have discussed in general the ways in which Faeroese attach themselves to the landscape and the landscape attaches to them. We have yet to take a look at the psychological and social "experience of place" and the intertwining personalities and sensoria of people and place. Space is not just physical, but also social: it is "socially constructed" (Rodman 1992).

The author Tony Hiss (1990:3–4) terms humans' sensory ability to be linked to their surrounding's "simultaneous perception":

> Both the pinpoint focus of ordinary perception, which lets us shut ourselves off from our surroundings, and the broad-based focus of simultaneous perception, which keeps us linked to our surroundings, are inherited skills built into each of us. People sometimes get so good at blotting out the sights and sounds and smells around them that simultaneous perception, when it resurfaces, can catch them by surprise . . . whenever we summon it, it's richly informative.

Thus people are not always fully perceptually aware or informed of their environs. Individuals often unconsciously follow the thinking, habits, and habitus of their culture in experiencing their environment.

People's awareness and responsiveness to aspects of the environment and the degrees of importance accorded them vary with the immediacy and obviousness of environmental features, methods of subsistence, and cultural preoccupations. Faeroese connections to their environs are enhanced and in part mediated by the abundant place-names. Thus names, when simultaneous perception is operating, help to invoke cultural experience(s) of various kinds, from the gustatory to the supernatural. A sheepfold at 'Sheepfold Point', for example, or a fowling cliff foothold like 'Big Ledge' can incorporate sensory relationships to landscape. Like the places they represent, names often emanate moods and feelings. They all contribute to the dominant aesthetic of place. Particular visual, auditory, olfactory, and tactile experiences affix to locations. In some places the sea air fills your nostrils, or the spray wets your face. Even flavor sensations can adhere to place-names—some sheep graze on certain guano-enriched pastures near bird cliffs and provide the consumer with sought-after tastes. The quality of skerpikjøt and fresh mutton, as with food everywhere, in part depends on the immediate conditions of their production. With the direct knowledge of one's dinner having originally grazed on a certain patch of ground, a man's family literally tastes meat from a particular (named) place. As we have seen, some shepherds even bid for a season's usufruct rights on certain pastures so that they can fatten their sheep to a prestigious size and prized taste.

Local sheep and birds not only provide Faeroese food but are, of course, the bases of cultural activities, beliefs, and rituals connected with shepherding, fowling, and the preparation of food. These ethnic activities, associations, and images derive from known places of their own environs. They literally and symbolically contribute to family, village, regional, and national identities.

Experiences in Place

The Faeroese ongoing use of place-names for people far surpasses the degree of significance in English last names like "Smith" or "Smithy," historically referring to the place of a smith's occupation, or "Highgate," deriving from a landscape feature. Faeroese names based on place are still very much "alive" in that people can see or pass by in their daily lives the places attached to people. At the simplest level place-names refer to what one visualizes as part of a landscape—the topography and architecture of the land. The same name also implicitly refers to the place's history and associated personalities.

An out-of-the-way place on Suðuroy where ▶
electric power is generated.

Some pieces of land, as shown, have individuals' first names attached such as the infields Símunfield and 'Haldan's Wife's Field' or the fishing bank 'Aksal's Spot'. There are many others that historicize events, with or without direct reference to the person. One man said 'Girl's Pool' is where a girl drowned and 'Maria's Chasm' is where a village woman met her own demise by jumping into the sea. 'Gormund's Chasm', another man affirmed, was "probably [named] after Gormundur, a sailor from another village who sought a calm shelter in that cove during some very difficult weather, perhaps one hundred years ago." And another place, 'Dog's Chasm', the story goes, is where a dog, thrown by a villager into the sea, escaped drowning through an under-island passageway. Naming associated with a place often freezes particular social moments.

In efforts to construct a place-name map of the Sumbøur area, I spoke, among others, with Albert 'in the High Cowpath', a knowledgeable, longtime former resident of Sumbøur who now lives in a neighboring village. With little prompting, he talked for hours about places and place-names—their etiology; the quality of land for grazing, planting, beauty, connected events; associated past and present people and their relationships to others; and so forth. It was just such an experience that led me to realize that simple words for specific locations brim with associations. Place-names are mnemonics of social knowledge. They bring social history to the present and help to understand and preserve relationships. They are forums around which to gossip and storytell and maintain social control. Meaning and social structure converge in the named partitions of the landscape.

Through names villagers externalize society, and degrees of familiarity with individuals and groups, onto place. 'Under the Bluff', for example, like any village section, has a unique variety of topographic qualities, social flavors, and social histories. There one finds the House of Egil, whose namesake, the hard-drinking brother of Jon, related through grandparents to Regin, is now married to Dagny. 'Under the Bluff' also contains 'House of George' and 'Stonehouse'. Also, Hjartvar's stubborn father, who lives in another sector of the village, shares grazing land in 'Pigeon's Shelter', the large expanse of outfield, co-owned with three other families, all of whom live in 'under the Bluff'. One could delineate and dissect kinship linkages, social ties, family histories, infamous

Gormundsgjógv ('Gormund's Chasm') along the coast southeast of the village. Like nearly every place delineated by a name, it too has its own history.

events and the like ad infinitum. Of course residents of 'under the Bluff' and others directly related or connected to those who live there have deeper, more complex associations than those who live elsewhere. One's information and experiences of place vary. But it is in just this varied overlapping and independent knowledge and experience of place and person that the environs cognitively and emotionally vibrate with ongoing meaning.

Furthermore, as people interact with the environment, places and their names take on added history. Local events and legends can further "locate" through association with known places. For example, 'Wide Chasm' is where the man Hjartvar played as a child and was hit by a rock that permanently damaged his hearing. Similarly 'Black Magic Rock', in addition to its original fame as a supernatural place, is also the location where Tummas tripped and broke his leg. Local history is an amalgam of tales associated with particular places.

Social Commentary

In everyday social discourse villagers sometimes directly or indirectly use place-names as symbolic statements about place and person. Often encoded in place-names and persons' names are various messages, especially in the ongoing social judgments and creative dialogue of everyday conversation. One might temporarily or permanently use someone's locational nickname like Egil 'up on the Bluff' to associate the elevation of the 'up on the Bluff' section of the village with the person's own "elevated" ego. Or a villager might say that someone acting pompously ought to live there. Sometimes the associations and meanings are multiple. One multiply meaningful appellation using place is the mocking nickname 'Landmaster', partly derived from a place-name. It literally refers to the owner of 'The Land By the Edge', a pasture on the outskirts of the village. Social commentary implicit in the nickname, though, alludes to both the fact that the man has larger landholdings than most other villagers and that he acts arrogantly, as if he is "master" over other villagers. Locational nicknames can be powerful shapers of social assessments.

Villagers may even use patronymics to make social evaluations. Sumbingar know a father's or husband's personality and reputation and can incorporate that knowledge in a patronym. For example, on the surface, George hjá Gunnar simply means Georg son of Gunnar or Georg 'at the house of Gunnar'. Yet in conversation it may also mean that Georg lives at *that* house and is the son of *that* Gunnar, a particular person known for foolishness. By saying Georg hjá Gunnar, a villager, knowing that the listener has similar conceptions of the father's behavior, may imply that as the son of a fool, living at the house of a fool, Georg is himself foolish. Especially if Georg has another, more popular name in village dialogue, choosing the patronym stresses the judgment of social characteristics of place and person.

With typical Faeroese pithiness and wry humor, nicknames, locational and otherwise, are often amusing and socially penetrating. Seemingly straightforward, 'Girl of the Cove' is the nickname of a lady who lives by the cove of a village section that is itself named 'Cove'. However, in addition to doubly identifying where the lady geographically lives, at the cove of 'Cove', one villager said that the name can imply that she is not only geographically but socially "a harbor to anyone," i.e., sexually promiscuous.

Individuals may either give places personalities and/or take on the personalities of places. For example, within the local peasant/fisherman worldview, post office work is not highly valued. It contrasts with the demanding physical activity of fishermen and laborers. Accordingly, the very name Leif 'Post Office' may carry with it a negative connotation, whenever a speaker wants to invoke that aspect of the name. On the other hand, Sigmund 'Stonehouse', raised in the village's oldest stonehouse, connotes tradition, strength, and "solid" character. Similarly a man from another village told me that Sumbøur's 'in the Rock' homestead produces clever people. Thus as individuals descend from particular houses and families, Faeroese note them for the peculiarities of where they were raised. This is a belief, in part, in the inheritance of psychological and social traits of place. So homestead names and patronyms can imply predecessors' traits—through generations some families are "good" or "bad" (Gaffin 1987:110–14). This can go on for many generations. One villager said that a man he knew was prone to violence because the man was brought up on a particular homestead of a nearby village. Reportedly the man's violent temperament descended from the sixteenth-century Faeroeman of the (now-written) legend of *Snopprikkur*.

And some place-names are created to make social statements and reflect egalitarian norms as applied to changes in the village. During the summer of 1984 the town council of Sumbøur employed local men to repair the village road and side streets. In one area workers widened and paved a dirt road. To prevent earth from coming down upon the construction site, they built a concrete retaining wall. The wall became known as 'the Berlin Wall' (Berlinarmúrin), reportedly because the construction took so long. The village wall, like the real Berlin Wall, took on emotional and social significance as the product of a "great," unnecessarily lengthy task. In a village whose people prize being *raskur* ("hard-working," "able," "quick") and where supervisors often have reputations for unnecessary assertiveness and "wasting time in talk," the nickname mocks the importance of the wall and the construction supervisor. In mentioning the name and recounting the wall's history, villagers exhibit their leveling techniques and powers of scrutiny.

Village and Island Reputation

Natives also attribute social characteristics and personality types to entire villages and islands. All over the islands Faeroese think that people from Suðuroy are more talkative and humorous than people in the north of the archipelago. A Faeroese friend of mine, who grew up on Suðuroy, yet now lives in the north, recently wrote me about humor in Sumbøur itself: "Again I must remind you that some of this [Sumbøur] culture is not so predominant in other parts of the Faeroes." Thus, like people, villages also have reputations: one is known for joviality, another for physical strength, one for somberness, another for contentiousness. Islands-wide belief also has it that Sumbingar are cantankerous. Some of these attributed traits of Sumbingar and others have ecological explanations (see Netting 1986). Cantankerousness, it appears, comes from their more than usual isolation from other villages over the centuries and their need to fend for themselves, even under the attack of pirates. Another trait of Sumbingar is their reputed quickness in wit and motion, ecologically derived from the need to negotiate boats in especially rough waters. One former resident of the village explains:

> People from other villages have always been slower. Slower in words and slower in turns. But Sumbingar have been very quick for turning [on their feet onto and off boats]. They don't need to look over things much when there is something to do. It has always been useful to be so because they have lived in a brimpláss (a village with dangerous landings], and also by a big cliff. It requires being quick—there is not a long time to look around when the surf comes in at a brimpláss. One must be quick and think quickly. And the same with the cliffs . . . They [Sumbingar] could manage themselves well. It was their distinction.

Even within a small landmass, geographic separations and minor differences in subsistence activities can distinguish inhabitants. Each village, each group, of the island is truly special, and part of that uniqueness is explained ecologically by natives.

The Characters of Place

In small communities like Sumbøur, where everyone to one extent or another is familiar with the names, background, personality, and location of others, each person becomes literally and symbolically rooted in common village history. Each person is a known element in the social system and the landscape. Individuals' physical characteristics, personalities, habits, and activities embed in the very associations of place and person and many of these conceptualizations are shared by members of the community. David Canter (1977) in *The Psychology of Place* uses the term "consensa" to designate these shared images or commonly held conceptualizations of a place. "They serve as clear symbols in the landscape of the beliefs and attitudes upon which place meaning is defined" (Jakle 1987:162). And being a Sumbingur, a true member of the community, entails common conceptual participation in a vast and complex web of knowledge and associations of the social (and physical) environment.

In great contrast to large urban communities, in Sumbøur each person is little differentiated by differences in clothing, economic status, education, nationality, religion, and so on. Any differences between villagers thus become crucial features of distinction. As in other communities, like monasteries, nunneries, parochial schools, or prisons, differences between Sumbingar revolve primarily around physical characteristics, habits, and personality.

Moreover, treeless landscape vistas, open ocean views, and the usually gray skies often make foreground and close-up detail much more observable. Contrasts between items and people close at hand draw attention and gain importance. People who grow up in small communities are often more familiar with the notion that each human is quite distinctive, in contrast to the near unnoticeableness of individuals in large enclaves. Perception of person is thus in part a consequence of settlement size.

In Sumbøur each person has substantial character, and people seem to be caricatures of themselves. Each person has strong mental images of who lives where and what their personality is like. Since place and local talk about others are so crucial, the socially discussed and created characteristics of individuals make life there an intense drama. Indeed, many of the originally oral, now-written, local legends tell how a feature of the landscape received its name or relate how a person's reputation and nickname grew from an event that occurred in a certain place.

John Berger (1979:8), in a nonfiction introduction to his short stories, explains peasant village culture:

> Most of what happens during a day is recounted by somebody
> before the day ends. The stories are factual, based on observa-
> tion or on a first-hand account. . . . Sometimes there is a moral
> judgment implicit in the story, but this judgment—whether just
> or unjust—remains a detail: the story *as a whole* is told with
> some tolerance because it involves those with whom the story-
> teller and listener are going to go on living. Very few stories are
> narrated either to idealise or condemn; rather they testify to
> the always slightly surprising range of the possible. Although
> concerned with everyday events, they are mystery stories. How
> is it that C . . . , who is so punctilious in his work, overturned
> his haycart? How is it that L . . . is able to fleece her lover J
> . . . of everything. And how is that . . . ?

Thus everyday life and person are partly mysterious. With a "surprising range of the possible" and with the tentativeness of activity
in the capricious Land of Maybe, Sumbøur—its people and its
places—takes on even added enigma. The environs are the sets and
the settings of distinctive spaces and individuals in a large mystery
and morality play.

My own notion that life in Sumbøur is an intense drama of
unique characters set on a remarkable stage seems not to be just
something that I perceived as a newcomer getting to know people
in a new place. Natives, as well as other short- and long-term
visitors to the Faeroes, have also remarked on the dramatic setting
and on the "basaltic solidarity" of the people (Brønner 1973). My
friend and informant Albert 'in the High Cowpath', mentioned
above, wove inseparably into his discussion of places and people
around Sumbøur the personality of its inhabitants. Jonathan Wylie
(1974:30–31) says that "One could practically write an ethnography
of a Faeroese village by following around the stories behind the
names of its places and inhabitants." Previously I (1987) have also
discussed how verbal caricature is very Faeroese.

Feeling Sumbøur to have its own dramatis personae when I was
there, I developed my own written character sketchbook of residents. I wrote down the names of many individuals, described their
look and their habits, and jotted down anecdotes and events about
them as I experienced them and as they were told to me by others.
Some sketches are a page or more long. At the time, I thought that
I would use the character sketches as material for writing a novel
about life in the village. Later I came to realize that in some ways

an ethnography like this one is much like a novel. This book, with its own intents to portray, highlight, and interpret the lives of a particular community, itself selects individuals and topics through which I dramatize and philosophize.

In my sketchbook there are written portraits of people like Ele from 'the House of Egil', who wears sunglasses, rare for a man, and a pair of old Faeroese leather sock-slipper boots. There's Jon 'on the Heap', a *pinkalitil* ("perfectly little") man who lives in the little red house at the corner of the one-lane road to Bartal's and the road coming from 'the Turn'. There's Anna Sofía, 'the Doll', with a golden complexion to match her hair, perhaps the only unmarried older woman in the village. There's Jutta, the false-toothed woman who keeps her house impeccable with her always-moving broom. She always refers to herself in the first person, as in "Jutta is fine, today, thank you" or "Jutta is going to the store now." Then there's Sigvarð, a grumpy man, who shares sheepfields with Sune, and the friendly Ole 'under the Smithy', the noted balladeer, who talks incessantly to me without prompting. And others. Like the observations of anyone, native or visiting anthropologist, my collection is a compilation of visual impressions, judgments, and consensa.

Each villager has such observable character and profundity. Each living out his/her life in an isolated wind-swept scene. A person's character, like one's geographic identity, is special, not lost in the crowd. Each experience of person, like experience of place, is unique. A whole book could be written or told about a person. And since each person is more or less equally part of the village scene, each potential life story is a meaningful portion of history.

With each individual as a larger-than-life feature and landmark of local history, a caricature of place and person, a kind of mystique and magicalness pervades village life. In its juxtaposition with the ordinary, each person, like each place, becomes extraordinary. Each person, of the present and the past, is a legendary figure. The legendary, surreal nature of each person contributes to the ultimately mysterious quality of Faeroese life and culture.

In the context of Western formal art, especially in surrealist painting, this phenomenon is termed "magic realism." H. Harvard Arnason (1977:314) defines it as

> a mode of representation that takes on an aura of the fantastic because commonplace objects are presented with unexpectedly exaggerated or detailed forthrightness. . . . precisely delineated

>recognizable objects, distorted and transformed, but neverthe-
>less presented with a ruthless realism that throws into shock-
>ing relief their newly acquired fantasy. (308)

In the lighting of the open ocean sky and in the light of Faeroese subsistence and society, there is a merging of the place and the person, the simple and the profound, the ordinary and the magical.

To Sumbingar the physical environment is a *vital* source of experience. Some modern architects and planners have generally investigated the characteristics of natural and built landscapes to try to help create such vital environments for people in cities and elsewhere. For example, Christopher Alexander et al. (1977) developed an extensive list of aspects of rooms, streets, and districts that link with joyful experiences, that "make people feel alive and human" (xvii). The experience of one's immediate environment clearly affects one's thinking, attitude, and aesthetic.

Faeroese conceptions of areas ranging from the archipelago as a whole to a particular house provide rootedness in space and society. And villagers' familiarity with much of other inhabitants' lives and histories contribute to how they paint intimate social and cultural pictures of one another that are significant to social identity. Villagers' portraiture and sculpting of covillagers is central to the culture. Berger (1979:8–9) finds similar words to describe French peasants:

>What distinguishes the life of a village is that it is also a living
>portrait of itself: a communal portrait, in that everybody is
>portrayed and everybody portrays. As with the carvings on the
>capitols in a Romanesque church, there is an identity of spirit
>between what is shown and how it is shown—as if the portrayed
>were also the carvers.

Unlike anonymous life in large urban settlements, each French peasant or Faeroese villager participates in the public arena and takes part in contributing to the characteristics of the place. Villagers are not sheltered from the trials and tribulations of life, the joys and the sorrows, the births and the deaths. Encoded in the landscape are the various possibilities of human behavior, although many are yet to be revealed. Faeroese people partake in the topography, architecture, and society that play off one another to create singular senses of social space. People *are* landmarks (Gaffin 1994).

Chapter Five
Proximity, Social Behavior, and Social Control

T he word *place* in English has many layers of meaning. It can refer literally to a general location, to a particular type of place like a village, and/or to a specific location with local connotations such as 'Black Magic Rock'. Over and above these territorial meanings, *place* can also refer to the "place" of someone in the community or the putting of something or some behavior in its proper "place." Belonging in the spatial order of things carries over into belonging in the normative order of things.

If a villager feels attached to the community as a physical or geographic entity, then one is likely to feel attached to and invested in the community as a social entity, since so much of villagers' social identities are bound to place. Faeroese village social control is also built into the cooperative work of subsistence. Communal institutions like whaling and shepherding help maintain social order in general. As cultural ecologist John Bennett (1993:187) concludes, common property institutions make for "high demands on conformity and austerity." As one becomes socialized into economic and social practices of a more or less single culture setting, phenomena like nicknames, local history, gossip, and stories subtly yet powerfully support and correct learning. Culture members come to internalize the worldview, the basic values and perspectives of the community. This is especially true in Sumbøur where the past plays such a major role in supporting a local identity and where the pace of change has been relatively slow, even compared with other places within the archipelago.

Spatial Proximity

In the isolated nucleated settlement pattern there is close observation of others' behavior. Most social contacts occur in the street,

117

in shops, or as part of work routines. Larger gatherings occur at religious affairs, dances, or occasional group social activities. In summer people gather casually by the harbor dock, or if there is a game, by the soccer field. Except for religious services, face-to-face meetings are informal.

The village has a post office; a mission house; two general stores; two kiosks for bread, coffee, candy, cigarettes, and so on, open only in the evening; two banks, one open only six hours a week, the other about fifteen hours; one communal activity house; and a small dance house. The stores, kiosks, banks, and post office are all parts of what were or are family dwellings. The village has no real center, although the two main shops are about in the middle. At one end is the small harbor and dock, at the other, the road leading out of town. The village is laid out generally along one long road with houses bordering both sides. There are also two or three short side roads with houses along them and two or three slightly more distant clusters of a few houses.

Sumbøur's post office is on the ground floor of this building (residents live above it).

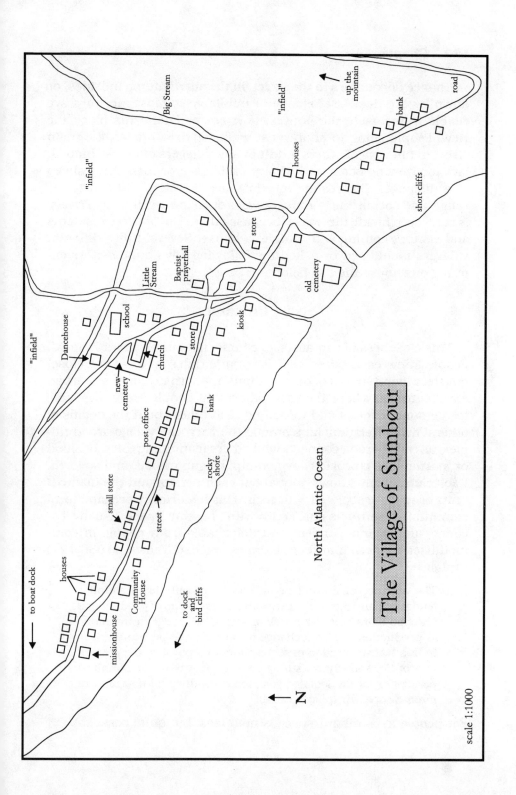

The Village of Sumbour

scale 1:1000

Chance encounters in the street, in the surrounding hillsides, or down by the dock are usually in public view. Most meetings are visible from inside the houses; no trees or landforms block the view. People going to shop must walk (or drive) down the main street in full view of others. Additionally, villagers often use binoculars for viewing boats and whales on the sea or identifying sheep at a distance. Clandestine meetings are therefore difficult to arrange, and socializing is almost always open to surveillance. Privacy is rare, even inside the house, because others can observe residents and visitors coming and going to a house. Several times different villagers mentioned or asked the following day about visitors entering our house the day before.

Social Proximity

This closeness of contact is, of course, not simply observational. People know each other well. It is quite different from the close-quarters living spaces of other nations' modern urban or suburban environments, where the vast majority of people are unavailable for personal contact and for telling each other about the details of others' lives. Relationships among the Faeroese village are multiplex, as each person connects with others in multiple roles, of blood or marital ties, cowork, coownership, neighborhood, and so forth. Each Sumbingur knows a lot about each person and the (named) units of space associated with each. This historically peasant, local community contrasts markedly with the way space usually becomes almost independent and detachable from people in commoditized modern market economies. Michael Taussig (1980:121) explains:

> The advance of market organization not only tears asunder
> feudal ties and strips the peasantry of its means of productions
> but also tears asunder a way of seeing. A change in the mode
> of production is also a change in the mode of perception. . . .
> In this transformation of society and metaphysics, the perception of the socially constituted self gives way to the atomized
> perception of the isolated maximizing individual as a unit of
> *mass-space*. (Emphasis mine)

For people in Sumbøur space is not mass, but quite personal.

Time has not dramatically changed Sumbingars' direct economic relations to the immediate landscape. In the Faeroes there long remained a mixed economic base without marked macroeconomic changes up until the turn of this century, and then mostly with respect to sea-going activities. Thus there has long been stability in both subsistence and in social order. (A 1973 study of homicides on the islands showed that there had been only two murders since 1877, one in 1967 and another in 1970 (Joensen and Hansen 1973).) Even if someone wanted to commit crimes of some sort, in the context of the topography and settlement pattern, villagers would have a very difficult time being unobserved and/or escaping quickly.

Distances between population enclaves, especially prior to the introduction of the automobile, made intervillage contact and travel somewhat difficult. Thus villages have come in great part to be social worlds of their own. Some villagers, especially women who generally do their work in and around the house, have hardly left the village. One older woman in Sumbøur said that she had left the village only twice, once to go to the capital Tórshavn and once to another village on the island. Her social interests and world, like that of many other villagers, is nearly 100 percent local. Even with the recent growth of a more cosmopolitan extravillage perspective, for many women especially, shopping at the local store, participating in local religious affairs and fishermen's dinners, and impromptu meetings at the kiosk in the evening become the focal points of social life and ground the person in local affairs and society. This intense localness deters social alienation that could otherwise lead to social disorder. Such a spatial orientation makes for stability and the maintenance of social control.

Travel within the village is mostly done on foot and permits easy visiting. Etiquette surrounding visiting is informal, like nearly everything in village life. Faeroese let people enter their homes with little, if any, ceremony. Knocking is not customary. Anyone may find someone else inside his home at any moment. Although locked doors are a little more popular now than years ago, many houses are left open when no one is home. Locked doors during the day could mean something unusual or secretive is happening behind them, like excessive drinking or sexual activity. Sometimes a villager might knock on an inside door to the kitchen or sitting room, if it is closed, or call out a few words. The visitor might wait for a response in the foyer. More usually one walks right into a room where people are sitting, eating, or working. Since the encounters are face-to-face in the house, getting rid of visitors is uncomfortable and unusual, unless the residents are obviously about to leave for work or shopping. Like meetings in the street, visiting is mostly unplanned and incidental. House visits may last for a minute or for several hours. Movement within the general physical and social landscape is quite informal.

Although people occasionally complain afterward about visitors who stay too long, guests are made to feel welcome despite any possible feeling of discomfort. A man complained mildly to me about a neighbor's lengthy visit that stretched into the early hours of the morning. One female neighbor of ours used to grumble that another woman occasionally stopped in with her knitting and spent all day in the kitchen. Another man, Sune, says Sumbingar generally know Marianna as a bad neighbor who does not get along with others because one day during a visit she put Sune's uncle out of her house. Sune proclaimed, "You don't put anyone out of your house." He delivered the line as if it were a commandment.

The longer we stayed in the village and the more drop-in visitors we had, the more I understood the consequences of permissive visiting. A few specific villagers often walked right into our house, expecting tea and a snack, along with a chat. We always, like villagers generally, made sure we had enough tea, coffee, crackers, bread, jam, and so on for a *temun* or *kaffimun* (tea or coffee klatch) at any time. However, we occasionally risked our social reputations by locking our doors during the day so that we could get some uninterrupted work done.

Children, who are generally indulged, come and go even more freely than adults and also contribute to the social proximity of village life. Children's freedom of expression permits an open inquisitiveness that adults do not publicly exhibit face-to-face. The young may see and hear things in people's homes and tell their parents about them. Consequently children's roles in the information network of the village are significant. Parents can rely on their children to keep them up to date on village events.

As Marvin Harris (1983) points out in his cultural anthropology textbook, one of the main reasons for the lack of full-time law enforcement specialists in small-scale, egalitarian societies is the densely interconnected kinship connections. The same holds true for Faeroese villagers, nearly all of them related.

Kin ties are a common topic of conversation when people discuss family history, visitors, and persons from other villages. Villagers pride themselves on knowing the kinship networks of the village and of the islands. When a person's name comes up, conversation runs like the following one, taken from an exchange I had with an older woman. I had mentioned a person I knew who lived in Sumbøur. She responded: "I know Mortan. He is "family" (familjia). My grandfather and the grandmother to his mother were siblings (systkin). So my mother and his grandfather were cousins (systkinabørn). So his mother and I are second cousins (trýmenningar)."

People quickly recite familial and genealogical connections. Through them people continue to piece together local history. As people are well-acquainted with kinship connections of others in the village, kinship becomes part and parcel of the mutual familiarity that dominates social life. No matter how tongue-tied a person may feel, he can always depend upon kinship for conversation. Villagers express their own individuality in their varying positions within the networks and their varying knowledges of the relationships. At the same time they verbally and psychologically reinforce their social connectedness to the community.

In their contact with other villages, the Faeroese desire to know about who is who and where others come from is especially evident. The appearance of an unknown person evokes villagers' avid curiosity about social and spatial connections. My journal reads:

> While waiting in Vágur [neighboring village] inside the summer public transportation van the driver, Arnfinn, observed a boy playing outside. He asked the woman passenger next to him "Who does he belong to?" (Hvør eigur hann?) [literally "who owns him?"]. She did not know. The woman, who had sat in the front seat with the driver three or four times previously when I had been in the van, had often asked the driver the same question about other people.
>
> Arnfinn said again, "Who does he belong to?" Puzzled, he then declared, "I will ask him." He opened his door, stuck his head outside, and yelled over the van to the eight- or ten-year-old boy 20–30 feet away from the side of the road. The boy came over. Arnfinn asked "Who do you belong to?" The boy answered

"Thorleif." The driver responded "So, so." Then Arnfinn asked
the boy to whom does "that other boy over there on the bicycle"
belong? The boy told Arnfinn the names of the other boy's
parents. After a few seconds silence while the boy waited,
Arnfinn said to the boy, "It was only that." Then the boy walked
deferentially away.

Sometimes Faeroese act as if they *have* to know who's who and
from where they come.

Frequently one hears questions like "Who is that over there on
the hillside?" "Who is that talking with Maria?" "What is Tummas
doing behind his house?" "Whose boat is that out east by the
rocks?" and "Where is Anna going?" Villagers stare and strain to
identify passengers in cars, walkers on distant hillsides, or unfamiliar faces in the village. They try to figure out what people are
doing, where they are coming from, and why they are going some-
place. As soon as onlookers identify the people and hypothesize
about their activities, interest wanes. I often observed workmen
and shepherds on mountainsides stop their work, crane their
necks to observe a car or person on the road below them, and then,
suddenly satisfied, return to their work. One can almost hear them
say some approximation of "*Jú* [Yes], that must be Sigvarð, coming
back with Mortan from their fishing trip on the *Norra*."

Men usually stay in their native village or move to a larger town
or the capital for job opportunities. Knowing that social life is
intricate and based in very local history and space, rarely does a
man move to a village of similar size or to a smaller village. The
one exception I knew of in Sumbøur was a young man who moved
into the village from a larger village, setting up a new household
with his wife, born in Sumbøur. But he had taken a job in Sumbøur
as a schoolteacher.

Marriages constantly relink and reinforce kinship connections.
Recent marriages or sexual unions evoke discussion of previously
existing relationships and stories connected with the (potential)
marriage partners. Indeed, any noticeable change in kin and social
relations—two cousins spending more time playing together, a
woman speaking more frequently than usual with her distantly
related neighbor, a man drinking again with his brother—precipi-
tate discussions of personalities and social relationships.

As each person can trace relationships in different ways and is
intimate in different amounts with the spaces and reputations of

individuals, families, and lineages, there is nearly unlimited fuel for conversation. Thus almost every social action can be located in the kinship system.

Everyday Talk and Gossip

Everyday communication and interest centers on others' behaviors. Local life is an ongoing portraiture of village events and relations. Most happenings in a day are told and retold to different people during the day and the days thereafter. The tellings are informed by observation of others as well as by second-, third-, and fourth-hand accounts. Details combine with people's already well-developed knowledge of individuals and places to produce gossip.

By *gossip* I simply mean talk about other people, regardless of the possible moral or judgmental content. Even in larger-scale communities and cities, much of everyday conversation centers on other people. The difference here is in the degree of familiarity people have with one another. In a city much communication is about others the speakers have never met or seen, like movie stars and politicians. And urbanites talk a lot about people met in single roles such as merchant, teacher, doctor, cashier, and so forth. In Sumbøur relationships are many-stranded.

Village gossip allows each and every person to contribute to the defining and control of local life. Social control occurs as people portray each other and discuss local events of the past and present. Gossip is vibrant and personal. As moral lessons are available in the carefully attended-to local talk, more formal methods of social control are less necessary. For example, as other social scientists have noted (e.g., Pitt-Rivers 1971), nicknames in general often comment on individual behavior. Such names point to behavior that if gotten out of hand would jeopardize social order. They also highlight the public scrutiny of village life.

In Sumbøur 'The Fast Walker' is a man who often hastens among a few different houses in a particular part of the village. He usually does not put on outer clothing when moving to and fro between houses. Also, according to three or four informants, he often scurries to these houses trying to cadge drinks to quench his excessive thirst for alcohol. 'The Fast Walker' explicitly describes a physical behavior (walking fast), implicitly describes a personal habit (underdressing), and indirectly refers to immorality (excessive alcohol consumption).

Moral and personality defects appear directly or indirectly in other names like 'Bottles' and 'The Clergyman'. Villagers think 'Bottles' drinks too much beer: he has a lot of bottles around. 'The Clergyman' is a tongue-in-cheek name for a man who is very active in the evangelist movement and thinks of himself, according to some, as very religious. Unordained, he is thought to be self-righteous and fanatical. One person said he is a "clergyman with the devil behind him." Even straightforward, descriptive nicknames can carry extra meaning. 'Fat Frida' literally describes a woman in town. In addition, one villager compared her to a formerly fat person who had "worked" to lose weight, implying that Frida is too lazy to diet. More than mildly derogatory nicknames are not used face-to-face, although everyone knows they exist.

The force of nicknames as warnings against nonconformity is clear. Some of their power lies in their usually untapped potential to make people show anger, itself a sign of weakness. Such lack of personal control can provide even more material for mockery. One man said, "If Mortan heard his nickname when he was drunk, he would get very angry: he wouldn't like it."

Moderate drinking is not uncommon, especially on weekends and holidays. When drinking occurs, there is the ever-present possibility that a temporarily uninhibited man might use a nickname to ridicule someone to his face. Such (rare) face-to-face mockery could lead to more ridicule and counterridicule, which would generally affect people's reputations as well as disturb community tranquility. As no one is immune to mocking names, people are careful not to disturb or anger others for fear of verbal retaliation, immediately or later on.

The informality of most names and the omnipresent possibility of ridicule generally support the nonhierarchical organization of economic and political power. Everyone more or less contributes to the social good and the definitions of "place" and community by being the possible butt of, and perpetrator of, social labeling. In this way everyone is important for a small community. In this virtually crime-free community daily talk levels each person through comments on his or her negative or deviant traits. The community's continuing narrative keeps people in their proper (equal) place. Set Faeroese names and nicknames also help deny human unpredictability, giving the impression that even deviations are foreseeable. They simplify and reduce behavior to controllable, identifiable stereotypes. Such a system works because of close spatial and social proximity within the village.

Villagers' knowledgeability and willingness to exchange information about others appears in many guises: readiness to answer anyone's telephone queries, drivers' stopping to chat on the road, constant talk among men in the baithouses. Sumbingar share information about many things. Common topics include peoples' work (fishing, sheep raising, housekeeping, etc.), romantic relationships, alcohol drinking habits, religious and social activities, holiday events, personality characteristics, and unusual behaviors. A person who fishes in a spot where fishermen do not normally fish, a suspected budding romance, a person's visit to an acquaintance or relative, or someone's loud clothing might provoke comment and discussion.

Often a person telephones someone else, even a stranger, to find a third person's whereabouts. Villagers do not view such calls as intrusive. The islands' telephone book lists the names, phone numbers, addresses, and even occupations of all Faeroese. The back of the book also lists telephone numbers in numerical order, so that anyone can find another's name, occupation, and residence by knowing his or her phone number. One man stated that he could "find out" about any of the forty-six thousand Faeroese by making only three phone calls! Faeroese villagers are well informed about each other and eager to demonstrate what they know.

Concern with collecting information is also observable in villagers' firm habit of listening to radio newscasts. It is especially evident at noontime. Lunch is always punctual, timed to coincide with the noonday news at 12:20 P.M. For twenty or thirty minutes the streets are empty and the shops deserted. Radios play throughout the village—this is the best time to find someone home. Those working too far away to lunch at home invariably bring a radio along. When the news begins, work and conversation cease as people listen. Faeroese are also avid newspaper readers, and, for the small population of the country, produce an astonishing number of publications. The thirst for social knowledge and input and the desire to convey information greatly accounts, I believe, for the large number of Faeroese writers.

Unlike official radio news about national and international affairs, however, local talk is news with no set schedule or formality. Face-to-face news is created by all villagers and is informal. The nonchalance of conversation is evident in how men lean on posts or fences during encounters in the street or in fields. They converse, often without much eye contact, and space themselves not too close and talk not too dramatically. Such social presentation and spatial arrangement seems to say that nothing very important, contentious, or intimate is occurring. The use of personal space in social relations, the proxemics (Hall 1966), thus also demonstrates and supports local ideas about social order.

The local desire to talk about others became quite evident during the language lessons I exchanged with one of the two schoolteachers in Sumbøur. The arrangement was that I was to teach the man English and he would teach me Faeroese. Initially our lessons were somewhat focused. But as we began to know each other better, the lessons turned into general discussions, usually on his part, about other villagers. Instead of learning English he seemed to prefer speaking Faeroese and telling amusing anecdotes and stories about local residents.

Everyday Comments and Deviance

Celebrating the distinctiveness of local life and the characters within it, villagers rejoice in making comments and telling anecdotes about local personalities. Such accounts usually detail or allude to deficiencies or unfavorable character traits. One often hears not so scathing remarks: "Andreas is always driving up and down the road." "Magnus drinks a lot." "Birgir never has anything to do." Or one villager may relate short incidents to another: "Eivindur, when he was pitching hay with his hayfork, stabbed his own foot." Villagers like to amuse each other with such third-person ridicule. Such remarks and other grievances marking more serious social offenses can be linked to values in various aspects of culture such as family, economics, politics, religion, and so on. Not only does each realm of culture have its deviant(s), but each villager is portrayed as deviant with respect to at least one cultural realm.

Some comments describe sexual, familial, or kinship-related activities. One man appeared several times in comments and anecdotes. I heard "Jens is a flirter," "Jens is a lady's man," "They say Jens slept with another woman while his wife was pregnant, about to give birth." Another man revealed to me that Leivur, a married man with three children, was not the "real son" of his father Hilmar. He was the product of a union between his mother, Alma, and another villager, Ólaf, who was married to Marianna. The man said that he thought that Leivur did not know that Hilmar was not his real father. Furthermore he commented that "Alma was all that Hilmar could get [for a wife]."

One day a neighbor of mine told me about Poulina. He said that she was temperamental and unsocial and that every villager knew it. My neighbor, then mentioning that there was a problem between Poulina and her husband asked, "You know that Poulina had a child by another man, a previous husband?" The interjection of the comment seemed to point to more evidence that Poulina was not a respectable person.

Sumbingar practice monogamy and prize female sexual virtue, and I had observed that male-female relations in the village were well defined. Men and women (other than engaged or married couples) would generally avoid being in the company of the opposite sex without a third person nearby. It may not be the case that Jens slept with another woman during his wife's pregnancy, but the searing story gives credence to the possibility that men and women are capable of infidelity. That comment, along with others attributing flirtatiousness to Jens, indicates that villagers notice such sexual antics, that they might lead to infidelity, and that such behavior is subject to public scrutiny and comment. Jens was the only person I had heard about with such a reputation.

The comment about Leivur's parentage, of which he is possibly unaware, is instructive about sexual norms and the desirability of mates with particular traits or stories associated with them. Women with less sexual experience are more desirable mates. Since Hilmar could only "get" a wife who had borne a child by another man, the story implies that he, too, lacks desirable social/sexual qualities.

The comments about Poulina also point to sexual norms and general social skills. Poulina not only broke traditional norms of monogamy and onetime marriage, but the comments imply that Sumbingar link sexual behavior with other personal characteristics. In this way it is possible for villagers to attach a person's deviance in one realm of culture (sexuality) to another (sociability) and in the process for such reputations for deviation to gain power and momentum.

Some comments discuss economic or workaday skills; statements I heard include "a sheep died at Poul's; I don't understand Poul, he is lazy"; "Johan couldn't take the life of the sea"; and "Gunnar is a good foreman, but he is too fiery-tempered." A schoolteacher, a fat person, and a handicapped person are often subjects for derogatory remarks about "not doing anything" or "having nothing to do." Publicly visible physical work—from men's fowling to women's knitting—prevents a man or woman from gaining a reputation for laziness, which wastes precious economic time and material. The comment about Johan also points to the local emphasis on hardiness and seaworthiness.

In the following story drinking alcohol becomes the forum through which storytellers hold forth about another form of socially disapproved behavior. One day Sverre joined a friend of his to buy two cases of liquor from Denmark. They divided up the liquor. After a few weeks Sverre went over to his friend's house to help his friend drink up his share. It seemed that Sverre had already drunk up his own share. When they finished drinking his friend's share, Sverre told his friend that he knew where they could get some more liquor. So Sverre went away and later came back with a bottle. He said that he and his friend had to pay a dear, inflated price because liquor was then scarce. Sverre's friend contributed his share of the price, and then together they drank the more expensive liquor. Later it was discovered that the expensive bottle that Sverre sold his friend was one of the same bottles that he had originally ordered with him. Greedy Sverre is the protagonist of a story that ridicules and complains about those who act against egalitarian and cooperative pursuits.

Other comments refer to the incompetence of town councilors, the fanaticism of those who belong to religious minorities, and the arrogance of particular individuals. People also like to talk about people who are inept in everyday social interaction, especially the shy and those who cannot control their emotions. Angerability is particularly disliked and offensive. "He always becomes angry immediately when someone makes jokes with him"; or "He does not know how to take practical jokes"; or "He is so ill tempered" are favorite comments about some persons. There is a local deviant called the *rukka* ("easily angered fool") who is said to exist on nearly every fishing trawler and exists in several stories about local villagers. Control of emotions is necessary for dangerous, confining small-group fishing, fowling, and whaling pursuits. In a land of self-control, emotional display is dangerous. The link between getting angry and being bad for the community is epitomized in the Faeroese word *óndur*, which means both "angry" and "evil."

The tales and characterizations of everyday conversation are grounded in known spaces and kinship connections. Here one man in his sixties speaks about connections and events a few generations back:

> Stórustova ('Large Sitting Room') and í Hamri ('in the Bluff') [homestead names/lineages] had nothing to do with each other. There wasn't any relationship between them. . . . My great grandmother 'in the Bluff' became a widow. Gamal Erling ('Old Erling') was somehow related to both [lineages]. He went with some dry fish, or rotten fish, to give the widow's family some food to eat, in order for her family not to die of hunger. And she paid him for it. And you can imagine the way she paid it. . . . So we became related through fish, through rotten fish. . . . Well, life is a funny thing.

The identifiable lineages and locations and 'Old Erling', with whom villagers are familiar, tend to make this story believable. They project credibility. Information about other persons can be told over and over again by different villagers, each adding or deleting details as events, memories, moods, or audiences change. In this way information becomes increasingly more public and simultaneously available for exaggeration and distortion. Each time a story is told, it becomes more and more a definitive part of local history. I myself heard villagers' repeated, similar stories and characterizations of each other. The variations added to an underlying uncertainty about what the full truth is/was in any account of the present or past. Yet this uncertainty adds to the ultimate mysteries of human behavior and the notion that there is quite a breadth in "the range of the possible."

Legal Culture

The nicknames, anecdotes, and stories of village conversation often ridicule others in an amusing way. But they are usually not meant to denigrate or be malicious. The tone and intent of such informal communications are crucial in differentiating this ordinary talk about others from the rare talk that is meant to scandalize. Gossip is quite different from scandal (Paine 1970).

Jokes about others are methods of social control. Such amusement acts to deflate the potential seriousness of breaches of cultural norms. They indirectly and informally point out social offenses and inappropriate behaviors. Thus, without official or confrontative actions, people in general receive frequent messages of how one is *not* supposed to act. Most legal, that is, conflict-resolving, methods anywhere utilize grievances as the initiating point of a problem. A grievance is "a circumstance or condition which one person (or group) perceives to be unjust, and the grounds for resentment or complaint" (Nader and Todd 1978:14). A grievance, a feeling of being wronged, may be a consequence of an action taken against someone, but may also, I suggest, be a consequence of any act that offends a person's sense of propriety, regardless of whether the act was done directly to that person. By so extending the concept of grievance, any inappropriate act can become an opportunity to express social values and to impose sanctions (Gaffin 1991). As a member of the community, a person may have a generalized interest in seeing that norms are obeyed. In this way, a person's personal and cultural values tie into general social control. Any act that threatens social order provides an opportunity for people to condemn deviation and express norms. Complaints about anyone's deviance become key to understanding the social order of a community.

Thus the very definition of a community rests in great part on the kinds of behaviors people encourage or discourage in their environment. As one legal anthropologist puts it, "The role of law is particularly apparent in the social construction of space. Law is self-consciously spatial in orientation, and its first concern is to define the boundaries within which it operates" (Engel 1993:130). Boundaries are not only of geography and political jurisdiction, but also of social behavior.

Even indirect ridicule of others is a sanction. Nicknames, gossip, anecdotes, stories, and so on are really forms of indirect conflict resolution and ways of defining appropriate behavior in local space. They function as phenomena of law in the widest sense of that term. That is, talk serves to maintain the social/legal order of the community and fits into the general informality of the local culture of controlling conflict. We can call the various methods of social control, and local ideas about controlling conflict, "legal culture" (Friedman 1969). Thus, legal culture comprises a variety of conscious (and unconscious) ways of dealing with potential or actual conflict. One of the major aspects of Faeroese legal culture is the villagers' own belief that direct, confrontative conflict—argument or aggression—is bad. In line with their preference for the informal, Faeroese try to avoid conflict in great part by focusing on harmony, or at least the outward appearance of harmony.

Thus Sumbingar prize agreeableness, even temper, amiability, and humor in great part because they avoid overt discord and support peacefulness. These are especially practical traits in isolated settlements where people have depended upon one another for their very survival.

One such method of promoting harmony is through repeated customs and conventions of agreement. This ritualized agreement depends upon repeated contact with people of close social and physical proximity, of people who frequently fish, fowl, hay, and play together. Thus we see again the overlap of the ecological setting and the maintenance of social order.

Ritual Agreement

Faeroese are eager to hear what others have to tell, although the rules of proper discourse forbid direct disagreement and dissection of what people say. Only amongst close friends or relatives will people venture to disagree with one another, and even then only politely and mildly. Sharp dissent, considered foolhardy or "stupid," is anathema in village life. Conversation should be pleasant and equable, and villagers specifically accommodate each other through particular uses of language, "fashions of speaking" (Whorf 1941).

Faeroese liberally sprinkle public and private conversation with ritual agreement. Such phrases include *ikki nei* ("isn't it so?"); *ikki sannheit* ("isn't it true?"); *so tann er* ("so it is"); *so er* ("so it is"); *eg meini tað* ("I mean it"); *hvat sigur tú* ("what do you say"); *álvaratós* ("real talk [this is]"); *soleiðis* ("there it is"); *soleiðis er tað* ("that's the way it is"); *ja* ("yeah"); *jú*("yes"); *so* ("so"); *nettupp* ("exactly"); *akkurat* ("just so"/"exactly"); *faktist* ("really!"); *hundrað per cent* ("hundred percent [certain]"); *tað er sikkur* ("it is certain"); and *tað er heilt sikkurt* ("it is quite certain"). Women and occasionally men sometimes use a dramatic pronunciation of *ja* (yes). At the same time as the speaker vocalizes *ja*, she inhales through her mouth. It sounds like gasping for air in accentuated agreement. All these phrases generally keep conversation harmonious.

These conversational expressions also stress the truth of what is said. They are akin to Canadian "ey?", the German *nicht wahr* ("isn't that so?"), and the American "you know." Many of the Faeroese expressions could gloss loosely as "that's the truth" or "isn't it the truth?"

Speakers request direct agreement during conversation by asking "ikki nei?" or "ikki sannheit?" A nod of agreement, or "jú," supports the query. At the end of short or long narratives, speakers use "so tann er," "so er," "soleiðis," and "soleiðis er tað" to mark the reliability of what they say. "Tað er sikkur" or "álvaratós" add emphasis when a person speaks with special candor or makes a point that might be construed as fabrication. Some young persons familiar with vernacular Danish (sometimes derived from English) use "faktist" and "hundrað per cent" instead of "álvaratós."

Listeners say "hvat sigur tú!" to emphasize that the information is novel, although indubitably true (a comparable use would be the American "What do you know about that!"). A speaker says "eg meini tað" rather evenly and slowly at the end of a conversation to emphasize veracity. It gives the impression that someone's information is the "rock-bottom" truth. When a listener has clarified, or put in different words, what a speaker just said, the speaker responds with "nettupp" or "akkurat," a Danish word, to which the American "you got it" corresponds. The speaker thus supports the listener's response. One woman I knew frequently sprinkled nettupp throughout her conversation, sometimes just to break short periods of silence.

Some individuals idiosyncratically use the same pet ritual expression over and over. One elderly woman in the village was renowned for her constant use of an odd pronunciation of jú. Villagers also imitate absent others by mimicking their pronunciation of eg meini tað or hvat sigur tú. Thus they note even the idiosyncrasies in others' ritual expressions of agreement.

In a humorous story about Faeroese who live in the north, reputedly less talkative and opinionated than southerners, expressions of agreement are central:

> Once there was a Faeroese couple somewhere in the Northern Islands who were quarreling one day. They were both sitting around the sitting room reading or doing something quiet, not talking. The woman said after a while of silence, "Eg meini tað" ("I mean it"). Then the husband replied "So er" ("So it is"). Thirty minutes passed by and the woman said again "Eg meini tað." Her husband replied "So er." Thirty minutes passed again, and the woman said "Eg meini tað." The man, fuming in anger, quickly stood up, shouted "I can't stand all this gossip!" and stormed out of the room.

The tale itself mocks local phrases of agreement.

In Sumbøur the word *bara* ("only," "just") also often crops up in conversation. "You have 'only' to go to the store" and "I caught 'only' one hundred kilos of cod today" are examples. Construction crew workers with whom I worked frequently used bara, for example, "Put 'only' ten shovelfuls of sand into the mixer." It seemed to diminish workers' potential sense that they were being asked to do too much work. Bara acts generally to prevent emotional reactions to requests, mitigates possible assertiveness, and implies mutual recognition that no one is overdoing anything.

In private conversation speakers also frequently ask their listeners to keep information secret. People might reveal a tidbit of information—"Hjartvar let a sheep die by not feeding it"—and then say "Don't say anything about this," "Don't tell anyone I told you," or "Say nothing [about this]," and so on. Such commands give the impression that information is true and that people are creating dyadic pacts of intimacy and agreement.

Earlier discussion of legend and history pointed to the insignificance of temporal exactness: when events were supposed to have happened is not all that important. Sumbingar are habitually vague about the timing of past events. When referring to the unknown past, villagers say *í gomlum dogum* ("in the old days"), *í gamli tíðini* ("in olden times"), or *fyrr í tíðini* ("in former times"). Accounts of events that may have occurred "in the old days" or recently also often begin with *einaferð* ("once"), as in the story just above. Villagers likewise frequently begin reference to their own activities with "once" as in "Once, when I went to Tórshavn" and "Once, I baited seventeen buckets of fish lines in one day." Sumbingar also make references to the general time periods *undir krignum* ("during the war, World War II") and *aftana kríggjið* ("after the war"). More than moments set in precise history, these indisputable, vague temporal references tend to create an atmosphere of agreeable certainty, of "the way things were," without leaving open the possibility of disagreements with any specifics. These and the other "fashions of speaking" act as vehicles of accordance about how to converse and share space with one another.

Contrary Opinion

Faeroese villagers, ready to talk about the weather or embroider extant information, eschew strong opinion. After greetings and comments about the weather, conversation often entails such questions as (1) "How are you doing?" (2) "Are you doing anything special this weekend?" and (3) "What do you think about the size of Johan's ram?" Respondents often begin with *Eg veit ikki* ("I don't know"), as in (1) "I don't know, not bad," (2) "I don't know, maybe I will go to the dance in Skálabøur," and (3) "I don't know, it's pretty big." Such tentative responses avoid dogmatism. Villagers might interpret sharp, unequivocal responses as potentially disputable. Cautious statements help prevent challenges and subsequent disagreements.

The undesirability of debate is also evident in villagers' direct statements about "opinions." One man, Karl, whom villagers know for his exaggeration, said with conscious irony, "Sometimes, one *must* have an opinion, ikki nei?" Another man, allegedly more level-headed than Karl, told me privately, "Sometimes you have to have an opinion." Both comments indicate that villagers are ambivalent about expressing strong opinions and make reference to the fact that Sumbingar generally avoid verbal competition. The first speaker apparently rebels mildly against the common reticence to speak bluntly; the other man seems to say that usually disagreement is dangerous, but occasionally you have to risk contention. On the surface running counter to the expectation that villagers should avoid brusqueness, both statements implicitly refer to the pervasive (perhaps confining) atmosphere of conviviality and caution. People generally try to avoid controversial areas in people's emotional space.

There are other indications that dissenting opinion violates Faeroese standards. Villagers call one man 'Big Mouth' in his absence because, some say, he is offensively opinionated and enjoys being contrary. One time a friend succinctly instructed me about contradicting others. While riding in his car, right after giving a lift to a then-drunk acquaintance from another village, my friend said, "One must never disagree with a drunk man." As if a formal law of daily life, the man's statement underscores how, if one person loses his inhibitions, others must be even more cautious to avoid contention.

Formal Law

Although the bulk of interpersonal problems, disagreements, and conflicts never come to direct confrontation or formal dispute resolving forums, conflicts do arise, as in any social setting. The ethos of Sumbingar, however, as mentioned above, has almost always been to avoid formal legal proceedings. They are proud of their ability to avoid trouble, police, and the courts. Villagers want to keep any interpersonal problems out of view and/or within local space—the immediate environment, physical and social, is more under the self-control of villagers. Airing one's grievances about local villagers in formal forums and to outsiders and officials is opening up social and geographic space to the outside world. Keeping control of local space and society means the community takes care of its own problems and conflicts. Ideas about addressing conflict internally, if at all, are social and spatial safeguards.

One sixty-two-year-old fisherman, making a complaint about a malfunctioning stove he recently bought outside the village, declares:

> I have been at the ting (court session) only once in my life. And I was sixty-one years old when I went with this matter about the kitchen stove. I have never been taken by the police, or anything. Not for anything, not for drinking or anything. The police have never been inside our house. The first time I ever had anything to do with the ting was over this kitchen stove.

Another Sumbingur, Róland, says:

> Here in the village, *being good is not to have enemies.* All one
> has to do to get any enemy is to say something bad to someone
> . . . I think that to get enemies two bad men must meet. *I can't*
> *think of any people in the village who are enemies.* (Emphasis
> mine)

Róland knows that some villagers do not speak to one another.
Thus the interpersonal conflict between silent quarrelers is not in
Róland's estimation between "enemies." Hence Sumbingar are not
"bad," that is, they do not incur hostility from fellow villagers, nor
do they fight in extralocal proceedings.

One must be careful not to say something that might provoke
another, and, reciprocally, one must be careful not to take offense
at what others say. Villagers generally prize emotional self-control
and discourage assertive or aggressive expression of opinion, as
rital agreement demonstrates. Residents of another village,
Alvabøur, likewise "go out of their way to get along with one another"
and find "open confrontation. . . . intolerable" (Wylie 1982: 439–54).
Sumbingar must redress any grievances or conflicts in ways that
maintain their own reputations as unquarrelsome and composed.
To quarrel with (*klandrast*) or yell at (*sjeldast*) others is deviant in
this context.

Similarly, disputes in other North Atlantic Scandinavian fishing
villages, (see, e.g., Yngvesson 1978:78), are not resolved directly.
Aggrieved parties and the community at large wait to see offenders'
subsequent behavior before taking action. Usually discord passes
away without direct confrontation of issues. This indirect, "nonac-
tion" form of conflict resolution depends on no overt response to
conflicts. In their everyday commenting and gossip, Sumbingar
relieve much of the tension of conflict and tightly knit village life.
Conflict avoidance is thus a common method of conflict resolution.
In ignoring offenses—sometimes called "lumping" by sociologists
of law—and avoiding conflict, villagers often fail to press directly
their claims or specific grievances against a person.

But sometimes people want or need some procedures to make
economic claims of various kinds or to go beyond the expression
of discontent about third parties in ordinary village dialogue. And,
of course, over the centuries the Danish, Norwegian, and Faeroese
governments have had courts and proceedings for the administration of justice and the ironing out of economic transactions.

Around the year 1035, Faeroe Islanders began to pay tribute to the Norwegian crown. Before then the legislative body was presumably an *Althing* ("assembly of freemen"), later changed to Løgting, which met at Tinganes ("Assembly Headland") in Tórshavn. Although few documents of the early Middle Ages exist, it appears, especially from references in *The Faeroese Saga* and other scattered written records, that the king's court, the Løgting, was long the ruling body (Young 1979). The legal code was the *gulathing*, the same law Norwegian monarchs applied in Norway.

About 1,100 Gudmundur of Norway established a bishopric in Kirkjubøur ('Church Field') at the southern tip of the island Streymoy, where the ruins of an uncompleted thirteenth-century cathedral can still be seen. Apparently the clergy were powerful, as they held large tracts of land. Young (1979:81) describes the church as a legal institution:

> There is no direct evidence that churches were used as lay courts in the Faroes but it is almost certain that the practice was no different in the Faroes in this respect than other Norse countries. This view is strongly supported by the fact that the space between the inner and outer walls of the churches was formerly used in the Faroes as local prisons.

Twentieth-century stories told on the island of Suðuroy attributed to the clergy the right to spend the first night of marriage with the bride (*jus primae noctis*), although Faeroese written records do not corroborate these stories. Two Sumbingar rather scandalously told me that until the end of the nineteenth century priests slept with brides on their wedding night. Although the Faeroese have long been reverent and religiously observant, the church as an institution has always been external and formal, and led by officials outside the village. These stories, true or not, may reveal perceptions of the church in past history as well as contribute to some of the general mystique surrounding the behavior of figures of the past.

The Sheep Letter from 1298, as noted above, has been the primary set of laws for the islands for hundreds of years. Particularly in the days when land was unevenly distributed, the resolution of agricultural conflicts and the application of land tenure laws were important. Applying the laws, however, was often complex because of the fragmentation of landholdings, especially in recent times. The increasing complexity of local holdings made any village disputes over land and sheep, or other matters, increasingly the province of local island officials and occasional village meetings.

Three formal settings have existed for settling disputes. The Løgting was the highest official legislative and juridical body before courts became separate institutions. It handled islandswide affairs and disputes. Secondly, each of the island's legal districts on the six major islands had an annual spring court session, the *varting* ("spring assembly"), a subordinate court, presided over by a løgmaður, with some of its members also sitting in the Løgting. It dealt with district issues reported by the *sýslumaður* ("district man/officer"). Today the duties of the sýslumaður are more like a sheriff's, and he is Faeroese. Today a ting meets quarterly in each district to hear regional civil and criminal matters.

Local Law and Procedure

The third, most local legal forum, is the *grannastevna* ("neighbors' gathering"). The district officer comes once a year to the local village to discuss and decide matters of local interest. Opinions differ as to when the grannastevna began. John West (1975) argues that it was not a regular event until the nineteenth century. G. V. C. Young (1979:88), however, believes that if the grannastevna was not widespread until the nineteenth century, then:

> one would expect provision of the grannastevna to have been laid down by statute, but there does not appear to be any such statute enacted in the last two or three hundred years. If the grannastevna is not a creature of statute then it must have been in existence for many hundreds of years, possibly dating back as far as the eleventh century.

Although few published records of the grannastevna predate 1800, Young (1979:88) shows some references to Sumbøur's grannastevna dating from 1708.

> The absence of such records is not, however, unreasonable as the grannastevna generally dealt with matters of a purely local nature, such as the division of pilot whales after a grindadráp, deciding how many animals might be kept by a farmer, decisions relating to the repair of boundary fences and to the division of wreck etc., which had been driven ashore. These are

matters on which decisions must have been required long before the nineteenth century. For example the number of stock which could be kept had, by virtue of Article 6 of the Sheep Letter, to be agreed by all the people concerned, and the obvious forum to decide that question was the grannastevna.

I am inclined to agree with Young about the antiquity of the grannastevna, not just because his historical research is more comprehensive than West's, but also because Faeroese conflict resolution at the village level seems to fit with a long-standing Nordic habit of self-control and self-regulation. People tend to avoid legal forums outside the village: participation in supravillage forums might demonstrate lack of personal coping skills or an interest in invoking hierarchical methods of decision making.

The grannastevna meets only once a year before the spring varting. On Suðuroy it meets in February. The district officer goes around to each village district with two court messengers, whose duty in older days was to summon people required to attend the varting. Today these same officials witness events or documents of the grannastevna. Young describes it thus:

> It is possible that the witnessing of decisions of a grannastevna is a development of the provision in the Rescript of May 11, 1775, requiring decisions relating to the number of horses which could be kept by the landowners in a bygd to be recorded by the *sysselman* [district officer] and witnessed by "some of the best men in the bygd." (Ibid.:88)

The fact that local witnesses have long been part of the grannastevna's procedures, perhaps as formally decreed in 1775, indicates long-standing recognition by Danish officials and villagers of the importance of local participation. It matters little now whether external law or villagers' pressure originated this democratic process. At times the Danish government ratified laws initiated by the Faeroese themselves or recognized local laws, especially after Denmark officially made the Faeroes a county (*amt*) in 1815. The interaction of Danish officialdom and legal procedure with village practice has kept Sumbingar more or less autonomous. Today a Sumbingur keeps the records of the official register book of proceedings and decisions of the annual grannastevna: my neighbor was a witness and keeper of the record book, which he lent out to interested parties, including myself. Thus villagers maintain checks on the powers of officials. Moreover, although the district officer can be appointed for life (although he might be shifted from one district to another), islanders maintain close scrutiny over his behavior. I asked the respected Suðuroy district officer, who had already held office on the island for twenty years, whether his position was for life. He smiled and responded: "Yes, if I am not thrown out of office!"

The grannastevna has never been a forum for what official Danish or Faeroese law considers criminal matters. The Althing or Løgting was historically the criminal court. Nowadays the quarterly official island court sessions (ting) handle criminal and civil complaints, brought by villagers or police. The grannastevna, despite the presence of the sýslumaður, is an informal dispute and decision-making forum for economic matters, not for matters between the state and the individual. As formal dispute and crime are rare anyway, it is just those local economic matters, along with violations of unwritten village codes, which concern villagers.

During my year in Sumbøur, I heard about only two cases involving Sumbingar who were scheduled to appear before the quarterly court session held in a larger town on the island. One involved nonpayment of debt by a Sumbingur to another village's storeowner. The debtor did not show up for his scheduled appearance: he was a fisherman then out on the sea. The judge who presided at that session later told me that he postpones many cases (and the same case many times) because fishermen scheduled to appear are often at sea. The pattern of livelihood even works against head-on dispute resolution. The other case I heard about concerned a dispute between two Sumbingar and a covillager who allegedly destroyed a boundary fence. One man told me he was going to the session to make a complaint. I went to the larger town to hear the complainant, but he did not appear. Almost three months later he told me he or his cocomplainant were going to the next session about the matter. I again went to the session, but again neither complainant appeared. Apparently, even when rare open disputes occur, villagers avoid formal procedures.

Criminal Matters

There is also little use for formal criminal procedures arising from village events. Little or no property or personal injury crime occurs in Sumbøur, or for that matter, around the islands generally. Even today there are only six jail cells in the capital. According to the only Faeroese probation officer, drunken youth from the capital or large towns commit the few crimes that occur, usually vandalism of store windows. A brief review of the role of formal criminal law will help to show how jurisdiction over criminal matters best lies in the hands of people who do not live in the village, thereby ultimately supporting village-level equalities.

Historically, in state criminal matters, the court of first instance was the varting, over which the sorinskrivari ("judicial clerk") presided. The sorinskrivari was a lawyer and a clerk who was to advise jurors but eventually became a judge in practice. In the Løgting each summer the prosecutor for criminal matters was a king's bailiff, a nonresident of the islands. Thus outside authority prosecuted crimes.

The main offenses during the seventeenth and eighteenth centuries, in the days of the trade monopoly, were property offenses, usually stealing sheep or dried mutton, or sexual crimes, usually adultery, punished by a fine (West 1972:26). The penalty for a fourth conviction for theft was death; officials hanged thieves in 1626, 1638, and 1657. Officials also punished persistent vagrants by sending them to work on chain gangs in the royal dockyards in Denmark. Danish officials banished troublemakers from the islands. Most crimes in those days of economic (and marital) restriction stemmed from poverty and social inequality. Minor crimes, the only kind really known today in the villages, included slander, assault, and trespass.

The other crime, a consequence of the trade monopoly, was smuggling. The southern islands, which have good ports of call and are furthest from the capital and centers of external social control, were especially noted for smuggling. Smugglers thus partially made up for externally imposed restrictions by bypassing the law:

> The penalties for trading with smugglers were, for a priest or official, the loss of his post, and for a peasant the loss of his farm, and that the smuggled goods should be forfeit; however, the court had ways of getting round the law. An accused person who could show that there had been no corn in the Monopoly at the material time would almost certainly not be punished for buying it from a smuggler. The priests and officials often evaded the law by sending their wives on board the boats to do the

> trading, especially choosing times when they themselves were
> away from home on business. (West 1972:39–40)

Since the lifting of the trade monopoly and the equalization of economic advantages, extensive smuggling operations have disappeared.

A minor form of smuggling begun in 1907 still persists. Heavy drinking was a problem after economic development following the lifting of the trade monopoly. I heard stories in Sumbøur about people trading land or money for liquor. Religious fundamentalists, along with others against liquor, organized temperance groups in the mid-nineteenth century, and, in 1878, the teetotal Thórshavns Afholdsforening. For almost thirty-five years beginning in 1894, the society published a journal, *Dugvan* (*The Dove*). In 1907 a referendum made local sale of intoxicants illegal. It remains so, and people must order their liquor from Denmark, although private clubs, using their members' liquor rations to circumvent the law, operate bars in the capital and large towns.

The law restricts how much liquor one person can purchase, and liquor is obtained via post. One's taxes must be paid to receive the documentation necessary to order liquor. But sometimes fishermen and merchant sailors smuggle in bottles on board ships, or Danish and Faeroese travelers smuggle in bottles on cruise ships or airplanes, although officials only confiscate the extra bottles they find. Also sometimes villagers, in violation of public drinking laws, carry pocket flasks and drink in public. Yet these offenses are not criminal matters of any gravity. Far more serious is the application of unofficial village norms to those thought to drink excessively or on inappropriate occasions. Villagers often discuss one another's drinking habits, and some heavy drinkers become closet drinkers to avoid the talk and loss of respect that follows from unrestrained drinking. Villagers' comments about habitual drunkards deter people who might be tempted to overindulge.

From the viewpoint of the official legal system serious village crime has always been rare. Danish and Faeroese official social control has evolved in such a way as to help people maintain virtually crime-free, self-regulating villages.

Documents gloss over village decision making, where informal Faeroese legal culture manifests itself. The fact that the grannastevna historically met and still meets only once a year and that district (island) court sessions meet only four times a year and outside the village, support the proposition that village social control of conflict is informal. No other formal legal institutions exist. Local conflicts do not erupt into public confrontation and rarely reach formal channels of redress. After all, bringing a dispute to Danish and Faeroese authorities would reinforce external powers and at the same time indicate to fellow villagers that the complainant could not be self-reliant.

Current governmental tax and social policies and laws also reflect the long-standing independence and egalitarian sentiments of these Northern people. Income tax is high. Thus the tax offsets differences in income. Nearly half one's income in excess of average income goes to the government and its social programs. This tax erodes incentives to try to become wealthier than others. Moreover, the annual taxes that each person pays are matters of public record and thus of popular conversation. Thus official policy from above and local village talk reinforce each other to prevent hoarding or hiding income. The tax monies provide villagers with equal access to and care from state medical and welfare facilities.

Village legal life is informal: Sumbingar are distant in space and sentiment from official Danish/Faeroese nonlocal systems of control. Formerly, before regular passenger boats and automobiles, storm and sea often interrupted journey to court sessions. But topographic obstacles aside, villagers have always been eager to manage their own affairs. Scandinavian formal laws and officials themselves have long reinforced local customary methods of social control, which appear mostly in informal communications.

Being a member of the social/spatial community of Sumbøur means adherence to a mostly local form of justice. Thus the egalitarianism of village practice and thinking appears in the invocation of popular, peer opinion rather than of officials of superior legal and political status. Sumbøur as a place is in great part held together by common notions of how to act, how to talk, and how to control one's own social environment.

Chapter Six

The Place of Individuals

Communicating Social Order

Village social control is primarily an informal matter enacted in everyday conversation. A good portion of the socially constructed aspects of any place is community members' overlapping ideas about what the characteristics of the people are and what they should be. This is the social order. All communities have ideas about behavior proper or becoming to their place. Violations of such behavioral definitions of a place often lead people in large urban settlements to send the nonconformists away to prisons, asylums, hospitals, or other specialized communities where aberrant behavior is expected.

In Sumbøur, to lessen the impact of the ever-present observation and possible criticism of one's behavior, comments about others are often indirect, about absent third parties, and/or intentionally amusing. When people complain about, ridicule, or condemn behavior, they are engaging in what Andrew Arno (1985:43) calls "control communication."

> Social actors do not always accept one another's actions without questions as appropriate, and when they explicitly invoke relationship categories in explaining actions or debating the propriety of an act, they are engaged in control communication. . . . Whenever accounts of problematic behavior are given, control communication takes place. There are prevalent and subtle control communication modalities in the everyday life of every society.

In the Faeroese village, control communication is much of everyday conversation. Names, nicknames, comments, anecdotes, and so on combine to comprise villagers' evaluations of one another. The various remarks transform individuals' personal histories into community folklore, commonly held stereotyped conceptions of the personality of a person. Such talk comments upon and criticizes anyone's behavior or personality, even those of close friends or kin. The caricaturing talk is not only about living villagers, but like folklore in general, about former villagers, dead or alive. They become part of a repeated, growing repertoire of historical information about villagers that adds to the "sense of place"—the interplay between person and setting (Steele 1981).

No Faeroese word corresponds exactly to English "gossip." All Sumbingar often engage in *prát* ("talk") and *tos* ("conversation"). Yet it is rare that villagers describe any speech as *slatur* ("slander," "character assassination") or describe individuals who *tosa ringt um onnur* ("talk bad about others"). Thus villagers' comments about third parties are well accepted and not thought to be out of order. Indeed they suggest a local preoccupation with conformity and deviance. Usually unknown to the subjects themselves, such simple comments as "Jon is always driving up and down the road," "Daniel is so stubborn," and "Ele was drinking Thursday night" contribute to a complex of statements and interpretations of behavior about individuals that construct social caricatures. With no direct check on the veracity of these normative statements, social caricatures seem to take on a life of their own.

Most interesting, however, is the fact that everyone appears to have a legendary reputation and is considered deviant in one way or another. Everyone is more or less both equally open to criticism and equally a participant in the leveling of others, in the keeping of everyone equal. Although evaluated according to communitywide norms, each person is also an idiosyncratic, unique individual analogous to the unique places from which he/she springs. The fine detail of Faeroese vision is not only topographic, but also social. Each villager "sees" peculiarities and distinctness in each person just as in the characteristics of places. Yet, as there are categories of places—chasms, coves, stacks—any specific one of which is unique, so in social life are there categories of personages. This chapter is about categories of Faeroese personality, of "human types," and the ways in which people come to be categorized. Thus the community of Sumbøur maintains and creates its localness and collective sense of place through the very discussion and creation of a social landscape of particular people who look and act in

Mr. and Mrs. Vestergaard, locally known as Mr. and Mrs. Steinhús ('Stonehouse'). Friends of the author and his wife, they provided them with fresh cow's milk and chicken eggs.

particular ways. The caricaturing of everyone helps to maintain the view that the village is both egalitarian and made of singular individuals, two major aspects of the local sense of place.

Getting Information "From the Sides"

My first inkling that villagers' information about each other was often not wholly accurate came after two or three months of fieldwork. I began to hear bits of what other villagers said about me and my wife. Some villagers said that I was an ornithologist. Others said that I was a Russian or American spy. One story concerned a noontime rendezvous that I had one day with a Russian submarine off the tip of the island. Reportedly, some people "really" believed that it was true. Other pieces of information proved to be misreports. A man was surprised to hear that I did not receive a present of fish from his brother-in-law, as it had been reported to him. A woman of a neighboring village had heard that neighbors of ours who were relatives of hers had given me a present of cakes,

Some of the villagers with whom the author worked on a construction crew.

although we never received any. Another story circulated about an illness that my wife had: the originator assumed the sickness because she had not seen my wife for a long time. Another villager heard that we had installed a shower in our house, where we had no hot running water.

I began to follow villagers' comments and anecdotes systematically, paying special attention to people frequently mentioned. It became clear that at least some of the stories did not match my knowledge of the same people. Although my experience was not as representative as Sumbingars', it nevertheless seemed to me beyond question that there was embroidery in many accounts.

After I had lived in the village for only a short time, a nearby neighbor told me about one of my neighbors, then away on a fishing trip. She said, strongly backed up by her husband, that Eyðtor was

Here a Sumbingur wears the traditional Faeroese hat, the høgva.

a terrible drinker. They stated that he would come over to my house nagging and searching for booze to satisfy his voracious thirst. He was a drunk, they said. I should hide my liquor, if I had any, and if Eyðtor ever asked me for some, I should say I didn't have any. Otherwise he would constantly be intruding in my house and cadging my liquor.

The starkness of their description made me glad that he was then away from the village. I had an amorphous image of this man as swaggering, frightening, and rude. He came home after a few weeks. He appeared at our doorway sharp and respectful one day with a present of fish for us. He was one of the first villagers to offer us a present. Surprised and relieved that this man appeared more neighborly than most of my other neighbors, I later wondered about the gap between our neighbor's description of the man and his actual behavior. Subsequently I learned that Eyðtor did have a general reputation for occasionally drinking to excess. I also discovered that my nearby neighbors disliked Eyðtor. I was never sure what the truth of the matter was or whether Eyðtor, given the chance, would have frequently intruded into our house. Nevertheless, the early warnings and embellishments created mental images of him that have always remained present in my mind.

Then there were the often volunteered descriptions of Vagnar í Kálgarði (Vagnar 'in the Cabbage Garden') as a *serlingur* ("eccentric") who "foolishly" believed in *gandur* ("black magic"). Several villagers said that he also had experiences with various imaginary beings including trolls and huldufólk. Many said that he was the only man in the village who really believed in these things. One young woman in her twenties told me about how she "knew" about Vagnar:

> He has probably had experiences that other people have not had. He probably has a reason for believing. Well, you know as people say, there is more between heaven and earth than we know. But with him, he imagines things, as far as I can understand. It is probably a combination of things, his beliefs and things he sees. . . . Well, he talks about this and that sort of thing. . . . Well, I don't know exactly, I have never talked to him about these things. Some people who have gone to his house to visit have talked to him, and they have mentioned it [that he believes in these things]. He [Vagnar] talks about it.

This woman's thirdhand knowledge of Vagnar did not convince me about Vagnar's beliefs. Besides, Vagnar was one of my primary informants, originally selected as one of two villagers reportedly knowledgeable in local history. Even after several intimate conversations, including discussion of how villagers criticize him, Vagnar said that he had never actually seen supernatural events. He did say that he often heard of other people's experiences with *ónaturligt* ("supernatural") things and that he did believe supernatural beings and black magic existed. But several other villagers, sometimes privately, sometimes publicly, told me about their own first- and secondhand experiences with huldufólk, ghosts, monsters, trolls, and black magic. Vagnar's villagewide infamy seemed a product of exaggeration.

Villagers generally tended to characterize their covillagers according to a single trait. Besides commenting about alcohol drinking and belief in the supernatural, Sumbingar often talked about various persons' quarrelsomeness, adultery, arrogance, heterodoxy, and stupidity. It did not seem to matter whether accounts were correct as long as they supported community caricatures of local personalities. People became manifestations of certain, known traits.

Similarly, in a small Shetland fishing community "whatever any person's *actual* attributes and almost regardless of the actual distribution of such qualities among the population, only certain people will be credited with them" (Cohen 1978:452; emphasis mine). Likewise with respect to people's reputations in a Scottish crofting community on the island of Lewis, Susan Parman (1990) quotes a resident saying, "What matters . . . is not what you do, but what people think you've done" and then herself proclaims that "the truth is irrelevant." Gossip inevitably tends to particularize and individualize both people's traits and personalities.

Much local concern, as noted above, centers around how well someone works and socializes, as well as about sex, family, and kinship. Some are thought to be lazy, some promiscuous, some alcoholic. Since description that belittles a person in one role may affect him in another, comments can taint a person generally. The man who lost a sheep to his own laziness, as the story goes, was also a member of the village council. There, too, he had a developing reputation for laziness. His laziness in sheep raising generalizes to his political sloth. Thus simple comments become multiply symbolic. Even if a comment highlights only one role a person fills, listeners can easily link it with other roles. In this way caricatures take permanent shape.

Although each villager might perform well in many activities and more or less live up to village ideals in areas such as verbal skill, hard work, holding one's liquor well, raising healthy sheep, or managing a family, village talk selects alleged faults to emphasize. No person can be the best fisherman, potato raiser, sheep shearer, and fowler. Thus no one can fully live up to village standards. And some values may even nearly conflict with one other. No person, for example, can always be jokingly critical and at the same time fully friendly and accommodating. Negative traits that villagers attribute to each other are often associated with one of a pair of such values. Thus no one person can strike a perfect balance. But this is not a contradiction in the culture—competing values and practices keep villagers striving for conformity and ideal behavior. Everyone seems singled out for one or more shortcomings for the purpose of egalitarian social control.

Some Sumbingar talk about how villagers gather and relay information and form opinions and conclusions about others. One man said that instead of asking unfamiliar persons where they come from, a villager is likely to "guess where they are from." Several times I did hear villagers speculate about the backgrounds and home villages of others. Later this man extended his analysis: "The Faeroese like to guess." Another man revealed a similar understanding in describing his uncle: "He makes conclusions very fast based on only a couple of facts or little data. If he says that a man looks like a criminal, he is a criminal."

One young Faeroese woman explained to me how it was that sometimes villagers' information was not "correct." She had been living in Denmark for several years but was then visiting her grandparents in Sumbøur. She said that villagers were telling her things about her own life that "never happened." She said, "People [Sumbingar] usually do not ask direct questions, but prefer to get information from the sides." Likewise, villagers rarely asked about my wife's and my backgrounds or work. Yet there were several theories about us in the village. The Faeroese avoidance of cross-examination generally contributes to the collection of "information from the sides." In this information gathering there is no direct intrusion or aggression into others' lives and no conflict between the frequent criticism and the general desire for face-to-face agreement.

One man told me that Sumbingar do not ask many direct questions because they are "embarrassed to ask a stupid question." They are afraid, he said, that others might speak of their "stupidity" around the village. Hence it appears that it is better to speculate and to say something that sounds credible than to ask a lot of questions and appear unknowledgeable. Since Faeroese villagers know that certain folks are certain ways, they can always contribute credible information that builds upon extant stories and images. Although the frequency and openness with which information is communicated does tend to produce some checks on what people say and will inhibit lying, the buildup of information makes for little built-in veracity.

One man describes how information and stories become "certain":

> It [information] becomes more and more true every time it is spread further and further. . . . It is only temporary that they [villagers talking about others] are saying *eg haldi tað* ("I think so"). . . . The rumor is spreading for a few days and the rumor is getting more certain. It is just in the first stages where they are using expressions like eg haldi tað or *eg eri ikki so sikkur* ("I am not so sure"). . . . I have heard that one person can manage to do all those three things after each other. The first time he tells you one thing, he says to you "I heard a rumor," "I'm not sure about it," or "I don't think it's quite true." And the next day he can tell you the same thing and tell you "eg haldi tað," and the third day he will tell you that it is "100 percent certain."

Reputations take shape from ordinary everyday conversation and in the process gain power and permanence. Information reinforces itself.

Indirect questioning and speculation about people and their activities lead to individual identities based on what people say. If someone says, for example, that Magnus was very drunk last night, the listener might later impart the information to someone else. Then that person might say that a few weeks before someone told him that Magnus had been staggering drunk. He might then respond with "I didn't know that Magnus had been drinking so much lately." Without substantiation of his claim or direct criticism of his statement, the inference might turn into a (mis)report that Magnus had of late been drinking heavily and frequently. In this way villagers establish for Magnus a particular social identity. Repetition and embellishment, short of intentional fabrication, perhaps spurred on by someone's grievance against Magnus for some other behavior, contributes to a communitywide caricature. This caricature results from people's readiness to criticize others and to apply community standards. As part of everyone's search for others' offenses, such ridiculing verbal caricature is an oral forum for agreement about local norms and people.

Perhaps the words of Sigga, a seventy-year-old woman who had spent only a few days of her life away from the village, best reveal the legend-making quality of village talk. I had asked her to tell me about conflicts between Sumbingar. Instead, she answered:

> Often it happens that a story is false, not quite correct. And that things really happened otherwise. That was so about Barbara í Geilini, that she was full of black magic. But the story remains, not what or how she was as a woman, [but as a witch]. She was a farmer's wife, a farm woman.
>
> *Ja, so tann er* ("Yeah, so it is"). There have been so many stories through the times from Sumbøur and other villages. *People take only certain stories away from the lives of men. And so the story becomes the person.* It can be a story that only one time happened. . . . There is much that is false. (Emphasis mine)

These are poignant comments on the nature of social identities.

Despite the fact that there clearly are personality differences in different individuals, I could not often distinguish fact from fiction in people's accounts of one another. My status as a stranger and my own culture shock added to the difficulty of separating myth from reality. But in truth such distinctions were often beyond the capabilities of anyone, native or anthropologist. It seemed that I was the only one really concerned with the issue of historical fact versus local folklore. During an interview, in response to a question about what a person does with information he finds out to be false, and what a person does about the person who gave him the false information, one man said, "Just forget it. The person won't take it seriously. One is so much used to the fact that maybe a half-part of talk is true and the other half-part is not true. . . . People just want to have a picture, an image of you, in their heads." Probably like most members of any society, villagers center "images" of one another around personality traits.

Personality Traits, Getting Along, and Belonging

Faeroese are most concerned with the attitudes, emotions, and behavior of others who threaten the egalitarian harmony of living in the close physical and social spaces of the village. Nearly all Faeroese, especially men in their cooperative subsistence pursuits, are interested in at least the appearance, if not the reality of getting along with one another. In other communities in the world where people are less consistently and directly dependent upon one another, as in large cities or scattered farm settlements, individuals probably have less need to monitor each other's sociability. The places where urbanites or dispersed farmers live and work are generally less personal and subject to scrutiny.

Thus villagers' personalities and behaviors are quite important to people in their own interpersonal lives and as communitywide concerns. Villagers individually and collectively have a stake in talking in ways that support village norms and popular images of others and the place where they live. Locally criticized emotions like anger, arrogance, and argumentativeness are (negative) "emotions of place"—they are sentiments that people do not want strongly associated with the local environment. Evaluation of others' emotional dispositions are assessments of others' positions in societal space, of others' connectedness to the village community. Social connectedness and spatial attachment converge in the notion of belonging, both to a geographic location *and* its human community.

Familial, economic, political, and religious spheres of village life all have social components. And the egalitarianism and individualism of village life—the lack of strong interest-group alliances—make getting along with each and every one a particularly important theme of village discourse. It seems that Sumbingar love to talk about how others interact. This appears dramatically in villagers' commentary on what others talk about and how unsocial, uncontrolled, arrogant, and contentious certain individuals are.

Naiveté

To talk about different subjects with fluency is something of which every villager is theoretically capable. In practice, villagers make many comments referring to another individual's unintelligent, narrow, and/or excessively single-subject conversation. Typical short comments run like "Georg is stupid," "Anna talks too much," "Hilmar always talks about money," "Andreas only talks about fish and sheep," and "Sjurdur is stupid, but he only hurts himself." One man laughingly said that one time he and Sigurd went to another village to rent a catamaran. Shortly thereafter he asked Thomas what he thought about the Ayatollah Khomeini: "Thomas thought that Ayatollah Khomeini was the name of the catamaran." By itself the anecdote may not be amusing, but in the context of Thomas's local reputation, it takes on much more (humorous) meaning.

Another amusing anecdote, mocking a villager's ignorance of a language, recounts the time a fisherman docked in a Norwegian port and went into a store. As the storekeeper spoke a language not unlike his own, the villager asked in Faeroese for a "bag." Unfortunately the Norwegian homonym means "whore."

Villagers also criticize those who constantly talk about only certain topics like religion, money, or local events. Thus the Hilmar who always talks about money and the Andreas who only talks about fish and sheep are examples of the heimføðingur (literally "home-born"). This untranslatable word, which I gloss as "local yokel," epitomizes the value put on knowledge of and connections to concerns beyond subsistence and into extravillage worlds. A heimføðingur rarely travels out of the village, is uninformed about the Faeroes and the world generally, and talks only about the weather, how many fish his neighbor caught, the size of the rams this year, the taste of whale meat, and other parochial topics. One villager describes a heimføðingur:

> He isn't aware that there are a lot of other things outside his home which are different and people who are different, who think different and who act different. He is a local, native person who is very special. He looks upon the world as if it was only his own hometown and he maybe thinks everybody from the outside is curious and funny.

A heimføðingur may be expert in traditional fishing or whaling methods, but he lacks full social integration in the village because he is not able to participate in all types of conversations and social interactions. He is naive. A neighbor laughingly told about a man who went to the movie theater for the first time to see an American western. When a gunfight broke out in the movie, he suddenly jumped out of his seat onto the floor to dodge the bullets.

Comments about some villagers' naiveté and ignorance about things such as the details of some subsistence practices warn younger villagers to broaden their interests and keep abreast of various practical (economic) skills. Yet, television, newspaper, and travel have expanded the amount and variety of information available. Increasing concern with modern Western trends in music, clothes, and technology and enhanced possibilities of livelihoods other than traditional ones have extended the repertoire of topics to know about. Some older folks think younger ones are now uninformed about local history and subsistence skills such as fowling, sheep raising, whaling, and so forth. Some younger persons think older ones old-fashioned and unsophisticated about the modern world. One younger person says, "all they [older villagers] want to talk about is fish, sheep, and gossip." An older man says, "Now there is so much from other lands. Now people know little about the old reasons for things." In both cases, one generation laments the ignorance of the other, just as peers criticize each other for being unconversant or unaware. So while modern information may replace some traditional lore, remarking on others' deficiencies in know-how remains a cross-generational social practice. Thus, while the cosmopolitanism of modern times has partly modified the definition of a heimføðingur, the term always marks a person with interests that are narrower than those of the bulk of the local population.

The ability to talk with people about various subjects appears unrelated to level of formal education. Although several older villagers have trouble writing or reading Faeroese, I heard no comments about them as educationally or socially deficient in that respect. Moreover, even though in the last twenty years more villagers have been going to gymnasia, high schools, special navigational schools, the Faeroese Academy in Tórshavn, or colleges on the continent, I heard no comments from young or old about the "stupidity" of the less educated. Intelligence, cleverness, humor, and narrative ability are traits of conversational virtuosity independent of formal schooling. While someone's naiveté may be comic and make him a less desirable social companion, he does not directly endanger group order. Comments about him instruct villagers to become involved in issues and concerns of other villagers and to function well verbally in diverse social situations. Oral skill and traditions remain dominant over the written word and continue to be the mainstay of educating children to local values, knowledge, and history. Belonging is much a consequence of becoming informed at the local level.

(Un)Sociability

Villagers also caricaturize those who do not socialize much, who seem socially inept, and who talk about unusual, unpopular topics. Examples of such commentary are "Delmar is a quiet person," "Magnus is *snedigur* (strange)," "Oda is a serlingur (eccentric)," "Soren's brother doesn't go out among people," "Elsebeth sits by her window all the time and never comes out among people," and "Jarmund always talks about trolls and gandur."

People who socialize little are said to lack the skills to be "out among people"; that is, they do not know how to act with others or are afraid to be in public. Shyness has consequences. One man said that young men who are not shy have "elbows" to push their way through others to ask girls to dance or to otherwise initiate contacts with women. They are the men who "get" the girls. The shy end up alone or, ultimately, as bachelors. Seclusion also reduces one's chance to gather information and often leaves one less informed about local events and personalities. A person uninformed about local news is usually not an "important" person to be with, having little to share. Villagers say those who stay home, do not go to parties or dances, do not converse when they go to the store, and so on, are *fólkasky* ("people shy") or *fyri seg sjálvan* ("[only] for themselves"). Such people are more mysterious than others and threaten to elude public scrutiny and control.

Villagers also call unusual persons (and events) snedigur or *snedugt* (neuter form). Behaviors as diverse as quick decisions to sell or buy a house, quietness on the part of a talkative person, or consistent staying home on dance nights are "strange." In Sumbøur, the use of snedugt to describe behavior can insinuate that the strangeness stems from a desire not to interact with others, being "snooty." The comment that someone is fyri seg sjálvan suggests a self-involved dismissal of the need to socialize with others. Self-centered people might be arrogant and unhelpful to others, thus challenging values on sharing and equality.

As alluded to above, villagers now also snicker about people said to talk frequently about unusual topics like supernatural beings. Some older villagers talk about ghosts, trolls, elves, huldufólk and gandur, usually repeating the stories others told to them. Indeed, accounts about such beings abound in village conversation. Although few narrators claim firsthand experience with them, one middle-aged man said, in front of several young men, that he had seen huldufólk on the mountainside one day. Two young men mildly pooh-poohed his story to his face, but later, out of his hearing, strongly criticized his contention.

Another man described a monster he saw come out of the bay when he was a child, although he asked me not to repeat the story to anyone in the village. Another man claimed one villager carried cemetery soil with him for good luck and another villager put cemetery soil into someone else's pocket to bewitch him through gandur. But villagers did not identify these men as strange or as serlingar. Yet Vagnar í Kálgarði, mentioned above, was mocked for believing in and talking about trolls, ghosts, and gandur, although he denied firsthand experience with such beings. Some villagers describe him as a serlingur. It seems that eccentricity and unsociability are attributed to those who are considered preoccupied with certain subject matters, even if they are capable of diverse knowledge and conversation.

Villagers' assertions that particular individuals are exotic in their beliefs and conversation are, I suggest, artifacts of local interest in those people and topics. That is, the salience of certain topics in association with certain people lead villagers to notice more when those persons speak of those topics. Villagers are also likely to lead people into conversations about the topics with which they are associated, thus having fun and further reinforcing caricatures.

Arrogance

As Sumbingar are sure to ridicule religious people who act "holier-than-thou," so they frequently make comments about people like Gunnar who "always put people down" or try to impress others. Thus, to get back at Gunnar, for example, and to demonstrate that arrogance gets its due and incurs deflating talk, villagers talk about the time Gunnar bought two chocolate bars and put them in his pocket. He ate one but forgot the other. After sitting around for a couple of hours, he remembered the candy. He stuck his hand in his pocket, and out came his hand full of melted chocolate. Another anecdote had Gunnar visiting another city, as part of his tour on a ship. He went into the red light district of the city with a friend, who made sure than Gunnar had enough money to procure the sexual services he wanted. The man watched Gunnar enter the whorehouse. Some time later Gunnar reappeared, and the man asked how much money he had left. Gunnar pulled out his wallet and showed that he still had all the money. He reportedly had not known what to do in the whorehouse! Portrayed as a bumbling, laughable figure, Gunnar epitomizes someone foolishly enamored with his own cleverness.

Another story involves the nephew of a man villagers believe to be generally self-righteous. Because the man was myopic, the nephew decided to play a trick on him. Wanting to pose as the boy who went around the village selling newspapers, he wrapped himself in them, so that he looked like a bundle of newspapers. Knowing his uncle was home, he knocked on his door and went right into the house to ask if he wanted to buy the paper. Without noticing anything unusual, the uncle bought one. Much of the humor here, as in other stories, is embedded in local experience and knowledge. Thus it is familiarity with individual local characters and the spaces they inhabit that provides much of the social depth to the places around the village. One could say that humor only comes to be fully appreciated—and located—in the context of particular spaces and places.

One favorite tale goes back to the 1920s. It concerns Bjarni, a man who walked barefoot in the snow one winter. He climbed up and down the rocky mountain paths to court a girl living many miles away. Villagers say he walked barefoot to show fortitude and impress the girl he was wooing. Fellow villagers, to discipline his arrogance, punished him by getting him stone-cold drunk and then putting him on an isolated offshore island with no boat to carry him home. When he awoke from his drunk, he did not know where he was or how he got there. In every direction he walked he quickly came to the sea.

In obvious delight in the event, several villagers told me this story of Bjarni, which was a rare example of Sumbingar taking direct action against an offender. Yet even this punishment was executed surreptitiously, seemingly more for entertaining villagers than for discomfiting the transgressor. No one even mentioned whether Bjarni ever learned that the prank was retribution for haughtiness.

Another story amusing to locals teaches abut self-righteousness and religious fanaticism. The story focuses on a religious man, Regin, formerly a heavy drinker who now drinks no alcohol at all. This man is quite active in the village's mission house. It is the prayer house and meeting place for *intermissionar*, a fundamentalist subgroup of the dominant Lutheran church who practice temperance and actively preach a conservative morality. There was a problem between another man, Thorleif, and his wife a few years ago. They were having marital difficulties, and Thorleif would sometimes come home drunk. One day the religious man, Regin, went over in his good clothes to the house of Thorleif's father to volunteer to go over to Thorleif's house to help him with his marriage and to talk about the evils of drinking. The conversation took place in the hjallur, while the father was slaughtering a sheep. After Regin offered his help, the father grabbed the shoulders of Regin's jacket and said "Out!" In taking hold of Regin's shoulders, he left bloody handprints on Regin's clean jacket.

As the end of the story is told amusingly, the bloodied jacket appears to be a sanction against the social sin of arrogance. The story also suggests that interfering in other people's personal and familial problems is wrong. As the storyteller explained, "One must be a good example, if one is to preach to others" and "Such interfering fanatics think they are nearer to God than us." To nominate oneself for leadership and morality is offensive. Being a "good example," or rather not being a bad example, is much more the philosophy of normative behavior in this village. Fundamentalists especially are deviant in their self-righteousness, assertiveness, and vocal nature: they challenge local values on reservedness. Bjarni, Regin, Gunnar, and others, acting as if they are better than others, threaten the village's unranked structure.

Contentiousness

Predictably, villagers also characterize each other in terms of agreeableness, an essential personal characteristic in the avoidance of direct conflict. One must, therefore, be careful in talking with someone who is *tvørur* ("difficult," "stubborn"). A difficult person is socially contentious and might bring up age-old disagreements between dead relations or might take offense at jokes. Or such a person will not give up old ways or will not admit himself wrong. Leif is allegedly tvørur:

> Leif can tell you that his cousin Jacob went to Tórshavn with his own car. And all the people on the bus going to Klaksvík say to Leif, "No, that is not true, Jacob went on the bus to Tórshavn from over there." There are 15 or 20 persons who have seen his cousin go onto the bus. But Leif, who has not seen his cousin go to Tórshavn with his own car, still says Jacob went with his own car. Leif, he is like that.

Such stubbornness threatens the congeniality and mutual accommodation of village life. The anecdote warns others about him and the danger of being pigheaded.

In the following case stubbornness appears in the form of rejecting "progress."

> And Jon is like that. He is so tvørur. Ja, he wants to be old-fashioned. In older days when he went to Skálavík he did not want a car. He wanted to walk. He wants to use peat for his oven, even if coal is cheaper. He did not want electricity in his house, and he didn't want a refrigerator. He eventually did get a refrigerator in his house, but he misused it. One time he wanted to make a fool out of his wife with it. In the older days fishermen used to take their fish whole without gutting or cleaning them and drop them in the hjallur. But one day recently Jon came back from the harbor with his catch and said to his wife, "Yes, now you have bought a new hjallur so I'm going to throw all this fish into it." And he emptied his whole catch into his wife's new refrigerator, because he was stubborn.

Jon's antisocial behavior, albeit minor and ridiculous, is not one of being reactionary so much as it is of being difficult. He wastes valuable time and energy. Such a contentious and impractical act and person make life unnecessarily difficult and disharmonious for others.

The sýslumaður, overseer of the grindadráp, described other "difficult" people.

> Many years ago, some thirty years ago, there was a grind in Norðavík, and I was there. It was often that there were several boats of villagers from Sandbøur [a village] and Dugvoy [an island] that drove the grind. It was after the kill, up on land that this happened. The dock was big. There were some twenty men standing on the dock, and we had not yet began to cut up the whales and portion them out. One guy stopped, and he said to me "I would like to take one whale back with me to Dugvoy immediately." So I said to him as sýslumaður that, since the weather was good, he could wait until after we mark the grind with numbers. Then another man came up right beside me and says, "We are from Dugvoy, and we would like our grind now."

This account illustrates how two men thought they could evade the communal procedures that entail orderly division of the whaling spoils. The busy sheriff's recall of a brief event years earlier shows how pushiness in attempting to overcome communal practice lingers in a man's mind. That experience of contentiousness adds to the reputation of those two men, and to those who live on Dugvoy generally.

Although villagers detest contention, they frequently refer to it or joke about it. One woman reported that two neighboring sisters who live together are "always quarreling." She constantly complained about how one sister would sometimes call her up to talk about her arguments with the other. Listening to angry people recapitulate their quarrels is upsetting, definitely not fun. But gossip about quarrels can be amusing as long as it does not rekindle emotions. It is much more entertaining to talk about how others not within hearing distance quarrel among themselves.

Children learn to avoid contention from their parents, families, and friends. They see their parents oblige each other and shun argument. They watch adult coworkers at sea, on cliffs, and around the fields cooperate smoothly. They learn through indulgent upbringing that they themselves get their way without arguing with parents or siblings. Covillagers display little overt anger and youngsters observe their own parents' face-to-face friendliness with villagers for whom parents might express dislike or harsh criticism in the privacy of the home. School-age children observe fellow students shying away from argument with teachers and hear others ridicule and nickname those who are stubborn. Thus, in various ways as they grow up, children learn nonaggression (compare Montagu 1978).

Niclas, a Sumbingur who no longer lives in the village, is a special legendary figure in that he offended the community in a number of ways. Niclas was lazy, "crazy" (svakur), and contentious. As one villager described:

> He was special, all right. He had little schooling also. He was special in that he was almost impossible. You could have him one day for work, and the next day he did not bother to come any longer. Jú, he also sailed as a fisherman up to Iceland with his cousin, but somehow he managed when he was on board ship, but he was a serlingur in that he didn't bother to work.

A younger villager, Johan, said that one time Niclas burned down part of his family's hjallur. Johan continued that when he was a teenager, Niclas came up to him by the village dock one summer day and told Johan that if Johan did not give him the fish he had just caught, he would throw Johan into the sea. Johan was so afraid he gave Niclas the fish.

Niclas is one of only two persons I heard villagers portray as aggressive. (The other was a drinker who hurt his wife.) His arson and physical threats radically violate village norms. Yet villagers do not speak of him as a criminal, but as a special, "crazy" person. Their analysis stresses local norms of hard work, fair treatment of others, and nonaggressiveness rather than the state's more formal prohibitions of assault and vandalism. Niclas's legacy reinforces local social control by keeping Niclas as a local legend rather than an incarcerated criminal. Ultimately he remains Sumbøur's "property," an epitome of the violation of local informal laws. I do not know under what circumstances Niclas left the village or where he resides. One man speculates about Niclas's current whereabouts: "I think he is in a museum somewhere on the island of Eysturoy."

During my first social encounter with one elderly man who knew I had been living in the village for several months, he asked, with obvious amusement, "Have you ever heard Sumbingar 'yell' (sjeldast) or 'quarrel' (klandrast)?" His penetrating question and smiling face suggested that yelling and quarreling were infamous, yet laughable. As central concerns of villagers, they were, it seemed, much more common as topics of conversation than as actual events.

Although Faeroese generally eschew aggression and quarrels, around the islands Sumbingar as a group have reputations for quarreling, although that may simply be a variation of the Sumbingars' reputation for greater than usual emotional expressiveness, their geographically based personality. Residents of other villages and some Sumbingar themselves say that they used to quarrel a lot and engage in barratry. But, almost always, villagers would relate the same story: the time different villagers claimed to own one ewe and took the ewe to court. Yet even (alleged) conflict and accounts of conflict can be material for fun. As one man recalls:

> And those persons who were taking others to court because of
> a ditch, or a ewe, or because of a ram, or fence or anything,
> they were talking to each other when they were walking to the
> court. And they were not more unfriendly than that . . . *I think*
> *they had it for some form of amusement* . . . And I think it was
> mostly the same persons, from the same families. Because they
> could always find something which the other family had done
> wrong. Then they would take them to trial, and the next time
> the other person. I don't know for sure. (Emphasis mine)

The sheriff, who was present at the ting for the infamous case of the ewe, says, "twenty-eight Sumbingar were there that day."

Quarrels, on the rare occasions they do occur, may not be grave matters even to participants. Even in dissension there can be amiability. Perhaps only silent quarrels, unvoiced resentments, are serious. With the emphasis on self-control, villagers do not want, especially in their rare quarreling, to be perceived as fools and hotheads. Therefore, they may downplay their emotional involvement in any particular quarrel.

Apparently only individuals and families known for their contentiousness quarrel. Reputations for contentiousness attach only to certain persons and ridicule of them aids in steering others from becoming troublesome. Although villagers create popular folklore around the "difficult" persons, they are, probably, like "crazy" Niclas, exceptional.

Drinking and Getting Along

Drinking behavior and talk about drinkers highlight a number of issues raised earlier about getting along. Excessiveness, unsociability, social isolation, and contentiousness are themes which appear and reappear in villagers' remarks about who drinks, how much they drink and how drinkers act.

Generally, drinking is fun and provides opportunities for people to laugh with and at each other. People can lightly ridicule each other face-to-face. At a village dance, one man, more inebriated than his listener, mocks another's false teeth to his face, a direct slur unlikely to occur at more sober moments. For a stoic community drinking provides welcome relief, social encounters, and conversation usually taboo. One young woman remarks about the widespread drinking in the village around Christmas: "Folks drink and are friendly and dance together and then the next day they go back to their rivalries." I have also observed many friendly encounters between drinking villagers who ordinarily do not speak or joke with each other.

Drinking is also a social affair in the household. Often two or three friends or relatives will drink privately together in the home on a weekend night or before a dance. Other times drinking with a friend or two leads the drinkers outside to romp and visit with others. Getting drunk is often a ritual of friendship. Acceptable drinking is social and occurs, as one man put it, "perhaps two or three times a month." So the amount drunk at one sitting is not a major concern, but quantity per month is. Solitary drinking, however, indicates to villagers that a person has an alcohol problem.

Thus, observed or suspected private and/or weekday drinking leads to criticism about others' drinking habits. Typical comments include such remarks as "Jon drinks too much," "They drink too much," "Jon was an alcoholic," "Magnus drinks by himself in the hjallur." "Gunnar must have drunk two bottles of Akvavit," "There goes Eyðtor stumbling down the road," "Georg used to drink *sprit* ('canned heat') during the war," "There goes Johan to buy booze from Tummas." "Johannes was out again last night," "Poul talks filthy when he gets drunk," "Don't let him see that you have alcohol," and "Don't tell anyone we were drinking." These communications speak to how alcohol should and should not be used and the notoriety of particular individuals for particular drinking habits.

Villagers know that others carefully watch drinking habits. Consequently people often hide some of their drinking by wrapping bottles in inconspicuous bags or containers, slipping into the hjallur, going for rides in cars to drink (drivers do not drink), and leaving the bottle in a cupboard so that uninvited visitors will not see it. "Don't tell anyone we were drinking," "Hide your liquor," and "Karl drinks in the hjallur" all allude to the need for disguising or hiding the degree of one's drinking habits. To avoid a reputation for excessive drinking, one must be careful not to obviously drink too much.

One night, two men, with a liquor bottle neatly hidden, came to visit at the house we were renting. They had begun their drinking a little earlier in the evening at a prearranged rendezvous in one man's hjallur. Upon leaving the house they offered me my last drink. As I was going with drink in hand to the open door to see them out, one man told me to stand away from the door so that no one would see us. He said, "Otherwise they will talk about us in the shop tomorrow morning." Such a popular understanding also demonstrates that the importance of behavior lies not so much in the (drinking) acts as in how villagers discuss and interpret those acts.

Fishermen, needing to keep their wits about them while fishing for long periods of time, often drink when back on land. But drinking behavior, like village behavior generally, must avoid aggression. Villagers do attribute the rare cases of theft and vandalism in big towns to drunken youngsters. And some comments suggest that certain sorts of people should not drink. Irascible people and those whose personalities change when intoxicated give rise to comments like "Jaspur changes when he is drunk" and "Valgerð is unapproachable when he is drinking." People also talk about one man who mistreated his wife when he was drunk; his wife left him, and they are no longer married. Such marital discord is unusual, and comments about it warn of the possible drastic familial and social consequences of excessive drinking.

One night a neighbor of mine asked me to help keep his uncle Jarmund, then drunk, from going out in public. He said, "When he drinks he talks filthy, and it's not good for other people to hear." Only later, after one Sumbingur told me the following about Jarmund, did I realize that the swearing and drinking were part of a larger problem of potential disorder:

> I will not go near some men when they are drunk . . . always they will have trouble. If one goes to talk with Jarmund, so he begins to talk about some oldtime folks, his family or great grandfather or something like that. And then he will say that

his grandfather and my great grandfather were enemies. And
such kind of things.

When someone, sober or drunk, is about to act offensive or quar-
relsome, villagers avoid him, or a friend or relative tries to keep
him under control. Drinking combined with argumentativeness
particularly affronts and endangers the public reverence for social
order.

Although some villagers must be careful to avoid contention
while drinking alcohol, drinking generally permits villagers to
review their work and life experiences in a more relaxed atmosphere. It is often when people drink that they tell little stories about
events and people of the week. While drinking helps villagers
release tension, be sociable and stand back from daily pressures,
it can also add some tension to village life, as it leads volatile and
cantankerous personalities to display themselves. There is always
a touch of unpredictability about what the effects of alcohol will be
on some people. For most villagers moderate drinking is not
shameful, but cognizance of the power of gossip leads most to be
furtive about some of their drinking.

Temperament

A sense of humor and emotional self-control—the avoidance of
anger—are important Faeroese personality traits. Irascible people
are óndur, *snarsintur*, or *illsintur*. Óndur is most commonly used
to describe temperamental persons. Other common phrases include *vera illsintur* ("to be ill-tempered"), *tað kom ilt í hann* ("it
comes bad in him" or "anger comes easy to him"), or the popular
bleivur óndur beinnavegin ("to become angry immediately"). Villagers say an irascible person has a *ringt sinnalag* ("bad temperament"). A person who is cool and collected is *sinniligur*
("even-tempered").

A villager might say "You can't joke with Johan" or "Niclas
becomes angry immediately." One older man says that Mortan is a
good fish-line baiter, but "he is so illsintur." The man who swears
when he drinks does so because he loses his temper. Another man
reputedly gets angry nearly every time he goes into a village store
because the storekeeper taunts him. Yet another, renting a house
to some visitors, became angry when a female store clerk said to

him, "So now you are a hotel owner," as he took offense at the possibility that she was accusing him of putting on airs. He walked out of the shop fuming. Recounting such incidents of the public loss of temper points up the value on composure.

Temperament is central in Faeroese appraisals of character. Villagers believe that every strong person consciously controls his/her emotions and is weak if unable to do so. Anger works against social accommodation and can upset the even-tempered-ness necessary for dangerous male work on the seas and cliffs. The concentration and cooperation necessary for Faeroese subsistence skills have always demanded that men especially keep themselves emotionally and behaviorally within bounds. An even temperament functions to keep fishermen, fowlers, and whalers alive.

Joking

Since ridicule is often the basis of most jokes, an individual's ability to entertain makes him a shaper of opinion and thus increases his prestige and power a little. A skilled talker and joker attains, at least for a short time, a degree of social preeminence in what is otherwise an egalitarian society. He helps to bind the group and express its collective values. Students of social life recognize the role of jokesters:

> the joker is not exposed to danger. He has a firm hold on his own position in the structure and the disruptive comments which he makes upon it are in a sense the comments of the social group upon itself. He merely expresses consensus. Safe within the permitted range of attack, he lightens for everyone the oppressiveness of social reality, demonstrates its arbitrari-ness by making light of formality in general, and expresses the creative possibilities of the situation. (Douglas 1975:107)

Sumbingar with skills of wit and humorous attack are effective agents of informal village social control, especially of anger.

Here a villager talks about such skills:

> Some people may not be clever when it comes to calculations and other things, but they can be very, very smart. When you ask them a question, they can answer you back so that you feel that somebody has kicked your legs out from underneath you. I remember a person on a ship where I was doing some work and I was astonished at his answer to a question. And I also

know he can do the same with someone from the Faeroese government. A tax collector came to his house; he wanted to get some old debts. And this guy he made a speech for five or ten minutes. And he made a speech before this tax collector, so that the tax collector went out of the house like a dog who has done something wrong, with his tail between his legs. And we are still laughing at his speech, it was very, very good.

I think they [such people] live on traditions, they know exactly what to say. . . . I think he is preparing himself ahead of time. Thinking and practicing in his mind. So he is always ready to answer back.

Wit is not only a method of personal and community social control within the village but a technique for preserving informal, local control in opposition to formal law imposed from above.

Some people are especially noted for knowing how to "hold [others] up for ridicule" (*halda fyri spott*). A "jokester" (*spaelopmakari*) is funny and skilled with "jokery" (*skemt*). A sinniligur person "knows how to tolerate," "knows how to take" (*duga at tola, duga at taka*) jokes or attempted "taunting" (*arging*) without becoming angry. He avoids becoming the frequent butt of "tricks, pranks" (*bragd*), "artful deceit" (*kunstgerð*) or "roguish tricks" (*skálkabragd* or *skálkagerð*). Indeed some councilmen, ring-dance leaders, and storytellers are also good at skemt and arging. Although these and other jokers and pranksters sometimes gain the upper hand, villagers rarely praise them, lest they become arrogant.

Jokes, although sometimes insinuating sexual liaisons between villagers, in typical Faeroese circumspection, usually avoid outright obscenity. A person whose jokes are irreverent or obscene is a "scoundrel" (*skálkur*). "Scoundrels" carry jokes and pranks too far. Yet no one in Sumbøur seemed to have that reputation when I was there. As long as no one is physically hurt, then such activities provide release and accepted amusement for villagers. But although everyone is open to verbal attack and ruse, some villagers are especially vulnerable to the witty.

As skilled talkers and pranksters operate through everyday stories, jokes, and tricks, they seek foils on whom to practice their skills. Although, like ballad singing and storytelling, jokery is a culturewide pattern that functions to encourage verbal facility and humor in young and old, men joke more than women. Because their lives are more public than women's, they most often bear the brunt of jokes as well as perpetrate them. Although some villagers noted one old woman for her cleverness and ability to talk about olden days, public display of verbal skill via jokes or storytelling is primarily masculine. Men and boys like to joke around and relay humorous tales of pranks they pull on each other.

The story that I was a Russian spy was told not only to mock others' "stupidity" but also to test others' gullibility. Most villagers thought it was a foolish idea and made fun of those who believed it. I told Niels that one neighbor of mine did not say hello to me for a long time because he thought me a Soviet agent. Niels reminded me that a few weeks earlier in December I had stopped at his house to visit him for a few minutes around 11:30 A.M. I told Niels that I was going for a walk to the tip of the island. After I left, Niels was talking about me to Heri. Niels told Heri that I had to be at the tip of the island at exactly noon so that I could rendezvous with a communist submarine. Just about noon, from a distance, a sea-going vessel could be seen rounding the point. Niels motioned there to Heri and said, "Look! There's the submarine." Heri supposedly believed it for a long time.

Jokes, Pranks, and Taunting

Faeroese value levelheadedness, self-restraint, amiability, and joviality: one should be even-tempered and able to tolerate all situations. It is important to be able to detect when others are joking or intentionally misleading. Additionally, one should be able to shrug off direct, potentially upsetting comments without becoming óndur. A middle-aged man discusses being inappropriately óndur.

> A man can become offended, for example, if he comes over onto my land where new grass is growing and I say to him that he shouldn't go there because the grass is growing there. So he becomes óndur. That is, he becomes offended over it, insulted. He tolerates so little. It is because he doesn't like what I said to him. Or, if a dog goes running after one of my sheep, and I go after the dog and put the dog elsewhere, the man might become óndur. There is much that one could become offended over.

Anger arises in those who take offense.

A boy of sixteen says a sinniligur person is

> a man with whom one can say everything, one with whom one
> can say most anything. If a man says something that he doesn't
> like, he doesn't make anything of it, *Hann dugir at dempa seg*
> ("He knows how to keep a lid on himself").

and a young woman adds:

> There are some people who never get angry, who are always in
> a good spirit. I think they are accepted more than others
> because *the person doesn't take anything seriously . . . And
> that is a good thing, that is about the best thing you can do.*
> (Emphasis mine)

There is a long historical tradition of ridiculing intolerant
Faeroese and pulling pranks on others, both on land and at sea
(see Joensen 1975:110–113). An older man recalls earlier days
when villagers composed *taettir* ("satirical ballads"), more:
"Sumbingar had taettir, but they do not have taettir so much in
these times. Most are gone. They were composed with skemt. But
it was not everybody who tolerated skemt. There were some who
couldn't tolerate it."

Taettir and contemporary everyday stories are especially aimed
at those who lack self-control because Faeroese believe that people
can and should control their emotions. And, as noted above,
drinking is dangerous for those who under the influence of alcohol
lose the ability to take joking around and become offensive. Lack
of self-control is to be contrasted with ridicule directed at villagers
who look or act odd for biological reasons. In the latter case, the
ridicule is less personal and harsh because it explicitly acknowl-
edges of its objects that *teir hava ikki skapt seg sjálvar* ("they have
not made it so themselves").

It is Faeroese men who ideally are supposed to be able to joke,
tease, and play pranks with one another without getting serious or
becoming angry. In accordance with Catherine Lutz's (1990) discussion of how Western culture generally associates women with
emotion, Faeroese males are the unemotional sex, or at least they
are less expressive of anger. Yet men from Sumbøur are supposed
to be adept at humor as seen in the very popularity of arging
("taunting"), a method to create humorous situations for those who
witness angered males.

As one astute observer of his own Faeroese scene put it:

> Arging is a kind of male humor. Women do not have the same kind of "training" in making others angry or making rukkir ["easily angered fools"]. Men's culture and women's culture are different. Trying to get others angry is not usual for women, among themselves or between a man and a woman. A man who tried to get a woman angry would be diminished, he would lower his reputation. Arging is men's sport.

The strong cultural value on male emotional control, as mentioned above, accords with the fact that traditionally it has been the man who works outside the home, often in cooperative, close-quarter efforts as well as in the village town council and other regulatory groups. An angry woman, working primarily in domestic spheres, does not greatly threaten economic and social order. The man just quoted also stated, "I have seen women angry more often than men. It is more permissible for women to become angry."

A man who loses emotional control damages his role as an effective unit of the economic group as well as a unit of the whole, and damages, at least symbolically, local social control. Again, as the last-quoted man stated, "If a person gets angry, he has lost control. Anger is the last way out of a situation." Anger is not being able to negotiate with others. From the observers' or group's perspective, anger is an individual's noncollective, noncooperative, antisocial posture. Anger is self-indulgent. Such negative traits are contrary to economic and social survival. In alignment with much of what we have discovered hereto, the ideologies about expected male versus female emotional expression and the actual differences between men's and women's emotional behavior surrounding anger and humor can be linked to the economic and ecological activities of the sexes.

There are two distinct forms of joking. The first, skemt, is mostly for fun, but the second, arging, deliberately tries to anger someone. One can be "joked with" (skemtast) without being subjected to arging. In arging, a person or persons intentionally "work on" (arbeiða uppá) someone. I have glossed arga as "taunt" but it is an untranslatable, quintessentially Faeroese word. The closest words in Danish are drille ("tease"), tirre ("provoke," "bait") and ophidse ("incite," "stir up"). Jóan Pauli Joensen (1975), writing in Danish about Faeroese rukkur, likens arging to the Danish til bedste ("to get the best of") and mobbing ("to gang up on"), a recent Scandinavian expression taken from the English "mob." A Sumbingur explains:

> There is a difference between skemt and arging. Arging is when someone is having a fiasco. Skemt isn't received badly; things stay pat. A man with whom you make skemt doesn't make anything with it and can wait until another time to get back at the other guy afterward. But the other, arging, that is something quite otherwise. One knows how to take skemt, but the other who is argaður ("taunted") takes it badly. Some know how to let being made fun of not get to them. Some men *tola* ("tolerate") skemt.

Unlike skemt, arging cannot be simply laughed off. Villagers recognize its purpose is to provoke. The villager continues:

> It is known if a man doesn't like what one will say. For example, it can happen that a man used a tool and placed it somewhere, and then doesn't know where to find it. Someone hid it someplace, and the man did not know that someone hid it. And they arga him about it. You could be aboard a boat or by the shore, and you use your knife to cut the line, and then you forget where your knife was. And then someone can argir him about it . . . And also you can be ridiculed up on land. If you were going up with the sheep you could have misplaced a sheep. You had set the sheep in a pasture, and all had slipped away when you got back, and people might ridicule you about it . . . And in the same way on the birdcliffs if you had caught birds and put them all up above on the ledge and then when you get up there were no birds. They would arga you about it. The most to be ridiculed about was work.

> They [villagers] arga mostly about happenings, or accidents. You were argaður over common, general things. There are so many other things to arga with. And that happened often.

> Some arga badly. So it was aboard the ships. There could have been ten, fifteen on board one ship for a year. So they could arga one who became angry. But the others didn't get angry. Arging was skemt that was not tolerated.

> In the village there are three things: gossip, jealousy, and arging.

Practitioners of this form of taunting included even the legendary *táttayrkjari* ("satirical ballad composer") Poul Johannes, the man known for his relatively "inoffensive" taettir. Allegedly, he told a friend on his way to visit their mutual friend Símun, that Símun recently died and was already buried. Believing Poul Johannes, the friend was surprised later to see Símun alive and well. Hence jokes, pranks, and taettir can be challenging trials to individuals' sensibilities. One villager even says "taettir are special ways to arga."

One man told me that villagers sometimes arga Peter "pretty badly" although Peter "doesn't get too angry" and "knows how to take it for the most part." Another case of arging involves Hans, a prankster "excellent at putting people on." Hans took out some pages of Georg's copy of *Reader's Digest* and put them back upside down and in the wrong order. Hans told Georg that the store where Georg bought the magazine had sold him a bad copy. Hans went to the store to get another. Here and in other tests of personality people engage in a form of "character game" (Goffman 1967).

Villagers become familiar with arging early in life. One eleven-year-old boy says with a frown that his friend from the capital who visits him and his family for the Christmas holidays sometimes "tries to arga" him by saying to him over and over "You are crazy, you are crazy, you are crazy." A young woman comments that children frequently taunt a man nicknamed Viðan ("Wide One") in the kiosk because they know he will "take things seriously." A boy aged sixteen said that schoolchildren used to taunt Anders because "he didn't go to school together with the boys; he went to school with the girls." The sixteen-year-old's knowledge of such matters already seemed well formed: "There is always something that one sees that a man does not do as the others. So he becomes argaður. It is always so."

When skemt becomes arging is sometimes difficult to tell, but joking and taunting generally test villagers' ability to tolerate ridicule and to see through put-ons. Jokers and pranksters may succeed in uncovering both credulity and ill-temper. Some "victims" are only temporarily credulous and learn later that they were fooled. Others never understand the joke, and they in particular may gain a reputation for gullibility. Some "victims," while naive, may react relatively calmly. But the prankster's true reward is to provoke a rukka—a person who is both naive and lacking in self-control. A rukka does "not know how to take" what people say or do and/or is singled out as especially ridiculous for some reason.

Both skemt and arging, like belittling generally, are public amusements. Individuals engage in such activity so that villagers may enjoy watching or listening to later accounts of others' anger or frustration. The victims themselves are thus less skilled than others at ridicule. In other words, villagers caricature and ridicule the very persons who are inept at ridicule. Unlike others, rukkur do not act well as agents of egalitarian, popular social control and are therefore made its subjects. Social control elegantly enforces and reinforces itself by caricaturing and mocking those who cannot perform its duties.

The Place of the Rukka

A rukka (literally "crease") is a laughable figure whom villagers describe euphemistically as a "certain kind of person." Different Sumbingar identify different persons as rukkur. Some villagers say that others are rukkur only in certain situations. The origin of the word rukka is obscure (Joensen 1975), but all rukkur I know are male. This fact lends credence to the possibility that the tradition of the rukkur originated aboard Faeroese fishing smacks. Many villagers agree that in the nineteenth and early twentieth centuries, every ship had at least one rukka (ibid.). Crewmen singled out regular butts of practical jokes, taunting, and face-to-face mockery. They were a means of entertainment during long, difficult, nerve-wracking sea voyages and may have started the notion of rukkur on shore: as one veteran seaman in Sumbøur put it, "in the old days they had no television, no radio. They made fun of each other. There was always one rukka."

Whether the concept originated in social life at sea and then became popular in the village, or whether it originally began as a notion within village life and then extended to a smaller society aboard ship probably will never be known. In any case, the rukka is a creation of group life and functions for the community as an epitomized object of social control. A discussion of rukkur and taunting helps to delineate some of the core values of Faeroese village society as well as emotional dispositions, personalities, and practices that are part of the socially constructed aspects of a place.

Sumbingar still talk about living rukkur aboard big ships:

> Eivind, he is always a rukka . . . Pápa and he were on a big ship. Eivind was the cook and he had a big mixer on board, and he was about to bake bread. But he only put flour in the

mixer. Pápa and several men went to talk to him so that he should forget to put water in the mixer. So suddenly the mixer became full, although he forgot the water. So suddenly it was all white snow in the mess, in the kitchen on board . . . Some things are done like this. It is to have fun, you know.

The narrator did not know whether Eivind ever learned that others had played a trick on him.

Mortan, an older Sumbingur, is also a rukka. Initially I did not know his reputation even though I knew him for several months and often saw him interacting with others. I had noticed a sparkle in people's eyes when they talked with him, as if their conversation were ritualistic rather than spontaneous. He used to come to visit workers in the buildings near a village dock. Several villagers, including teenagers, would talk to him tongue-in-cheek. They would ask him silly questions about his activities or about his younger days and seemed to know that his answers would amuse them. I later found out that Mortan was known to have been a ship's rukka during his days as a fisherman. One man said that Mortan was forever having his sweater knotted up as a practical joke: "Mortan is an expert at unraveling sweaters." One time his ship-mates allegedly sewed Mortan's sweater sleeves together and put sticks in it, so that he had to cut his sweater apart in order to untangle it.

Playing jokes and pranks on rukkur is also an activity ashore. One veteran sailor explains:

> there is a community of twenty-five men aboard and they point one [rukka] out immediately, and he will be the same one all through the trip. . . . And if he changes to another ship [after coming back to land], it is mostly the same because he will be the one who fits into being like that. . . . [Ashore] it is almost the same. It is just not as concentrated as it is aboard ship.

An older fisherman tells a story of making a rukka, someone who "gets really mad," out of another villager, to whom "they did so many things":

> I remember one Jacob Pauli, he was an old man. Well, he was a kind fellow, but he was one all the youngsters liked to do some nuisance to at the house. He lived alone and had a little store. . . . And it was fantastic. I remember he had been in Tórshavn one day, and he had brought back some caramels. The pieces

were wrapped in some sort of paper that looked exactly like paper money. And it was exactly the same size as the one-krona paper note. When you finished the caramel it looked like money. . . . Well, he could not see well, and it was dark, there was only one little light, and so the boys, Ólavur was one of them, asked Jacob Pauli for some caramels. "OK, take some, and put the money for them in the drawer." And so all the youths did so. And when Jacob Pauli came down to count all the money in the drawer, he found caramel paper.

The fisherman continues:

One day this kid, Jarmund, he was about the same age as I, was going to make some trouble at Jacob Pauli's home. Well, he broke one window. And Jacob Pauli went running after him. . . . Well, Jarmund knew Jacob Pauli would run after him. Jarmund was very nasty. He was standing at the door to get Jacob Pauli out to get him to run after him. Jacob Pauli began to run after him and was just behind Jarmund. But Jarmund kept control of the distance between them; he knew he was just about in front of Jacob Pauli and so he moved a little further forward. Jacob Pauli had come outside with only underwear on, and then he came out by the hamar. Then they stopped him. Then they took every piece of clothes off him, and then let him run home. And Jacob Pauli was crying like crazy in the middle of town. . . .

Once they put castor oil, to move your bowels, into the liquor he was drinking. So he was drinking—he drank a lot—and they put it in a beer, and most of it was castor oil, he couldn't see it. And he was shitting in his pants right there while drinking.

One man describes rukkur "temperament" (sinnalag) and talks about a particular rukka:

it is the sinnalag, not the mind, the psyche. You can't bear it, you become angry right away. And so one with a strong psyche is not a rukka. I mean, one must also be smart to know that they are "working on" you. You must only tolerate it, and not answer back. . . .

Eyðun. It makes no difference what you say to him. He is made into a rukka. It is one hundred percent certain. The people from the next village who know him often come over to him and "work on" him immediately. He becomes completely angry.

> Although he is quite smart, he is not a person like others. He
> lets himself become teased. He just can't control himself.

Wit, intelligence, and an even temperament can be separate
traits. Objects of jokes need not be "stupid," nor do verbally facile
jokers need be intelligent: one villager declares "even stupid people
can make smart people into fools. . . . People are used to having
stupid people make fools out of smarter ones." It seems that
avoiding the status of rukka is more important than being "smart."
Some Sumbingar say Eivind the cook is generally a rukka.
Another fisherman, more seasoned than Peter, says Eivind is a
rukka only aboard ship and in a unique manner, while Sigmund
appears always to be one:

> He [Eivind] is almost made for being like that [a rukka], but in
> a special way. He can answer, he can answer very fast. He can
> take the jokes. He even likes it. . . . But the other guy, Sigmund,
> he gets mad, and then he is lost. . . .
>
> Sigvard, he is almost made for being a rukka, . . . Poul, he fits
> more to be that kind, . . . Oh yeah, Sigmund, he is one, he is
> very suited for being that way.

Sigmund is apparently more of a rukka than Poul, and Poul more
than Sigvard. Only Sigmund seems to be a definite rukka. He often
appears in lively village talk, and one man says that two village
shopkeepers "always make fun" of Sigmund. Although many villagers believe a few individuals are rukkur all the time, they say others
only act like rukkur in certain situations. Jakup was only a rukka
when drunk, even though one man said he was "always famous for
being a rukka." And Peter himself does not talk as if he knew that
people called him a rukka. So, some people some times, and some
people consistently, are (potential) rukkur, and there are different
degrees of being a rukka, different types of rukkur, and different
definitions for a rukka.
Rukka labels a social identity assigned by others. Watching a
good soccer player fake out an opponent so that he misjudges,
stumbles, or lets him by, villagers say things like "He made a hell
of a rukka out of Johan" or "Sofus knows how to make rukkur out
of the other players." A rukka is the result of action around him,
as much as he is a product of his own character.
One local philosophizes:

> People . . . are more scared of being ridiculous than they are of
> dying. They are not afraid of being killed in an accident if they
> are doing something very, very dangerous, but they are much
> more scared of being laughed at.

A villager's concern is not whether there "really" are such people
as rukkur, but whether in the view of his neighbors, he might
sometimes be one.

Although some people have more skill at control communication
and more ability to laugh off pranks and shrug off comments and
stories, no one is immune to the collective narrative power of the
community, and everyone wants to avoid being the verbal prey of
others. When a person becomes an individual object of social
control, a legend is often made out of him. And in the Faeroes a
particular type of personality, singled out, named, and scrutinized
by the community is the rukka, a special social type, a special
caricature, of a special place.

Talk about anger is a crucial way people discuss how well others
fit in community life and exemplifies the ever present concern in
cultures generally of the relation of the individual to society. One's
conformist or nonconformist position in Faeroe society is greatly
determined by one's emotional reactions to jokes or taunts. Thus,
taunters represent, at least symbolically, the community at large.
The purposeful creation of anger in others and talk about taunting
and rukkur are components of the "rhetoric of control" (Lutz 1990),
not only of emotion, but also of society. Such practices define the
very place of emotions in the community and the very kind of
emotional landscape people want to live in.

Joking, taunting, and pulling pranks can on the surface seem
uncaring or unnecessarily nasty, but they also function positively
to keep the community viable, cohesive, and fair. Arging, in addition
to releasing tension and incorporating values on wit and leveling,
particularly points out Faeroese values on even temper and equality. Teasing ultimately helps people cope with the physical and
social environment.

All the foibles and gullibilities of an alleged rukka or, for that
matter, any individual subject of ridicule, might at first seem trivial.
But the belittling builds upon the fact that every individual is
vulnerable and implicitly shameful. Sumbingar display little concern with assessing the exact seriousness of norm violations.

People joke about the two or three "fat" people more or less in the same way they talk and amuse themselves with accounts of the one or two persons who have physically harmed property or people. They condemn what outsiders might consider trivial as vigorously as the serious. If seriousness of offense were truly an issue, villagers' equality would be jeopardized, for people might begin to rank themselves and others as better or worse citizens. Each "crime" is to some extent serious and each person is in some sense "criminal." Such a system is fair, attributing nonconformity to all and preserving both the individuality and the commonality of community members.

Chapter Seven

The Art and Arts of Place

Á Beinisvørði

Poul F. Joensen

Eg av Beinisvørði sá ein blíðan summardag yvir Føroyaland,
oyggj við oyggj, sum víkingar í herferð silgdu fram
gjøgnum sólarbrand,
túsund bjartar litir yvir land og sjó
lívið lívsins drottning bar sítt takkarljóð,
sael lá dýrd yvir land og stað,
foldin var von sum heimsins fyrsta dag.

Undan havsbrúgv upp á himin reina sum eitt skot
mjørkaflóki sprakk,
streyk á veldis veingjum gull og smaragdlitir út,
sól í dimmið sakk,
tokuskýggj í klingur mólu yvir grund,
sum í rúmd ein sól á síni føðistund.
Brátt var grátt, har við eyga bar,
eina eg tá í oyðumørkum var.

Eins og Ódins villa fylgi goystu flókar fram,
trøllskir uttan ljóð,
feldu alt, ið forða vildu teirra veldisferð,
rok um bygdir stóð,
sum tá Timur Lenk alt javnaði við jørð
og Artala oyddi land við eld og svørð,
sum ein dreki mjørkin goysandi
slúkaði sól og heim og sjálvan meg.

185

From on Top of Beinisvørð
Poul F. Joensen
Translation by Jaspur Midjord

From Beinisvørð I was overlooking the Faeroes one mild
summerday,
island by island, like Viking ships in campaign
sailing through through the fire of the sun,
a thousand brilliant colors over land and sea,
the queen of life sang her thanksgiving to life,
blessed splendid weather over land and place,
earth was beautiful like the world's first day.

Out from under the sea's horizon on to the blue sky
a bank of fog jumped,
spread on wings gold and emerald colors out,
the sun in twilight sank,
clouds of fog circled over ground,
like a sun being born in the universe.
Suddenly I could see only gray around me,
I was alone like in a desert.

Like Odin's savage flock gushing patches of fog,
silent like magic,
destroyed everything that would halt their mighty advance,
even village smoke stood,
like when Timur Lenk leveled everything to the ground
and Attila devastated land with fire and sword,
like a gushing dragon the fog
swallowed the sun and earth and me.

Europeans, and Scandinavians in particular, have long been students and preservers of oral folklore and legends and have often used later written versions as a conscious part of national and ethnic consciousness. This is especially true for the Faeroese, whose language has a short history of being in written form. Although Venceslaus Hammershaimb published a Faeroese grammar in 1854, it took a number of years for there to come to be an accepted standard and practice in Faeroese orthography. In 1881 the orthography was republished with an accompanying Faeroese-Danish glossary by J. Jacobsen. Thus Faeroese identity even until fairly recently centered greatly around oral traditions, particularly in regions away from the capital. It was not until around the turn of this century that local literature and political writing blossomed. Propelled in great part by Jakob Jakobsen's 1898–1901 collection of Faeroese folktales and legends, many of the publicly known and often-told stories came into written form.

In keeping with the importance of oral literature and in the absence of many historical records, scholars and writers have used the content and style of legends and folklore in the reconstruction of Faeroe history and culture. John F. West (1972), author of one of the few English-language histories of the Faeroes, writes in a case study in Faeroese oral tradition (1982–83) about the importance of the legend of Beinta and Peder Arrheboe. Jonathan Wylie's (1982, 1987) and his and David Margolin's (1981) cultural histories extensively use legends and huldufólk stories as central to their history and anthropology of the islands. Moreover, in the last seventy-five years or so, numerous locally published books, journals, and newspapers have appeared in the Faeroes that utilize and preserve the local stories and folklore of numerous places around the islands. Such writing and its reading reaffirm Faeroese history and cultural identity in general and solidify the islands as a special place. Vagn Wåhlin (1989:25) proclaims that "The spoken language, the printed word and the broadcast word in the local radio, útvarp, is the backbone of Faroese national identity today." He quotes a Faeroese citizen as saying "the language is our national identity." Thus oral and written formats for telling local stories are still central to Faeroe culture and natives' own senses of where and who they are.

A common conception of tradition and history creates unity, consensus, and continuity. Such ideas and sentiments tend to override divisions or conflicts between people. Thus popularly known stories, often repeated, act as social glue and sources of collective pride. Together with already well-established geographic identities, they contribute to a durable sense of shared, egalitarian place. This kind of approach to the study of ecology and place falls in line with the geographer Yi-Fu Tuan's (1991:695) urgings to study "the varying ways by which different societies use speech and/or the written word to realize place."

Faeroese locational names and narratives of place communicate about places and their associated events and thus solidify individual parts of the geographic and social landscape as unique. Each topographic and historical spot is a singular setting and place of experience. Each inhabitant or visitor to a place can come to know a place through its name, the folklore surrounding it, and through hearing others' accounts, and yet still have his/her own firsthand experiences and interpretations.

In accordance with the nation's language and subsistence history, specificity in space seems always to have overshadowed specificity in time. I have said that villagers relayed to me events of the Middle Ages, like Sneppan í Hamrabyrgi, as if they were recent history. And in the space-full, yet timeless landscapes of the Faeroes, phrases like "in the olden days" seem to mean anything from fifty to a thousand years ago. This contrasts markedly with the usual temporal fixation of American history in which students are taught to memorize names and dates of presidencies, capitals, wars, and so on to the neglect of experiencing places themselves. This linear orientation often bypasses an understanding that places and their "real" histories associate with many persons. Place, contrary to the famous names and dates approach to history, is meaningfully constructed by different individuals and groups with their own varying interpretations. That kind of public belonging of Faeroese places to people and people to places is not usurped in the Faeroes by academic history. Faeroese history is a congeries of experiences, the relating of those experiences by word of mouth, and, recently, by art forms discussed below.

Some scholars have argued that the preservation of Faeroese culture and national identity—and the islands' ultimate political strength culminating in home rule in 1948—derived from a conscious preservation of language and oral tradition. Similarly, and more particularly, I suggest that islanders' local and national consciousness and control were especially enhanced through indigenous expositions about and identification with local place and local places. Margaret Rodman (1992:651) explains how people, places, and narrators at the local level conglomerate into a culture pattern:

> Each teller and each mythically charged stone is part of a social landscape whose horizons overlap other social landscapes. Individuals are most strongly attached to particular named places, and can speak of those places (and their pasts) with the most authority. But the story and its larger landscape binds them to other experts and other places.

In the Faeroes oral, written, and visual arts are simply different forms of the general idiom of place that pervades the archipelago. Place-names, in the contemporary vocabulary of ethnography and cultural studies, are themselves, I suggest, short "texts" of geography, history, and social landscape. Place-names merge with stories of names' origins, which themselves trail into longer stories. Such stories culminated in written formats during the twentieth century, and many of them were transformed into contemporary literature, as with William Heinesen's (1983, translated by Hedin Brønner) rendition of the *grýla*, a folkloric being. Thus verbal and written arts seem to be only different sides of the same phenomenon of place embeddedness in the Faeroes. Whether the details of a story or legend are completely true matters little (except to historiographers). Truth shades into legend in a land where almost anything seems possible.

Storytelling and Balladry

Traditionally villagers often worked well into the evenings. Particularly during the long nights of the colder seasons, indoor work, a respite from the harsh conditions of outdoors, often combined with oral entertainment. Families and friends would gather inside to spin, weave, knit, and to tell stories and sing songs in gatherings called *kvøldsetur* ("evening sittings"). It was especially in these forums that village folklore and oral literature persisted.

Folklorists and historians have collected and discussed many Faeroese folktales (aevintýr) and legends (sagnir) relayed during these group gatherings. The stories' subjects range from supernatural beings like ghosts and elves to true-to-life heroes of local life.

Villagers often told and retold popular local and regional narratives. Storytelling (and more recently, story reading) were both entertainment and methods to teach history, values, morals, and generally to transmit cultural concerns.

One Sumbingur relates:

> I remember going to houses to hear stories. Andreas's father, he was working in a place called Hvalnes. He came home once every month or two and then left home again. . . . But there were always some who told stories and read stories. We had here one [a villager] called Maynard. He died a couple years ago. He was a wonderful storyteller, a very good one. We would listen and listen. He read book after book. He was very good. Before he died, he was reading on the radio.

Today, radio stories are popular. No one seems to tire of hearing the same stories repeated on the air year after year, and new ones continue to be written and circulated.

And on holiday nights and special occasions villagers chanted Faeroese ballads (*kvaeðir*) and danced the now-famous medieval ring-dances. Although kvøldsetur diminished considerably around the turn of the century, what with economic conditions favoring pursuits other than working with wool at home, dancing and ballad singing are still relatively common affairs.

Most folklorists are familiar with the Faeroese ballad-dance, a medieval ring-dance performed without accompanying musical instruments. It is a unique phenomenon within Europe, now maintained only in the Faeroes. Ring-dancing originated in France in the fifteenth or sixteenth century and became part of other Scandinavian cultures for a while. The leader of each dance (usually male) leads the chanting of ballad verses while participants lock each other's arms in an undulating circle around the dance floor. Each dance may have a different leader, as each leader has his own repertoire of songs. Dancing and dance leadership are open to all, although a few individuals are the most regular dance leaders because they are the ones who best know the ballads' stanzas—each kvaeði sometimes has a hundred or more. Insofar as anyone who knows a ballad well enough may lead, the social structure of dancing and balladry is nonhierarchical. Moreover, anyone, male or female, old or young, can break in and out of the dance chain at any time, at whatever place he or she pleases and without regard to whether he or she joins arms with a man or woman. Thus there is a casual openness to these social gatherings, additionally lubricated by the use of alcohol.

As a special folkdance performed by anyone and everyone and unique to the Faeroes, the kvaeðir tradition and practice marks the Faeroese culture as a special place with a special reputation. Moreover, since the ballad-dances often go hand-in-hand with whale hunts as a celebration of success, the art form also adheres to this activity as part of the islands' particular ecological setting. To both natives and outsiders this oral art serves as a text and symbol of the islands.

In many historically isolated villages, these traditions have survived fairly well. The Sunnbiar Dansifelag, the Dance Society of Sumbøur, is quite active and skilled in balladry and ring-dancing. Its members have traveled to other European nations and in 1977 won an international European folk art award, the Freiherr Von Stein award. Sumbøur, comprised of especially active and skilled

Sumbingar of all ages, most of them in traditional folk dress, chant ballads and ring-dance in the village's own Dancehouse.

singers and dancers, has even more fully than other parts of the islands gained identity in this way. Yet in traditional informal communicative fashion, one needs to be told of or read about this. There are no obvious signs or plaques in the village that attest to the award.

There are three types of ballads. Two are epics: Danish ballads (*vísur*) and Faeroese ballads. Both ballads refer to individuals and events in Viking and later historical periods. Faeroese ballads are sung in Faeroese and Danish ones in Danish. Danish ballads are usually about heroes from Scandinavia or the continent, whereas Faeroese ballads are typically about Faeroese heroes. The Faeroese folk ballads have formed the bulk of Faeroese oral poetry and, unlike those of other Scandinavian countries, they are chanted especially to go along with the dance. There are also the *dansipol*, "dance games," which are similar to the singing games in other parts of Scandinavia, in which the dance circle changes shape into a row formation, and hand-holding changes as people pass between each other. Sometimes the dance step changes. They are still performed to ballads, both short ones and some of epic length.

Collectors have counted 236 types of Faeroese ballads, with approximately 44,000 stanzas; there are no doubt more. Mortan Nolsøe (1977:31) divides Faeroese ballads into different genres, including "ballads of supernatural beings, legendary ballads, historical ballads, ballads of chivalry, heroic ballads, and jocular ballads." Among the ballad heroes, Sigurd from *Sjurðar kvaeði* and Emperor Charlemagne are popular, and they appear in several different ballads. Although there were some formally educated ballad collectors who traveled around the islands—for example, Hammershaimb (1819–1909)—most of the collectors have been local persons who copied down the folk ballads in their own villages or islands. Thus the ballad books, in typical Faeroese style of local association by place-name, have taken the place-name of the location of the collection, as in the *Fugloyarbók* (Fugloy island book), *Koltursbók* (Koltur island book), and the *Sunnbiarbók* (Sumbøur village book).

Faeroese ballads and poems are still written. In 1983 "Suður-oyarkvaeðið" appeared in *Varðin*, the islands' literary magazine. In it Mortan Hammer of the village of Froðba extols the virtues of the different villages and places of the island of Suðuroy including

Two villagers dress in
national costume on a
night of ring-dancing
and ballad-singing in
Sumbøur.

the mountain Beinisvørð near Sumbøur and how Sumbingar are
noted for their very own ballad singing. Through such formats
Faeroese demonstrate how they are intimately tied to their locales
and that they are proud of their ties.

As ballad variations within and between nations have long fasci-
nated folklorists, students of folklore are generally familiar with
Faeroese ballads. They treat the ballads not only as unique phenomena, but as evidence of historical linkage (or lack of it) to other
parts of Europe and Scandinavia (see, e.g., Nolsøe 1977 and
Conroy 1979). Perhaps one of the most remarkable aspects of this
local, oral tradition is that some of the balladeers knew thousands
of lines of verse by heart. Nolsøe (1977), using the documents of a
collector interviewing one balladeer in 1821, estimates that the one
man knew twenty-five hundred quatrains!

The third type of ballad, and the most Faeroese in character, is
the satirical ballad (táttur), although it is less openly discussed and

documented than the others. Earlier I discussed taettir as a method of social control, closely tied to the traditions and personalities of individual villages. They satirize local (and occasionally national) Faeroese figures. These ballads are a completely indigenous form. "It is likely that this type of poetic composition has older [than the Reformation] roots in this country . . . no Faroese satirical ballad has travelled outside the Faroes" (Nolsøe 1977:33). Taettir are quintessentially Faeroese.

Nolsøe summarizes:

> The satirical ballads are, in most cases, aimed against matters in a Faroese village, the persons there, and their faults. Jens. Chr. Svabo mentions, inter alia, the following as examples of satirical ballad material: sponging; unmanliness (effeminacy) or awkwardness in man's business; uncleanliness and vermin of the head; being present when a bitch whelps; a woman consorts with Hollanders; the eating of crows; boasting; poor housekeeping resulting in begging; a sheriff's bias; excessive miserliness; a suitor who is refused because of incompetence; sheep stealing. (Ibid:33)

This litany reads like a contemporary list of informal crimes of village life.

Many taettir have never been put to paper: they tend to embarrass and ridicule. Composers and repeaters of satirical ballads must be careful not to do obvious damage to others' feelings or to be too boisterous. Otherwise offended parties might then humiliate the balladeers. Consequently, most written taettir speak of former villagers or mildly of contemporaries. Two Sumbingar particularly knowledgeable in local taettir were reticent to repeat them, for fear they would receive retaliatory ridicule.

One of the most famous satirical ballads is the *Fuglakvaeði (Ballad of the Birds)*. It portrays ballad characters as different Faeroese birds that match the different personality and social traits of people. Some of the humans in this case are Danish bureaucrats and others who interfered with Faeroese matters during the trading monopoly.

Despite the fact that the few ethnographic studies of the Faeroes give little sociological attention to taettir, Nolsøe himself (ibid:33) recognizes that "they give . . . a very interesting insight into old village life and ways of thought in the Faroes and have great value as documents of cultural history." Taettir are forms of verbal ridicule and public spectacle, and, as such, are musical, poetic counterparts of nicknames, gossip, and social commentary. Like much Faeroese speech, taettir are acts of verbal virtuosity and control communication embedded in particular physical and social landscapes of the islands.

Villagers, mostly young, sometimes also gather for dances and music imported from outside the Faeroes. All non-Faeroese dancing and singing is collectively known in Faeroese as *Eingilskdansur* ("English dance").

Legends

While taettir as a folk art form attest to the humor and social control of local village life, sagnir additionally epitomize the Faeroese penchant for telling stories and for merging place with person, past with present, truth with uncertainty. John West has translated a number of Faeroese folktales, legends, and supernatural stories into English. In the introduction to his collection he comments on traditional oral Faeroese literature:

> In my opinion, the most outstanding of the Faeroese traditional stories are the historical legends. It is, of course, questionable how much reliance can be placed on the legends as historical sources in the absence of documentary confirmation, but they are a wonderful source of social history for the Faroe Islands in former centuries. (1980:iv)

He defines a legend as "a story about some village personality of former times, believed in the main to be true" (iv), although one kind of legend he says are folktales about witches, giants, and so on, and another kind are about huldufólk. Thus it is not only that after centuries of handing down legends by word-of-mouth that it is unclear where the truth lies, but also that legends themselves range in subject matter from the purely human to the supernatural. And, perhaps most to the point, villagers themselves do not clearly differentiate between types of legends.

Historical legends include ones such as "Snaebjørn," the story of a villager who accidentally killed a bailiff and spent his days living on cliffs (see Wylie 1987); "Beinta and Peder Arrheboe," which details a woman's destruction of her several husbands, including a priest; "The Turks in Suðuroy," an account of villagers' struggle against Turkish pirates; and "Regin of Toftir," about the settlement of village boundary disputes on Suðuroy. They and others now appear in Danish and English as well as in Faeroese. Sagnir, written or not, retain their charm for villagers. In my early fieldwork discussions with Sumbingar several different people told me about events in the history of Sumbøur, like the attack of the Frisian pirates, which I later discovered in a book of legends set on Suðuroy, *Suðuroyarsagnir*. Whether such events actually took place as portrayed is a mystery, but villagers savor the information.

Sagnir contain many nicknames, often with still extant place-names. For example, nicknamed characters appear in "Regin of Toftir," dating from around 1450. This legend tells of wrestling matches between two men of the (still thriving) villages of Sumbøur and Vágur. The men wrestled to determine animal grazing right boundaries between the two villages. The Sumbøur man is called "The Sumba Splitter" (Sunnbiarkleyvin). Another major character is "The Hook" (Krókurin), whose name derives, states the legend, "because he was always trying to get his hook into more than he rightly owned" (West 1980:11). Other legends in Jakobsen's collection contain numerous nicknames, as do many Faeroese stories written in the last hundred years.

The following short legend, originally collected by Jakobsen (1898–1901:163–164), is typically full of the flavor of Faeroe geography, naming practices, and history.

The Koltur Lad Who Swam to Hestur

There was once a young man on Koltur who was courting a girl on Hestur, but her father would not hear of their meeting. The lad thus had to visit the girl in secret, and he did so in this manner, by swimming across Koltur Sound (the strait between Koltur and Hestur), choosing the tidal current, a late ebb tide, to swim south by; the ebb tide when it is half run sets directly towards Hestur Point at the northern end of the island. There she would come to meet him, and he would swim back north-wards on the flood tide; for the flood tide sets directly across the sound towards Koltur Head. It is 120 fathoms between Koltur Ness (the southernmost point of Koltur) and Hestur Point. At Magnus's Ness, at the northern end of Hestur, he was accustomed to swim ashore, and this headland is said to have been named after him. The lad was supposed to have been called Magnus. There the girl waited for him with dry clothes. There is a little cove directly in from Magnus's Ness, called Lovers' Creek after the two of them. This continued for a time, but in the end her father noticed her absences and became suspicious. Then one evening, when the lad came swimming up, this old man, her father, met him with an axe in his hand, and threatened to kill him if he came ashore. Then the lad had to turn northwards at once, and afterwards nothing was heard of him again. The probability is that the current caught him and he drifted out to sea.

The story goes that when this Koltur lad was drowned, the current called The Pigs began, up through Koltur Sound. This was supposed to be in revenge for his death. (West 1980:15)

West (15–16) explains that

the drama of this story is heightened if one appreciates the violence of the tidal currents round the Faroe Islands, which even today sometimes cause the smaller inter-island post boats to modify their routes and timetables . . . the action of the girl's father, in compelling Magnus to swim back to Koltur against the tide, was indeed as homicidal as killing him outright with his axe.

Here is another short legend of the islands:

The Wild Boys of Viðareiði

In Wild Sheepdale Fell, north of the village of Viðareiði, there are many shelters, caverns, and dens, so it is very easy for folk to hide there.

In the Wallside hamlet of Viðareiði lived a poor man who had two sons. Sickness began to range around the village, and both the lads' parents died at once. They were then quite small and unable to do any work. Nobody took the trouble to foster them up, so the two boys roamed about begging or stealing. Then they vanished. Folk thought they must be dead, probably by climbing on the cliffs and then falling into the sea.

Later, food was stolen from the storehouses [hjallar], of various people in the village. But it was so usual in those days for everyone to steal from one another's storehouses, people were little concerned over that. But things got worse and worse as time passed. Men lost sheep wholesale, year after year. They often went up into the hills to make an investigation how this could come about, but all to no avail.

Then finally, after many years had elapsed, they met two men up on wild Sheepdale Fell. They were both troll-like to look at, with shaggy hair and beard, and they were clad in sheepskins. The villagers tried to capture them, but could not reach them. The wild boys were up in the cliffs, throwing down stones and straining their feet against great boulders, so that it was dangerous to approach them. Then the men began to speak kindly to them, promising that no harm should be done to them, and at length they were induced to rejoin other men. These were the Wallside boys, who had been living in the hills, and now were grown men.

Jóanis' Gully is the name of a gully on the western side of Wild Sheepdale Fell. It is extremely well sheltered up there. There are caves into the fell on both sides and the soil has fallen down from the cliffs above. The gully is named after one of the wild boys, Jóanis, who was said to have lived there with his brother. (from Jakobsen 1898–1901:245–246, translated by West 1980:53)

In the extremely geographic Faeroe Islands, names, places, and people merge with the arts of the culture. Geography *cum* legend, legend *cum* geography, are fundamental.

A Note about "Telling Stories"

Faeroese use the verb *fortelja* ("tell") in the past tense, as in English, to say things like "he told" me that my mother was at your house (*"hann foralti meg at mama mín var hjá tikkur"*). In the present tense without an object, however, *at fortelja* means "to tell stories." For example, "he doesn't know how to tell stories" is *hann dugir ikki at fortelja*. The use of the word "stories" (*søga*) is unnecessary to complete the thought. Thus, like others, Sumbingar use the same verb both to refer to others' simple everyday oral statements and to refer to storytelling. Folk stories and storytelling are ever-present aspects of local culture and identity.

According to W. B. Lockwood (1977:237) søga is Faeroese for "story," "legend," "history," "tale," and "saga," although *sagnir* are more specifically "legends." Perhaps the best gloss of søga is "account," connotatively neutral on the issue of veracity. The word søgn, "legend," implies that the events are based on actual history, which, while perhaps exaggerated or distorted, is not supernatural. Yet some so-called legends involve the interaction of local persons and huldufólk.

A Faeroese folktale is an aevintýr, "one of the North European stock of stories of witches, giants, trolls, and the farm lad who wins the princess" (West 1980:iv). Sumbingar did not use the word *aevintýr* when telling me about trolls or other supernatural beings, and thus local language is often unconcerned about, or does not clearly differentiate between, the meanings of the English glosses of søgur into "stories" or "legends" or "histories" or "tales."

West uses legends as material for historical reconstruction. He analyses the tale "Beinta and Peder Arrheboe" in the "hope that this case-study will aid others in the difficult task of distinguishing the possibly true from the definitely false in the wealth of historical legend in Scandinavia and elsewhere" (1982–1983:32). Yet such historiography is difficult and often tentative, more the concern of the outsider and/or scholar than the local person for whom the stories are whole and alive, not scientific objects to be dissected.

Wylie and Margolin (1981) and Wylie (1987) use legends to try to reconstruct Faeroese life in earlier times. But Wylie uses the seventeenth-century legend of "Óli Jarnheysur," a story of relations between farmers and hired hands, less for traditional historiography than as material for what he calls "legendary historiography." His is the study of what legends reveal about the previous Faeroese worldview. His chosen task is

> to make more explicit sense of what a legend says *about* events, whether these are "historical" or not, in terms that seem congruent with the principles by which its authors have already undertaken to organize experience.
>
> This means, for example, that apparent flights of fancy will prove more important than "sticking to the facts"; that precise dating, with which legends are little concerned, will be less important than the geographical details that do abound in them; and that the decisions of courts and kings will be less important than the actions of huldufólk. (Wylie 1987:50)

As pure entertainment, semihistorical accounts, or as folklore, sagnir are particularly Faeroese expressive forms. Legends are familiar, public possessions of egalitarian-minded communities embedded in familiar public places.

Folktales and Huldufólk Stories

Faeroese folktales include stories of types of beings found in other Scandinavian and European tales, for example, dwarves (dvørgar). Known in much of northern Europe, dwarves live in boulders or in mounds under rocks; there are many such dwarf stones around the Faeroes. (Dvørgasteinur [Dwarfstone] is a place just outside the village of Sumbøur.) More indigenous and common to the archipelago are stories and experiences of huldufólk. Some villagers say that the huldufólk left the environs of Sumbøur in the 1950s, when electricity arrived, suggesting in effect, that electricity was the literal and symbolic beginning of "modern" times in the area. Many villagers I interviewed often were ambiguous and non-committal about huldufólk, yet I did construct a place-name map of the village environs with the reputed, traditional haunts of huldufólk, dwarves, and trolls. There are numerous huldufólk stories, some collected and written down, many others passed on orally.

Jakobsen's collection has several stories about huldufólk. Here is a short one.

Glove Friend

A farmer on the island of Great Dímun was out on the hill pasture one day. As he was walking along, someone spoke to him and bade him give him some wool for a pair of gloves. He answered yes; but he saw no living creature however much he looked around. The next day he went out into the pasture again and put the wool down where he had heard the voice. When he went that way once more, the wool was gone. Some time afterwards the farmer was out fishing; a storm broke out, and the men were in peril. As they strove to row for land, they heard someone cry, "Glove Friend! Row eastabout, for westabout is impossible!" The usual landing on Dímun, known as The Gully, is on the west side of the island, but another landing place is on the eastern side, called The Breast. The farmer did as this same voice told him, and came safely to land. (Jakobsen 1898–1901:205, trans. by West 1980:87) same voice told him, and came safely to land. (Jakobsen 1898–1901:205, trans. by West 1980:87)

Hammershaimb's (1891) anthology of Faeroese tales describes huldufólk:

Huldufólk are large in build, their clothes all grey, and their hair black. Their dwellings are in mounds, and they are also called Elves. An 'Elves Howe' is to be found in north Streymoy, south of Haldorsvík. They live like human beings, and have sheep and cattle which go amongst the other animals in the hill pastures. Huldufólk can make themselves and all that they own invisible to human beings, and it is often said of something that one is looking for, that "the huldumenn have hidden it." They like to take unbaptized babies from their cradles and put their own in their place, but these latter then become simpletons among men. Small children who go out alone often disappear, and then it is the huldufólk who have gone off with them. Sometimes they are found again far from the village and have then told how a big man gave them food whilst they were away.

Huldu maidens often take a fancy to Christian lads and then try to tempt them and entice them into their homes. If they go into the hill pastures to look after the sheep, and are tired and thirsty, the mound will open, and the maiden will come out and offer them drink, either ale or milk. If they do not blow off the froth, they drink themselves into forgetfulness, for in the froth lies witchcraft, and by this the maidens ensnare them, gain power over them and keep them with them in the elves' howes. (327, trans. by West 1980:103)

Huldufólk can be both helpful and mischievous.

During long wintry nights, walks in the foggy mountains, and in ordinary conversation in the street Faeroese perennially have shared stories that attest to the ever-present mysteries of humans and other beings. Even a fifty-year-old man who told me that he did not believe in huldufólk said that when he was young there was an old woman in Sumbøur who always "saw" before it happened the death of a local man through disaster. This included the speaker's own relative who had fallen from a cliff. The "range of the possible" in a small, far-off community is quite wide.

Bygdarsøgur

The bygdarsøgur are twentieth-century forms of local Faeroese history. They are local accounts of events and places in and around a specific village. As a vernacular genre, written by anyone interested, these histories express a commonality of village sentiment, a generally held desire to communicate about and record the past, and a relishing of local culture and history. Predictably, many of the histories use places and place-names as the foci for chronicling the local community.

One of the more popular bygdarsøgur is *Miðvinga søga*, set in the village of Miðvágur ('Middle Bay'). The author, Mikkjal á Ryggi (1965:5–6), explains his own work:

> About 25 years ago the society Solarmagn asked me to write down the placenames of Miðvágur and record them on the map. I went to the old and knowledgeable men, and all of them were enthusiastic about telling me names or going into the outfield to show me the places. With some of the old men it was rather slow work at first, but I was very soon amazed to see the way the life entered into them when they called the old names to mind; it seemed to me as though they had grown young once again—and perhaps they felt the same too. I did not need to ask for information; when they knew anything about a place or a name, they came out with it quite spontaneously. Usually it was something short, and then I wrote it down with the name. But sometimes there were whole stories, and then I would ask them to save the information for me until I had a better opportunity of writing it down. Yes, they would agree to tell me again later, but in the meantime they would not remain silent—the flow had begun, and would not cease till all was out. (trans. by West 1982–1983)

J. Símun Hansen (1971, 1973) has written a whole series of books on the northern islands organized by island, parish, village, and homestead. (See also classic bygdarsøgur by Edward Hjalt (1953), Jóannes Patursson (1966), and Jóan Christian Poulsen (1947).) Indigenous Faeroese literature seems only a written extension of their sensory and verbal aesthetic of geography.

The popularity of this local literary form is revealing of the Faeroese people's strong interest in storytelling and in embedding themselves in local space. Not including unpublished accounts, approximately twenty bygdarsøgur exist in about twenty of the eighty different villages. That is 25 percent. (Imagine if in the United States one-quarter of all settlements had local residents whose local histories were published!) Despite the small market of potential buyers of a book, islanders are quite interested in writing, publishing, and reading about their local communities.

Sumbøur also has its own kind of bygdarsøgur, *Seggjasøgur úr Sumba* (Tall Tales from Sumbøur) by native Poul F. Joensen (1963), also a prolific poet. It contains eleven different chapters set in and around the village. They range widely in time and in content. One recounts the legend (originally collected by Jakobsen) about the Frisians at Akraberg near Sumbøur during the 1700s. Another is a story with a *huldumaður*. Others speak about memorable persons and events of the nineteenth and early twentieth centuries. The latter include an account of men stranded by weather and tough seas on the islet Sumbiarhólmur not far from shore. There is also a story of a man who fell to his death from a bird cliff. Another entry entitled "Rivastakkur," the name of one of several nearby sea stacks used by fowlers, tells of Sumbingar and their adventures catching hundreds of birds. In all the stories there are familiar local place-names and locational nicknames. Among other characters, Jakup í Kvidni, Paul uppi í Kvíggi, Pól á Ogrum, and Símun undir Hamri appear bearing the place-names still used in the village today and still attached to current residents.

Elsebeth Vestergaard's (1975) book, *Feðgarnir Miðgerða Poul og Poul Johannes*, contains vignettes, short tales, local taettir, and short personality sketches about people and places of the southern half of the island of Suðuroy, mostly around the settlements of Sumbøur, Akrar, and Vágur. Some of the people mentioned and described in it, and in other local works, like Maria í Kálgarði and balladeer Albert í Høgeil, were villagers with whom I spent considerable time learning about Sumbøur. Yet neither of them, in typical Faeroese modesty, mentioned to me that they were written about in local books and publications.

Modern Literature, Place, and Character

Although officials used Danish for formal legal matters and the Faeroese were probably nominally literate in Danish since the mid-1900s, for centuries villagers exchanged information without their own everyday language available in written form. However, since the advent of written Faeroese, population growth, and the nationalist movement (including mandatory school instruction in both Danish and Faeroese), Faeroese have been prolific writers. They have held the distinction of being the country with the largest per capita output of written works in the world. There are over a half-dozen weekly newspapers and more than twenty magazines of various genres. Forty or fifty books are published in Faeroese each year. This wealth of printed information is quite an accomplishment for a society with a history of only 140 years of written language, with only about the last 100 or so of concerted writing. Some say that the abundance of literary talent on the islands derives from the strong sense of belonging felt by members of a small nation and from the associated feeling of responsibility of those capable of such writing. Over and above the long-standing importance of oral traditions, the Faeroese sense of place and belonging function to promote written artistry.

Hedin Brønner (1972:3), literary critic and translator of Faeroese works into English, connects Faeroese geography with themes of communication in Faeroese short stories:

> The problem of access and communication has therefore always been an essential element of Faroese life; one must understand this in order to appreciate the preoccupation with it in Faroese stories. Some landing places are hardly more than narrow ledges washed by the sea and useless when tides and currents are unfavorable. Once a boat has successfully negotiated these hazards, its occupants may have a dizzying climb along narrow paths and ledges till they reach the farmlands at the top.

Villagers say that in older days men used to talk in loud, bold voices to each other. One person pointed out to me two elderly Sumbingar who still talk like that. He said the loudness derives from the fact that fishermen and shepherds needed to shout to each

This stack, a free-standing pinnacle of rock, sits a few hundred feet off Suðuroy's tall cliffsides. The stack is called Rivastakkur ('Split Stack'), and Sumbingar climb it in order to catch puffins. Rivastakkur is also ▶ the title and setting of a story published by Sumbøur's own Poul F. Joensen.

other in wind and storm. Many times a few words could be crucial to the survival of sheep, fish, harvests, boats, or the men themselves. Such climatic and geographic variables may also contribute to the descriptive, poignant Faeroese speech and ultimately to the conciseness of Faeroese writing.

Transposing oral culture into "written" culture, Faeroese novelists, poets, dramatists, playwrights, satirists, and journalists have thus helped to preserve much of what it means to be Faeroese. They have collected local stories, woven legends into new works, documented traditional folklife, and written the local village histories. Wylie (1987) argues that Faeroese literature is a conscious attempt to maintain cultural distinctiveness and demonstrate to other Scandinavian and European peoples the Faeroese ability to produce works of literary quality as high as anyone else's. A benchmark in this development was Hammershaimb's 1891 *Faerøsk Anthologi* (Faeroese Anthology), quoted earlier, which contained collections of ballads and folklore along with his own descriptions of village life. Other significant products include Fridrikur Petersen's 1877 poem "Eg oyggjar veit . . ." ("I Know of Isles . . ."), which later became the national anthem.

Numerous poets, including Poul F. Joensen from Sumbøur, have used the seemingly natural poetry of the pithy Faeroese language in verse form. The poem that opens this chapter exemplifies Faeroese concern with place, orientation, and weather and, in this case, describes the very mountain that stands above Sumbøur. The title of the poem, "Á Beinisvørði," with Á meaning "From on Top Of" also demonstrates the difficulty of getting the full feel of the poignancy and indigenous meanings and rhythms of Faeroese. Faerose poetry (*skaldskapur*), as in other languages, uses the various poetic conventions of rhyme, alliteration, simile, and so on, nearly impossible to preserve while translating into another language. Moreover, without actually seeing and feeling Faeroese geography, Faeroese poetry about the landscape is not able to be fully appreciated. As the translator of the poem, my friend Jaspur Midjord, told me, "it's impossible to translate and still get the dramatic effect and to convey how Faeroese poetry about the land is itself nationalistic."

The novels are somewhat more accessible. The first Faeroese novel was *Bábelstornið* (*The Tower of Babel*) by Rasmus Rasmussen, published in 1909. The next major novel of significance was Heðin Brú's (1930) *Lognbrá* (*Mirage*). Then came *Barbara*, by Jørgen-Frantz Jacobsen, published in 1939, since then translated into several languages and made into a German movie.

With the Faeroese language having a short history in written form one could say that all Faeroese literature is modern. Yet "modern" in this setting is still in many ways quite traditional in flavor and style. As one might imagine, local legends and folktales have often been bases or jumping-off points for much writing, and originally oral accounts shade off into written ones, as in some of the bygdarsøgur stories. Indeed, the legend of Beinta and Peder Arrheboe formed the basis of Jorgensen's *Barbara*. In the legend a magistrate's daughter married three clergymen one after the other and made life difficult for all of them. The novel details one of the marriages, Barbara's (Beinta's) early relationship with her third husband. Among other traditional tales, the legend of "The Koltur Lad Who Swam to Hestur" was the basis of a play, "Magnus," written in the 1890s by R. C. Effersøe.

The importance of place-names and place experiences of bygdarsøgur and other written or verbal communications are also echoed in short stories and novels. In his own novel *Fastatøkur*, Heðin Brú (1935:134), perhaps the most noted Faeroese writer, describes the discourse of local attachment to the landscape.

> Høgni listens to him, not out of necessity, but out of interest. And he gets the impression of how much *at home* his father is up here in the mountain pastures. Not just because he knows all about the sheep that live up there, but he knows every stone, every hollow, every hummock. Some have names, and some have no names, but it is all the same to him, every little thing has as it were its own life for Sakir, reawakening for him particular thoughts and feelings. Every time something happens on the mountains, a stone, a tussock, or something like that will take it to itself, and preserve its memory. The generations carry this forward from father to son, the places constantly increase in number, and before you realise it, the mountain is quite alive. (trans. by West 1982–1983)

Saying it another way elsewhere, through the words of a character in his short story "Fair Play," Brú describes his own people as "this home-loving way of [Faeroese] people who have been living in the same spot all their lives, where they know every person, every animal, every pebble, every tuft of grass—where everything talks to you and feels a part of you." In the lives of his literary characters we see Faeroese life as deeply situated and oriented in place. We read of the natives' attitudes to their environment, their mental ecology. Written literary and (oral) cultural themes seem to be one and the same.

Brú is popular not just for his ability to put his finger on the Faeroese aesthetic of geography and on the strong relations between human beings and nature, but also for his portrayal of a community and the social landscape. He writes about unique, colorful everyday characters and traditional village livelihoods. The mayor of Sumbøur once said to me that Brú's most famous and widely read work, *Feðgar á Ferð* (*The Old Man and His Sons*), together with the Bible, are the most important written works in Faeroese.

The Old Man and His Sons, translated into several languages since it was originally published in 1940, sketches classic economic activities like whaling, sheep raising, and fowling, along with the social dimensions of village life. It is the story of a man, Ketil, and his sons who struggle to come up with the money for whale meat he hastily bid for at an auction after he had drunk some liquor.

Ketil is one of the Faeroese men that Brú describes as:

> sturdy old men clad from head to foot in their thick homespun, their heavy whaling knives at their belts. These are the men who grew up at the oar, and trod out the mountain paths. For them, all journeys were long journeys and risky ones. They are all keyed up to meet any problem, and they take life very seriously. These men stride onwards with ponderous footsteps—strong men of few words. (1970:3).

Ketil, like the older generation of Faeroese, prides himself in not having debts and living meagerly. The novel is much about the younger generation's desire for goods and how some economic and moral values have changed during the twentieth century.

Brønner summarizes Brú and his work:

> Not alone his language, but his style and thinking as well are Faroese to the core. All the characteristic features are there—the slow and rugged strength, the terseness, the irony, the outward resignation, and that immense reserve of unspoken thought that forces the listener into active participation in the communicating process. . . .

> [his style is] one of monumental, biblical simplicity—rough-
> hewn, earthbound, compact. It builds on visual qualities inher-
> ent in the Faroese language itself. Its economy of words leads
> the reader to search between the lines. . . . (1973:81–123)

Another internationally known Faeroese novelist is William
Heinesen. He wrote in Danish, like Jørgen-Frantz Jacobsen,
because traditionally many Tórshavn families, although bilingual,
chose to speak Danish in the capital. Heinesen's often surrealistic
works are more popular among more formally educated Faeroese
in the capital and among continental Scandinavians than among
local villagers. As one man from Sumbøur said, he and fellow
villagers do not like Heinesen so much because he "does not write
of real things." Quite accomplished, Heinesen in 1981 renounced
a campaign to nominate him for the Nobel Prize in literature
because he felt a writer in the Faeroese language would be more
appropriate.

Heinesen, (also a noted painter), like other local writers, very
much envisages Faeroese culture as a cast of characters and a
landscape of unique personalities. He highlights the role of the
individual in society in a fantastic way in a short story, "The Night
of the Gryla." Ordinarily the grýla is a Faeroese "being" who appeared traditionally on Grýlukvøld, ("Gryla Evening"), the first
Monday in Lent when children dress up in costumes and enter
people's homes seeking presents. (In earlier days poor folks visited
farmers' homes soliciting gifts of food.)

> The grýla itself is a rather mysterious creature which appears
> to be a "fikt" of much the same order as the English "bogey-
> man"—a "fikt" because no grown-up really believes in its exist-
> ence, but cherishes it as an invention which prevents children
> from doing harm. . . . Faeroe children are warned that if they
> misbehave the grýla will get them. (Williamson 1970:247)

Heinesen's story concerns an ordinary Faeroese man who un-
controllably and agonizingly turns into a creature, the grýla. One
night of the year he becomes a kind of exhibitionist:

> Dunald is the only one who is on personal footing with the
> Gryla. But the exact nature of his standing with her is hidden
> from the world. It is known that in moments of weakness he
> has been deeply unhappy about her and has called her a burden
> and a curse. And indeed, many people are greatly surprised

At a spot along Eggjargarður ('Edge's Wall'), the mountain ridge above the village, a shepherd's gate surrealistically looks out over the North Atlantic Ocean.

that he has anything to do with her at all. In his daily comings and goings Dunald's manner is quiet and a bit shy, his speech is sad and dispirited, and his eyes are honest and melancholy. His whole demeanor makes people forget that he has anything to do with the Gryla. He is liked by every one on the island. Helpful and trustworthy, he lends the farmers a good hand, particularly with outdoor work—a great toiler. Since he is a poor man, nobody begrudges him what he gains from the Gryla. Nor does anyone try to tease him about anything, for though he may not be a bright light, he is nobody's fool either. His memory is as good as anybody's, he knows as much as the next fellow about ancestry and family ties in the village, and he knows a number of old ballads. But in spite of all these good traits, Dunald is an odd character. He is not like other men. He is a loner and an outsider. All because of the Gryla. (trans. by Brønner 1983:16)

Sometimes a "creature," Dunald is nevertheless like a common man with ordinary talents of cooperation, balladry, knowledge of kinship relations, and so on. Dunald epitomizes how the Faeroese individual remains true to the identity, "the burden," which life and others have given him. This story, like much of local literature and philosophy, portrays the joy and the pain of being a character within a community, the burden of self. The individual character, greatly controlled by fate and society, appears to be a general theme of Faeroese discourse, written or verbal.

There are many other Faeroese poets, novelists, short story writers, and playwrights. M. A. Winther, Sverri Paturrson, Martin Joensen, Jens Pauli Heinesen, Karsten Hoydal, and Hans Dalsgard are a few whose work has been translated into English. Here Brønner (1973:122) summarizes Faeroese approaches to fiction:

> Except for Heinesen's rare and whimsical excursions into the style of the eighteenth-century novel, Faroese fiction allows characters and events to unfold without visible aid from the author. The reader is not usually informed what kind of person he is about to encounter, what is going on inside that person's mind at a given moment. More often he must make his own character analysis with the help of action and conversations. This is in the best tradition of the sagas and of the modern Norwegian novel. The epitome is reached in Heðin Brú's short stories, many of which recount external events whose sole purpose is to support character portrayals.

This sounds remarkably analogous to village talk in Sumbøur. As the Faeroese depiction of characters in novels calls for interpretation, so do the images constructed by villagers' spoken words.

As mentioned, the Faeroese produce a large number of newspapers, periodicals, and journals. The postsecondary institution Fróðskaparsetur Føroyar (Faeroese Academy), and the Føroyar Fornminnisavn (Faeroese Museum) are also active producers of historical, cultural, and folkloric works. They follow the general Scandinavian penchant for the study of language, folklore, history, and nature and thus have produced over the years a number of serial publications with many entries written by Faeroese and others. Publications have included *Fróðskaparrit*, an academic journal; *Mondul*, a history magazine; *Varðin*, a magazine of local literature; and the *Faroe Isles Review*, an English-language journal for tourism and trade.

Despite the wealth of local literature, few full-length academic accounts are set on the islands. Most scholarly works about the islands have been in *Fróðskaparrit* or continental Scandinavian journals, such as *Ethnologica Scandinavia* or, recently, *North Atlantic Studies*. Other than the British, who occupied the Faeroese during World War II, not many long-term foreign-language visitors or students have entered the Faeroe scene. Other than the Danes who vacation there or settled there for employment opportunities until the recent economic crisis of the 1990s, the islands remain relatively untrammeled by outsiders.

One English-language travel writer, Lawrence Milliman, includes a chapter on the Faeroes in his 1990 book about places in the North Atlantic. While he calls Faeroese nature "positively surreal" and describes the islands visually as a place "wherein familiar objects take on richer colors," his commentary fails to see those traits as relevant to the social landscape. Thus he is often brash, arrogant, and ethnocentric about Faeroese culture, preferring to make not infrequent derogatory comments like "In the worldwide sweepstakes for most boring town, I'd place Tórshavn directly below Guaranda, Ecuador" (41) or, in reference to the nearly primeval, mountainous landscape, "I'm installed in a land that's dead with the absolute death of the stillborn" (39).

In the same year also appeared Susanna Kaysen's *Far Afield*, a novel set on the archipelago. It is in quite a different vein than the travel account above. It is an account of an American anthropologist doing fieldwork on the islands and echoes much of my own experience there. Kaysen obviously lived there for some time. By the end of the novel she portrays the protagonist, Jonathan, as similar to a Faeroeman and especially perceptive of fundamental issues of place and of life. On one of his final evenings after a year or so of residence there

> He was looking at light he would never see again. The ocean that was a dark reflecting pool, the earth polished by new grass to a silver surface, the latitude, all bent light and beamed in sideways, condensed it into a new substance in which every house, electrical pole, and rock on the streets of Skopun seemed the essence of house, pole, and rock, absolutes planted in more than three dimensions . . . he was convinced: here at the top of the world reality was visible, and he was looking at it. (320)

In the last paragraph, Jonathan, about to lift off in his departing airplane flight, is:

poised in the moment before it was all reduced to an illustra-
tion, a topography only hinted at by light and shadow, he felt
the hills, bays, and fjords with their wave-embroidered out-
lines, the very rise and fall of the fields, in the rise and fall of
his pulse. And his footsteps on that country—though they went
round and round in circles—were each precious, each tread
known to him and, annealed by memory, visible at this and
greater distances. (338)

Even after several years I, too, still see and feel the details of the
Faeroese landscape in my blood.

Visual Art

Traditional Faeroese visual art involves women's needlework
and knitted sweater designs and, in applied art, men's construction
of boats, houses, and churches. Karsten Hoydal (1976:18–19), a
Faeroese author, speculates why, until the turn of this century, there
was little painting and sculpture:

> Some critics have inclined toward the slightly deprecatory
> opinion that a lack of imagination was to blame. Closer to the
> mark, probably, are those who believe that the Faroese lived in
> an area which, in terms of climate and natural conditions,
> provided only the barest means for subsistence level living; that
> every day had to be used either at sea or in agriculture, in order
> to maintain an extremely modest standard of living. . . . The art
> of poetry enjoyed a better environment under these conditions
> as it could be pursued during both indoor and outdoor work.

Here, too, we have an ecological explanation for a local culture trait.
Nevertheless, Faeroese have quickly grown fond of visual art. The
first noteworthy Faeroese painters were self-taught. Their painting,
like later artists', usually depicts scenes of nature, especially the
changing weather and light conditions on the sea, in the mountains,
and in the villages. Some also rendered huldufólk. There are many
accomplished painters now, and Faeroese are eager to buy and
display native painters' works. Noted artists include Niels Kruse,
C. Holm Isaksen, Jacob Olsen, Sigmund Petersen, S. Joesen-
Mikines, Janus Kamban, Stefan Danielsen, and Frimod Joensen.
Exhibitions of Faeroese art have appeared in Scotland, Denmark,
Iceland, Norway, and elsewhere.

A fairly common form of visual art, which I suspect predates modern Faeroese painting, is caricature. Scholars have paid little attention to it. Yet one finds caricatures of people, real and imaginary, in local newspapers and journals, on signs, and in Faeroese books. Perhaps in days before the printed Faeroese page, some villagers drew humorous caricatures, as if visually creating a nickname or táttur. During my first month on the islands I met a young Faeroe man in Tórshavn who said that he would like to compile a collection of caricatures from various works in the national library. I made no mental note then of the significance of his interest. Only later, after I began to understand the role of villagers' character sketches, did I realize this man was telling me something revealing about Faeroese pleasure in character depiction.

Newspapers often carry political cartoons and humorous caricatures, and publications put out around the time of the national holiday of Ólavsøka sometimes appear with humorous caricatures depicting the events and personalities of the year. Politicians are especially subject to public surveillance and control. Such mocking and amusement accords with the leveling characteristic of the egalitarian ethos and structure of village life. William Heinesen's paintings also include a number of dramatic caricatures. Like all Faeroese forms of communication about people, caricature is a very Faeroese art form: it pokes fun at individuals and depicts characters in realistic, yet exaggerated detail.

Chapter Eight

Faeroese and Fate

An Ecology of Survival

The geography, topography, and climate of the Faeroe Islands have provided a remarkable ecological setting for human beings. Surrounded by poor soil, jagged coastlines, high cliffs, powerful winds, and violent ocean, Faeroese have had their work definitively cut out for them. The capriciousness of the sea, weather, and harvests further tests their ability to survive, physically and emotionally. In such a locale life probably could not be anything but dramatic. Yet the Faeroese make it even more so with their pithy speech and individuality. Thus it seems that not only the mountains, but also the people, are prominent features of the landscape.

The archipelago is a good place to examine the interdependence of human and natural communities. Sumbøur, one of the historically more separate settlements, personifies much that is particularly Faeroese. In such a location, at the end of a mountain road near bountiful fowling cliffs—some of the highest and steepest in the world—we have been able to glimpse how living off whales, birds, fish, sheep, and a few imported goods has led to a kind of life in which getting along with nature and with other humans is critical.

In this context especially, a traditional village or community study, limited to the location of dwellings and the social interactions of people, would do injustice to the notion of "place." It would also do injustice to the now-popular notion of sustainability, wherein humans strive for a long-term approach to dependency upon their environments. In Sumbøur, like other communities in the Faeroes, inhabitants still slaughter their own whale meat, hunt for their own seabirds, raise their own sheep. This parallels nonindustrial subsistence activities carried out for millennia in many parts of the world. Faeroese knowledge of currents, winds, animal behavior, and so on—and their possible unpredictableness—is necessary for their living within nature.

Commercial fishing is now the backbone of the national economy, but villagers still participate in a plural domestic subsistence pattern that keeps them multiply linked to their environs. In other parts of the industrialized world urbanites and others often forget their ultimate dependence on nature, or at least act as if their places in nature are assured. The Faeroese know better. They have lived through times when seaweed was important food. Their experience reminds them and us of the delicate balance within nature and of the need for sustainable livelihoods. They teach us about our own peasant roots. They teach us that one's diet *is* ecology. That one coexists with nature, the environment, the landscape. They teach us that people need to work hard at relationships with nature and that each place is special and that each person is special.

With the taste of skerpikjøt from a certain, named pasture or the flavor of a man's personality associated with a uniquely named homestead, subsistence and society, spatial and social order, are densely intertwined. In this postpeasant fishing society there still is a direct sensuality of place and person, an aesthetic of local physical and social geography based on the traits of the landscape and of the people within it. Thus this book falls within the general study of "landscape," now blossoming in the social and physical sciences.

The landscape concept embraces "material practices as well as aesthetic forms, underlining the convergence between economic structure and cultural project" (Zukin 1991:22). The Faeroese landscape is essentially egalitarian. Even its emergent middle-class economy is not linked to the presence of, or need for, poor people, or degradation of the environment. As a basically undifferentiated one-class society with a Scandinavian-socialized social welfare and medical system, this society has in the twentieth century reduced the amount of economic difference of earlier times in which landowning versus landless families was a major division of the social economy. Elsewhere today, human relationships to the land and to each other are often asymmetrical and revealing of power differentials between subgroups, each with its own "habitus."

The notions of "landscape" or "place" or "nature" are not, for Sumbingar, bourgeois concepts alluding to pretty scenery, weekend outings, or even artistic representations in "high-culture" art. To the Faeroese villager, ecology is not something to be studied or formally schooled in or "aware" of, as something separate from everyday life. It is the experience of the everyday. It is in trying to comprehend this experience and way of seeing that I delineate innumerable names and notions of places and people.

Faeroese demarcations of the landscape, of itemized portions of their environment, and of the environment as a whole, are things to be worked with and identified with. The infields, outfields, coves, and chasms are actively involved with the humans and they mold the human experiences just as the humans mold them. The process of adaptation is two-way. For humans it is cultural—they nominalize, categorize, utilize, and alter their physical environment. On the other hand the physical environment adapts and changes to activities of the humans, as in the fluctuation of fish and animal populations, in the introduction of plant species for cultivation, and in the addition of human-built forms like houses and sheepfolds. Cultural ecology encompasses the ways in which the human use of nature and place—subsistence practices, values, and worldview—influences the physical and social environments and how they in turn influence nature. This falls in line with the need to describe the "community as an ecological system" (Redfield 1960 (1973):32).

Part of the reason that Faeroese linkages to the land and sea are so strong is that the amount of visible human changes to the environment is relatively small. There are few architectural and industrial constructions that separate and segment people from their knowledge of their dependence on nature. Villagers' judicious harvesting of numerous seabirds, fish, whales, and sheep also mostly permits natural regeneration of species without permanent scarring or obscuring of nature. Sumbingar seem just as interested in using their physical environment as in incorporating their physical environment into their culture through names, associations, stories, and folklore. Their ecology comprises physical, social, and conceptual relationships. In this way place, history, and cultural identity remain relatively stable and preserved. Geographic knowledge and experience represent as well as support the social order of an intimate community.

Despite their currently heavy reliance on commercial harvesting of the seas, it makes sense that the primary conceptual focus is on land rather than sea and that land is the major metaphor of community and geography. After all, knowledge and use of the sea are for support of the community based ashore. One can also count much more on the solidity, the terra firma, of the land, than on the temperament of the sea. Thus this book primarily focuses on landscape rather than seascape. Place is the study of how people convert their physical environs, their "space," into social and cultural experience.

Faeroese are stoics, modestly proud of their ability to manage the harsh environment in a setting remote from other parts of the world and to survive the social conditions of the community. Villagers are acutely aware that outside forces mold their lives. "You have to be made special to live in a small village," one villager exhorts. Another Sumbingur describes why he thinks Niclas drinks a lot: "One can well say that he is a kind of eccentric. He has been made into one by the conditions (*umstøður*) that he has lived in. So he drinks every weekend." Another man captures this general Faeroese perspective in its proverbial form: *Umstøðunar skapa alt* (The conditions of life shape everything).

An older man, one of the more frequent butts of village ridicule, philosophizes in his own story below. He switches back and forth between using "I" (*eg*) and "one" (*man*). Villagers frequently use the Danish impersonal pronoun *man* ("one" or "you") instead of the personal Faeroese *eg* ("I") or *tú* ("you"). It attests to islanders' depersonalization of self and general philosophical understanding of "the way things are."

> I have survived many things. Many of my relatives are dead, both from accidents and other things. We were six brothers. My father died in 1929. First his brother died out there on the cliffs, looking after sheep in the night. Then there was my brother, the next oldest, he was out sailing and had an accident. He died. . . . My mother was left alone with four children, and one of my brothers died on a boat during the war. . . . And then my mother got sick.

> So I have survived so much . . . I have been a seaman for a great part of my life. So it was that I worked for much of my life for this house and for food. And it was a difficult life, because one had always to take care of things, one had to take care of the peat which one burned, and the sheep, and to take care of . . . yeah, everything. One survives a changing life. It is too long to talk about.

> And so one sits today. I have heard about others criticizing me.
> . . . But one needs to live, to survive, at any rate. One has
> survived much of everything, both good and bad in the Faeroes.

This man, like every man, has had to adapt to the capricious power
of the wind and sea, the accidents of fate, and his peers' gossip.

Within the whims and follies of physical and social forces,
Faeroese try to make life as certain as possible. Eager to avoid
contention, which challenges the way things are, and eager to avoid
the unpredictable outcomes of quarrels, they are quick to agree
with one another. Ritual forms of agreement ("Isn't it so?"), criticisms of others' alleged anger and quarreling, and the stress on
peace and equality demonstrate a strong desire for social accommodation. Making sure that there is constant talk about other
villagers' wrong ways of acting—about people who could possibly
upset the daily order of social life—almost everyone seems to focus
on third parties' behavior. Little that deviates from ordinary behavior goes unnoticed or unmentioned. No one can live up to all the
norms in all ways. In this way villagers deter potentially disruptive
behavior, and, like the named stepping-stones on the ledges of bird
cliffs, the right paths for behavior are not forgotten.

Belonging and Identity

The Faeroese belong to the geography around them, and the
geography belongs to them. This is very much at the heart of the
culture. Villagers belong in the literal, fundamental sense of dependence, of not being able to exist without it. They belong in the
sense that one's family, one's kinship grouping, and one's covillagers historically resided in their community of people and places.
The homestead, the village, the island is where one belongs if one
is to remain a product of one's history and heritage. Numerous
literal and symbolic geographic and social attachments via name,
experience, and tale represent that belonging. They also belong to
the community of people and places in the sense of feeling a part
of it, of having emotions attached to it. They belong to the community as a social entity, involving the community's general understanding of the proper way to think and to do things. They belong
in the moral sense of being socially responsible. Ultimately they
belong because the "place" is where life and destiny have put them.

Functional on the one hand, together these senses of belonging also comprise an aesthetic of life.

This belonging provides individual and group identity that helps regulate behavior and functions to provide an equilibrium within the changes of nature and the changes brought in by a modernizing world. Each person is meaningfully an expert in local geographic and social knowledge. The very philosophy, worldview, and meanings of life for Faeroese are linked to the landscape. Such local knowledge and expertness is what anthropologists see as crucial to understanding culture.

Faeroese senses of belonging are composed of membership in parts and in the whole of landscape/community. They range from membership in Sumbøur (sub)culture to membership in Faeroese culture at large. Sumbingar are familiar with Gormundsgjógv ('Gormund's Chasm') as a particular place with a particular feel, history, and social life as well as with chasms as a general type of Faeroese topography. Some places in the Faeroes even have exactly the same name like Dvørgasteinur ('Dwarf's Stone'), but villages' own histories greatly distinguish them.

It is this active membership and participation in the environment that is the experience of place and culture. And more than a static sense of belonging, we have seen how Faeroese actively produce, create, and support geographic embeddedness and social order through ongoing names, talk, and stories and their added variations and interpretations. Verbal virtuosity and new experience enable places like the 'Post Office' or the 'Cabbage Garden' and people like Albert 'in the High Cowpath' or Maria 'Stonehouse' to have added characteristics attributed to them by individual or group practice.

The shared knowledge and intimacy of places and persons—where they are located, how they look, whom they relate to by kinship, what social and historical associations are attached, and so on—provide security and orderliness. This contrasts with settlements elsewhere in the world without community in the sense of belonging, where even a village is only an "artifact, a tool for production and profit-making which has outlived its original purpose" (Nadel 1984:113). Faeroese villagers not only inherit but also grow up into a security of emplacement. Each person's identity is dictated greatly by his/her own geographic embeddedness and social history. Each person is in name and in reputation landscaped by the environment, physical and social—by the cultural landscape.

Regardless of the sometimes confining socialization of people, or the ridicule of deviation, each Faeroese individual has his or her own unique place. This Faeroese characteristic well accords with Nordic individualism, which has been remarked upon by natives, scholars, and travelers alike. Geography and place-names support the self as the "identity of a person wholly within the skin" (Shore 1982). They also support personhood as a product of social life created by the individual and for the individual by the group. Both inward and outward identities rely on knowledge about particular places, their whereabouts, and their specific topographic, genealogical, and socially imbued traits. Faeroese orientation and connectedness to physical-social environments—what could be called "individual ecologies"—hinge on places and their associations.

Sumbingar negotiate and reaffirm their belonging by expressing knowledge, sentiment, and loyalty to place. People activate both their individuality and their commonality by using and remarking upon kinship names, place-names, nicknames, local stories of place, and so forth. Some Faeroese even have legally changed their formal surnames to include locational names like 'Three O'Clock Rock'. Such names, formal and informal, mix nature and culture together. Such identification with place is profoundly penetrating to identity and culture and links place and person within a matrix of natural and social order. Just as people's relations to one another are multiplex, so are people's relations to place. Sumbøur's tentacles reach out to mountaintops and to the bottom of the sea. Place is multiply meaningful. Place *is* culture.

And in the village setting, relationships between people are solidified in the joint and equal uses of space. The public access to place, knowledge, and experience legitimizes the power relationships and reinvokes the egalitarian social order. And people become emotionally attached to these certain ways of living and seeing things. They become attached to the landscape, communal activities of shepherding and whaling, and to the form of socioeconomy. They like the smell of certain pastures, the feel of certain sheep, as well as the knowledge of equal status with fellow villagers.

As part of that social geography villagers revel in describing and caricaturing others' personalities. Local talk focuses primarily on social qualities, the ability to get along with one another. This discourse transforms personality traits into important social concerns. Indeed, one expresses oneself as an individual *and* as a member of the community in relaying descriptions, anecdotes, and stories about fellow villagers. Depictions of geographically embedded persons as lazy, temperamental, drunken, stingy, blasphemous, and arrogant permeate village life. These concerns highlight the social ecology of the community.

This matter-of-fact self-regulation of village life contrasts with formal externally imposed Danish hegemony and formal Faeroese law. Consciously or not, Faeroese preserve their cultural identity and the informal egalitarianism of village life through the everyday talk about people everyone knows. Local social control depends on character images that people create. Reputations and caricatures comprise an informal system of justice unavailable to outsiders.

Space, Time, Truth, and Order

Village social life is the collective composition of raconteurs, each and every member of the community. Nicknames, reputations, events, and stories blend truth and imagination in social caricatures, social points of view. Consequently Faeroese social control is far from a materialist, legalistic process. Everyday anecdotes and stories carry meaning independent of the issue of verifiable accuracy. Hjartvar's punching of his own foot with a pitchfork and the drunken rage of Georg exist outside time in the linear, positivist sense. Such things take on immediacy whenever they occur in conversation, regardless of when they allegedly took place. So people interpret new events and people's actions with preexisting as well as ongoing images in mind. Dated events serve mainly to establish the continuity of the moral order through time. What lasts are the accounts' symbolic meanings. The legendary names and talk put events and people in opposition to ordinary time and the tasks of daily life. Like pictorial caricatures, such verbal living legends emphasize enduring images and norms, not transitory moments.

Thus villagers' observations and descriptions of others in mundane activities like cleaning the hjallur or baiting a fish become part of remembered and reproduced accounts through which villagers make social and legal statements. Talk entertainingly transforms behavior and character traits into cultural guidelines. In this way villagers constantly give life normative meaning. Faeroese thus mark the social world not so much by calendrical dates or specific events but through timeless, mythlike caricatures.

On the surface, to the outsider, the legend-creating process might appear to be about minor matters and "nosy." But it functions to highlight values, deter offensive acts, and make people aware of their own behavior and their responsibility of how to belong to a specific community in a specific place. Especially as a respite from the concentration, sobriety, and requisite cooperation of fishing, fowling, whaling, and living in a close-knit community, humorous belittling relieves accumulated tensions. Moreover, caricature of absent others prevents direct adversary behavior and maintains equality by leveling anyone and everyone. It circumvents state involvement that could otherwise upset egalitarian relationships by emphasizing rank structures and deciding upon winners of disputes. Winners could become arrogant, anathema to social structure and cultural value. Cautionary tales and criticisms of third parties seem far superior to the direct, after-the-fact, and vengeful aggression of more formal systems of justice.

Despite the value on egalitarianism, Sumbingar tease the rukka. This seems a contradiction, but talk about ideal behavior in every culture probably surpasses people's actual behavior. Among the Faeroese, the social emphasis on each person's human fallibility is part of a process that uses individual deviance to foster general conformity. Villagers are able to simultaneously criticize and cooperate, to ridicule behind the back while remaining friendly face-to-face. Thereby they modulate conflict and maintain peace.

Thus daily talk and the heightened focus on the physical and social place of community members obviate the need for much open dispute and formal law. Grievances manifested as names, anecdotes, stories—talk in general—are fundamental forms and forums of social control. The formal legal system outside the village solves regional and national problems while the informal process of caricature in the village manages local problems. Law construed in its widest sense is a common, everyday affair.

Image and Mystery

I have explicitly and implicitly argued throughout this book that positivist approaches to ecology, while helpful, do not go far enough. When scientists measure caloric inputs and outputs, determine oxygen and carbon dioxide flows and concentrations, count species members, and generally use quantitative methods to assess populations and their resource utilization, they often do not penetrate deeply into culture. They sometimes overlook or minimize human groups' own conceptualizing of the environment. Understanding human-nature relations is not simply an issue of material forces and factors, but of cultural ones as well. Likewise, legalistic approaches to social order often fail to address the subjective, meaning-laden aspects of social interaction. I have suggested that both the landscape and the legal order are actually compilations of remembered sentiments and images that carry personal and social meaning. Landscape and law in the broadest senses are symbolic processes based, like myth itself, on "a condition of newness where neither stories nor rites are properly fixed and everything still vibrates with the event or emotion which gave it birth" (Leenhardt 1947:28).

And among the Faeroese, with their own unique approach to the surroundings, there is a merging of landscape and order, environment and social control. One modernist author, pleading for such a cultural approach to the environment, urges that there be "landscape unity between community and territory" (Olwig 1993:339). In a similar vein Barbara Bender (1993:2) suggests:

> Landscape has to be contextualised. The way in which people—anywhere, everywhere—understand and engage with their worlds will depend upon the specific time and place and historical conditions. It will depend upon their gender, age, class, caste, and on their social and economic situation. People's landscapes will operate on very different spatial scales, whether horizontally across the surface of the world, or vertically—up to the heavens, down to the depths. They will operate on very different temporal scales, engaging with the past and with the future in many different ways. Even in the most scientific of Western worlds, past and future will be mythologised. (2)

We have seen how nicknames, place-names, taettir, legends, bygdarsøgur, and other verbal and written communications of Sumbingar figure in the local social and mythical landscape. They act as grids for placing people into the natural and social environment. Sumbøur is not unlike another Faeroese village, Alvabøur, where the past is a topic of general interest and "the social order is construed in terms of such portions of reality as historical truths and the order of nature" (Wylie 1982:439).

Although the culture clearly delineates places and rules for locating oneself in both space and society, there still remains much mystery and unrehearsed drama. Despite, or perhaps because of, the openness of the sky, panoramas, and village events, the mystery of life remains. Existence in the Faeroes is a unique blend of the finely detailed with the indefinite, of known elements of nature and humanity with the ultimately unpredictable and enigmatic. Heðin Brú is perhaps the best-liked author among villagers not only because he represents a simple, poignant style of local life, but also for his "fascination with the mystery of life, the miracle of nature, the wonder of the shifting seasons" (Brønner 1973:109).

We have seen how the truth about human and not-so-human beings can be elusive. It is elusive for a number of reasons. In the uncertainties of weather and subsistence activities in a "Land of Maybe" there are often guesses about others' behavior. There is little historical documentation about the past. And even in the present people interpret and reinterpret words and deeds in different ways. In the Faeroes the very process of oral communication about the past and present—through gossip, legend, ballad, folktale—tends to edit or embellish facts. And of course the truth is elusive because some of the inhabitants, like huldufólk and dwarves, are able to disappear—and some people are not sure that they were there in the first place.

We should note that this lack of local positivist truth, the prevalence of life as legend, of people as living legends, is not a problem. On the contrary, it makes for a creativity and a common participation in the ongoingness of culture. Villagers' image-creating approach to history in the past and history in the present is much the reason for my own ethnographic urgings here to study ecology and social order from a perspective of aesthetics. In more technical terms this kind of approach and methodological orientation are consequences both of the objects of investigation (the Faeroese) and of the methods and views of the scientist (me) who creates the subject matter. Scientific results are, in part, designed by the scientist's own personal and cultural landscape. Ultimately, a recognition that the truth is escapable and mysterious can, like nature itself, humble the native and the anthropologist. In a world that can be molded but never mastered, humans live with, and within, the environment and unattainable truths.

Village life is a storybook of characters (and I was/am one of them). Faeroese daily life, even to locals, seems in great part a mystery. Relayed by word of mouth, much of living in Sumbøur is like a series of episodes, a saga where each page and chapter, each day and each person's life, is wondrous in its unfolding. The setting is half of it, what with its natural drama, its rugged, ragged mountains and stormy seas, its ubiquitous sheep, its cairns, its fog. The Faeroe Islands also maintain an aura of mystery to the native, not just to the outsider unfamiliar with this remote, volcanic archipelago somewhere near mythical continents like Atlantis.

Exactness in space is a primary frame of reference for Faeroese, much more than exactitude in time. In daily conversation about place and genealogy, villagers effortlessly skip back and forth through hundreds of years. Their temporal orientation is fluid, but deep, like the sea around them. With history alive in the very names and places around them, villagers are in a way living supratemporally, above time. Each place is encoded with numerous events of different days, years, centuries. The connections are mainly spatial. One is Faeroese not simply because a person now lives in a nation of Faeroese people, but because one's ancestors, special-named and located individuals, are animated in the hillsides of specially named Faeroese places.

This type of ultimate meaning-centered approach to culture and landscape and social order provides the possibility that people anywhere can understand and change their own views and practices. Not fully controlled by external environmental constraints, people(s) can come more into an awareness of sustainable livelihoods, of the importance of place and past, of linkages to the land, of an aesthetic of landscape, of the specialness of a personal econiche. Groups can rise above the deterministic or strictly materialist approach to space. They can embrace what one sociologist describes as the

> phenomenological view of social space as problematic rather than simply physical and objective; as being subjective and experienced; emergent and invested with sociocultural meaning in the minds of members; learned, and thus potentially variable from person to person, group to group, and situation to situation. (Ball 1973:7)

Or as Christopher Tilley (1994:67) concludes, after a review of the social construction of landscape in small-scale societies:

> It appears to be evident enough that the significance of landscape for different populations cannot be simply read off from the local 'ecological' characteristics of a 'natural' environment, whether desert, Boreal forest, rain forest or tundra. Nor can it be related in any simple manner to the mode of subsistence . . . or pattern of dwelling . . . It, rather, *cross-cuts* these determinisms and distinctions. A much stronger argument can be made that, in all the social contexts I have considered, landscape is intimately related to myth viz metaphor, allegory, synecdoche etc. (Emphasis mine)

And it is here, in the possible negotiation of culture and landscape, that environmentalism fits as an opportunity to change others' concepts and practices surrounding human relationships to nature.

Changes and Lessons

The Faeroese have recently run into some financial trouble. Long supported by their own village-level subsistence activities and the commercial fishery, as well as through substantial financial support from Denmark, the Faeroese have generally been prosperous in modern times. But inflationary economic trends in the 1990s, changes in the availability of lucrative fishing grounds, and the cessation of most support from Denmark have led to some unemployment, heretofore mostly unknown. The current use of commercial fishing as the primary basis of support for a relatively large population, (until the mid-1800s there were only a few thousand Faeroese), has made the national economy highly dependent on international markets for fish. This is quite different from the relative self-reliance of traditional village existence before the rise of the commercial fishery.

This parallels the situation of the modern American family farm, which has increasingly become overly dependent on the production of one crop, often milk, beef, corn, or wheat. Family farms have been forced to bail out when market prices have fallen and/or debt increased. Monocropping and the lack of a diverse set of harvests make survival questionable in difficult or changing times. The earlier, multiple economic pattern of Faeroese peasant village life,

In the town of Vágur, women fillet fresh fish caught by locals, including Sumbingar. Some of this fish is frozen and exported to the United States.

like similar patterns in many other nature-based subsistence ecologies, provides a good model for those who derive their livelihoods from the land and sea as well as for developers, economists, and planners. Consumer capitalism and Western popular culture, which tend to promote buying, even conspicuous consumption, can erode subsistence practices and landscape knowledge.

With the increase in "Danish food," technological conveniences, urban culture, and continental fashion in the Faeroes, there has come to be some displacement of some people's traditional personal niches in the physical and social environment. Relative affluence has permitted some to purchase imported synthetic fiber, for example, rather than continuing the age-old reliance on local wool, yarn, and hand-knit items. With more financial and social contact with other Europeans, the Faeroese view has begun to expand. Some local dress, behaviors, and values have begun to be

replaced, as some young people attend to continental and general
Western trends.

Globalization has changed some things about Sumbøur. In 1983
villagers started watching television programs, taped and flown in
from Denmark. They would sometimes sit in the evening watching
shows like "Dallas" and "Dynasty" in favor of social visiting with
friends and relatives. Now television is more common. Some patterns of verbal communication and consumer behavior have begun
to change.

Of course prior times brought change also. Even Ketil, protagonist in Heðin Brú's famous novel *The Old Man and His Sons*, set
early in the century, berates the consumerism of his eldest son:

> But you all demand so much from life—you're never satisfied.
> In the old days, a poor man was content if he had something
> to eat and a roof over his head. Nowadays, everything has to be
> so high-and-mighty. Everything you set your minds on, you have
> to have, whether you can afford it or not . . . And everyone's up
> to their eyebrows in debt. A fat lot of use it is having schools,
> books, and I don't know what! In the old days we used to be a
> lot more reasonable. (West 1970:117)

Perhaps there are some ecological lessons here also, about demanding too much of, and being in debt to, the environment.

Some of the older folk have begun to lament that some of the
youngsters no longer know many place-names and their histories
so well. Thus some persons' conceptualizations of space begin to
expand in size, but diminish in depth and detail. The "placeless-
ness" of much urban culture elsewhere in the world in great part
derives from a lack of consciousness of local history and culture,
from constant movement, and, perhaps most of all, from preoccupation with class positioning rather than positioning in the landscape. Attention mostly to externalities often leads to diminishment
of local power and control, as media and global forces come to
define the important physical and social reference points for identity and culture. Yet, the strong geographic embeddedness of
Faeroese and literary and folkloric traditions have helped to maintain cultural distinctiveness in the face of these factors.

Fortunately, the Faeroes' relatively late economic development,
coupled with a high value on tradition and independence, have
permitted change in the last half of the twentieth century to be not
so obliterating of the past, as it has been to some other nations and

cultures. The demographic change in the Faeroes, with one-third of the population now living in the capital, has still not dissolved the associations and cultural rituals—sheep slaughter, bird fowling, whale hunting—of village life. During my short, initial stay in the capital prior to living in Sumbøur, I observed a grindadráp in the main commercial harbor of Tórshavn. Shopkeepers and businessmen quickly ran out of their offices and buildings to jump into their boats and into the water to participate!

And most changes have been in the capital and two or three large towns. Even with satellite television and some emigration (and return visiting) to Denmark, no class system has developed to substantially threaten the egalitarian mindset of villagers and the general culture of their community, what Faeroese, especially those in Tórshavn, call *bygdarmentan* ("village culture"). Even with television's portrayal of the scenes and activities of urban industrialized society, Faeroese villagers still ply the local sea and bird cliffs for fulmars and puffins. Sheep still wander all around. Despite financial problems of a modern age (with an 8 billion kroner foreign debt) and even with the recent discovery of offshore oil, Faeroese generally maintain their distinctive localness of culture and activity. Sumbingar still know how to be self-reliant and to concentrate on local affairs. The Faeroese can rely on that. It may be key to their long-range viability as an independent nation.

In the increasing regionalization of Western Europe, in which the European Union, some say, slowly erodes national and ethnic differences, the Faeroese, I suggest, may have an advantage in continuity and stability. Modernization around a group does not necessarily mean the dissolution of most traditional patterns. Identification with local physical and social landscape, folk styles of interaction, communal practices, and "prebureaucratic" values can well persist. Witness Portuguese fishing-village society (Brøgger 1992) and the American Amish, among others.

The proximity and intimacy of isolated Faeroe island village living, the inextricable connections between spatial order and social order, strong egalitarianism, the emphasis on emotional and social self-control, and the arts of place may well withstand external economic and social encompassment. If nothing else, the ocean, the high cliffs, and the stormy weather, alongside natives' strong sense of place, will help to maintain their distinct boundaries and identity. People with a strong sense of place contrast sharply with "powerless people [who] have no place at all" (Rodman 1992:650).

The geographic embeddedness and aesthetic of Faeroese culture remind us of the different possibilities of human-nature relations. Their attachment to the landscape demonstrates that ecology is the study of values, sensibilities, and attitudes, as well as practices. Faeroese incorporation of nature and landscape into names, personalities, and the built environment helps to provide a sense of security in an ever-changing world. Indeed the "symbolic organization of the landscape may help to assuage fear, to establish an emotionally safe relationship between men and their total environment" (Lynch 1973:303). Faeroese geographic and aesthetic energy" does not invoke New Age spiritual and naturalistic sensitivities nor the now-popular social scientific concern with the notion of place. The islanders do not feel the need to join the Western "current wave of environmental awareness [that] was invoked more by pathology, by a sense of loss, grief, guilt, shame and outrage, as by curiosity, celebration and wonder" (Bishop 1994). Faeroese personal and community econiches have always been spirited.

These topics are not just academic. Anthropologists, geographers, architects, planners, and others increasingly play directing roles in economic development planning schemes. Applications of analyses like the ones in this book and familiarity with a holistic approach to spatial and social orderings of communities are on the rise. A "policy relevant cultural ecology" (Bennett 1976) is increasingly in demand. As Robert Netting (1986:92) suggests:

> The understanding of local ecosystems already achieved and the models proposed for the interaction of landscape, subsistence techniques, population, and social organization are clearly basic to any advice and predictions the anthropologist can offer.

The formation and maintenance of identities within Europe and elsewhere will likely become an increasingly important subject both for smaller cultures, as well as for ethnic groups and nationalities of much larger size (see, e.g., McDonald 1993).

Many observers and cultural historians have pointed to a demise of community life in many parts of Europe and elsewhere. Even many Danish think that Faeroese village society is unnecessarily "backward," albeit also romantic. Yet that so-called "backwardness" is now what many frustrated urbanites, landscape theorists, and postmodern travelers now seek.

With their enhancement of spatial and personal differences, with numerous narrative accounts referring to local groupings (as in bygdarsøgur) Faeroese—a European people—still stand in marked contrast to many thoroughly Westernized urban Europeans and Americans with standardized landscapes (e.g., shopping malls) that diminish differences between places. One author sees American regional identities as "out of place" (Hough 1990).

Faeroese conceptions and utilizations of geography, nature, and landscape are reminiscent of other indigenous peoples whose relationships to the land and sea are deep in practice and sentiment. Many modernists and postmodernists are beginning to recognize the physical, social, and spiritual "power of place" (see, e.g., Swan 1991). It is ironic that one must go to or read about a remote archipelago to come to realize that people back home may not really be at home. Perhaps communities like Sumbøur may teach us about how to cope with the twenty-first century.

Despite the creeping qualitative change in the Faeroes from a landscape of production to a landscape of consumption, in which economic markets challenge notions of place, there is a strong conservative and conservationist emphasis in Faeroese culture. Villagers, as well as those in Tórshavn, have not given up their cultural emphasis on pilot whaling, despite the attack of Greenpeace and others on Faeroese whaling practices. Local pride and use of whales, still strongly regulated by local officials and islanders' own sense of respect for nature, epitomize how the external world can never fully comprehend the local.

The Faeroese seem to cull their wisdom, their experience, from identifiable places around them. Place-names themselves are a relational system binding nature and society together. Like traceable links of kinship, different places and peoples' experiences with them provide personal and cultural grounding. Faeroese villagers' identities do not spring simply from spaces called 'Stonehouse' or 'Under the Bluff', but from a whole literal and metaphorical interlocking system of relationships and associations connected with such places. Each time a Faeroese utters or thinks a place-name, he/she metaphorically re-places culture onto and into the environment.

Place-name use and geographic sentiment is landscape conservation, the preservation of natural and cultural history. And each
villager is an indigenous naturalist, knowledgeable in the ways of
sheep, grass, birds, whales, fish, weather, tides, and the names that
encode that knowledge. The places of culture, and the culture of
places, are the foundations of a conservation ecology. One writer,
as if speaking of the Faeroese, says of the Irish residents of Ballymenone that "Place is space rich enough to provide travel for the
mind while the body sits still, space so full of the past that it forces
people to become responsible for its future" (Glassie 1982:664).
Localness has immense value. Not prey to external forces, much of
the coherence of Faeroese community and landscape has survived
through modern days because its spaces are so densely packed
with culture.

Glossary

Below are words found more than once or twice in the text which are not defined after their initial appearance. The list includes some Danicisms that have been incorporated into the local Faeroese vocabulary.

Aevintýr Folktale(s)
Arga, arging, argarður To taunt, taunting, taunted
Bøur (bøar) Infield(s)
Brimpláss "Surf place"; settlement right next to the open sea
Bygd (-dir) Village(s) and infields
Bygdarsøga (-søgur) Local village history(ies)
Eyknavn (-nøvn) Nickname(s)
Familjia Family
Feitilendir "Fatlands"; the proper name of an area of grazeland
Fleyga To fowl for birds
Fortelja To tell (a story)
Gandur Black magic
Gjógv Chasm
Grannastevna "Neighbor's gathering"; village annual legal session
Grind A pilot whale; school of pilot whales
Grindadráp Whale kill
Hagi (hagar) Outfield(s)
Hamar (hamrar) Bluff(s); a stretch of rock on a hillside
Heimføðingur A "homebody"; a local yokel
Hjá Of or belonging to; at the house of
Hjallur (-lar) Wind-drying shed
Huldufólk "Grey people"; elves who live in the countryside and who can disappear at will
Ikki nei? Isn't it so?
Ja Yes
Jú Yes (definitively)
Kommuna Village council; a village council's area of jurisdiction
Kvaeði (-ðir) Faeroese ballad(s)
Kvøldseta (-setur) Household evening gathering(s)
Mið Fishing spot(s) in the ocean

Nes Headland
Ólavsøka Faeroese national holiday
Óndur Angry; evil
Rukka (-kur) Easily angered fool(s); brunt(s) of jokes and pranks
Serlingur (-gar) Character(s); an eccentric
Seyðamaður Sheepman; shepherd
Sinnalag Temperament
Sinniligur Even-tempered
Sjómal "Sea language"; seamen's special vocabulary
Skemt Jokery
Skerpikjøt Wind-dried, cured, raw mutton
Slatur Slander
Slekt (slektir) Lineage(s); descent group(s)
Slupptíðini "Sloop times"; the days of commercial sloop
  (sailboat) fishing
Snedigur, snedugt Strange
Søgn (sagnir) Legend(s)
Staðanavn (-nøvn) Place-names(s)
Suðuringur (-gar) Residents of island of Suðuroy
Sumbiarkommuna Political jurisdiction and town council of
  and around Sumbøur
Sumbingur (-ar) Resident(s) of the village of Sumbøur
Svakur Crazy
Sýslumaður District officer; sheriff
Systkin Siblings
Systkinabørn Cousins
Táttur (taettir) Faeroese satirical ballad(s)
Ting Assembly; court session
Tjaldur Oystercatcher, a seabird; Faeroese national bird
Trýmenningur Second cousins
Tvørur Stubborn; difficult
Umstøða (-ður) Condition(s); life's way(s)
Vaettrar Pixies
Varting Spring legal assembly
Vísir Danish ballads
Ytir Positions on land or sea triangulated through landmarks

References

Alexander, Christopher, Sora Ishikawa, and Murray Silverstein, with May Jacobsen, Ingrid Fiksdahl-King, and Shlomo Angel. 1977. *A Pattern Language: Towns, Buildings, Construction.* New York: Oxford University Press.

Andersen, R., and C. Wadel. 1972. *North Atlantic Fishermen.* Paper 5. St. John's: Institute of Social and Economic Research, Memorial University of Newfoundland.

Arnason, H. Harvard. 1977. *History of Modern Art: Painting, Sculpture and Architecture.* 2d ed. Englewood Cliffs, NJ: Prentice-Hall.

Appell, G. N. 1967. Observational Procedures for Identifying Kindreds: Social Isolates Among the Rungus of Borneo. *Southwestern Journal of Anthropology* 23:192–207.

Arno, Andrew. 1985. Structural Communication and Control Communication: An Interactionist Perspective on Legal and Customary Procedures for Conflict Management. *American Anthropologist* 87:40–55.

Babcock, William H. 1922. *Legendary Islands of the Atlantic: A Study in Medieval Geography.* New York: American Geographical Society.

Ball, Donald W. 1973. *Microecology: Social Situations and Intimate Space.* Indianapolis: Bobbs-Merrill.

Barnes, J. A. 1954. Class and Committees in a Norwegian Island Parish. *Human Relations* 7:39–58.

Bender, Barbara, ed. 1993. *Landscape: Politics and Perspectives.* Providence, RI: Berg Publishers.

Bennett, John. 1969. *Northern Plainsmen: Adaptive Strategy and Agrarian Life.* Chicago: Aldine.

_____. 1976. *The Ecological Transition: Cultural Anthropology and Human Adaptation.* Oxford: Pergamon.

_____.1993. *Human Ecology as Human Behavior: Essays in Environmental and Development Anthropology.* New Brunswick, NJ: Transaction Publishers.

Berger, John. 1979. *Pig Earth.* New York: Pantheon Books.

Bishop, Peter. 1994. Residence on Earth: Anima Mundi and a Sense of Geographical 'Belonging.' *Ecumene* 1(1): 51–64.

Blehr, Otto. 1963. Action Groups in a Society with Bilateral Kinship: A Case Study from the Faroe Islands. *Ethnology* 2(3):269–277.

_____. 1964. Ecological Change and Organizational Continuity in the Faroe Islands. *Folk* 6(1): 29–33.

_____. 1976. Social Drinking in the Faroe Islands: The Ritual Aspect of Token Prestations. *Ethnos* 39(1–4): 53–62.

Blom, Jan-Peter, and John J. Gumperz. 1972. Social Meaning in Linguistic Structure: Code-switching in Norway. In *Directions in Sociolinguistics: The Ethnography of Communication.* Ed. John J. Gumperz and Dell Hymes, pp. 407–434. New York: Holt, Rinehart and Winston.

237

238 References

Blum, Jerome. 1982. *Our Forgotten Past*. New York: Thames and Hudson Publishing.

Bourdieu, Pierre. 1984. *Distinction: A Social Critique of the Judgment of Taste*. Trans. Richard Nice. Cambridge: Harvard University Press.

Brøgger, Jan. 1992. *Nazaré: Women and Men in a Prebureaucratic Portuguese Fishing Village*. Fort Worth, TX: Harcourt, Brace, Jovanovich.

Brønner, Heðin. 1972. Introduction. In *Faroese Short Stories*. Ed. and trans. Heðin Brønner. New York: Twayne Publishers and American Scandinavian Foundation.

_____. 1973. *Three Faroese Novelists: An Appreciation of Jørgen-Frantz Jacobsen, William Heinesen, and Heðin Brú*. Library of Scandinavian Studies, vol. 1. New York: Twayne Publishers.

_____. 1983. Introduction. *The Wingéd Darkness and Other Stories* by William Heinesen. Trans. with introduction and notes by Heðin Brønner. New York: Irvington Publishers.

Brú, Heðin. 1930. *Lognbrá*. Tórshavn: Felagið Varðin og Merkið.

_____. 1935. *Fastatøkur*.

_____. 1970. *The Old Man and His Sons*. Trans. and with an introduction by John F. West. New York: Paul S. Eriksson.

_____. 1972. A Summons for the Blacksmith (Onnur hersøgan). In *Faroese Short Stories*. Ed. and trans. Heðin Brønner, pp. 175–189. New York: Twayne Publishers and American-Scandinavian Foundation.

Canter, David. 1977. *The Psychology of Place*. London: Architectural Press.

Cohen, Anthony P. 1978. 'The Same—But Different': The Allocation of Identity in Whalsay, Shetland. *Sociological Review* 36(3): 449–469.

_____. 1987. *Whalsay: Symbol, Segment and Boundary in a Shetland Island Community*. Anthropological Studies of Britain, No. 3. Manchester: Manchester University Press.

Conroy, Patricia. 1979. Ballad Composition in Faroese Heroic Tradition: The Case of "Hernilds kvaeði." *Frodskaparritt* 27:73–101.

Davies, Dewi. N.d. Welsh Place-Names and Their Meanings. Aberystwyth, *Cambrian News*.

Debes, Hans M. 1969. (1932) *Føroysk Bindingarmynstur*. Tórshavn: Føroyst Heimavirki.

Djurhuus, N. 1953. Gjørðið—Steinurin í Akrabergi, urrit av listanum fra nr. 1–928. Fyri Dansk Stednavnenaevn. Unpublished manuscript.

Djurhuus, N., and Christian Matras, eds. 1951–1972. *Føroya kvaeði: Corpus carmimum Faeroensium a Sv. Grundtvig et J. Bloch comparatum*. 6 vols. Copenhagen: Einar Munskgaard (vols. 1–3), Akademisk Forlag (vols. 4–6), and Universitets-Jubilaets Danske Samfund (all vols.).

Douglas, Mary. 1975. *Implicit Meanings: Essays in Anthropology*. London: Routledge & Kegan Paul.

Engel, David M. 1993. Law in the Domains of Everyday Life: The Construction of Community and Difference. In *Law in Everyday Life*. Ed. Austin Sarat and Thomas R. Kearns, pp. 123–170. Ann Arbor: University of Michigan.

Engel, David M., and Barbara Yngvesson. 1984. Mapping Difficult Terrain: "Legal Culture," "Legal Consciousness," and Other Hazards for the Intrepid Explorer. *Law & Policy* 6(3): 299–307.

Fatelewitz, Madelynn. 1988. Knitting in the North Atlantic. *Threads*, no. 16 (April/May): 50–55.

Føroya, Landsstýri. 1967. *Seyðamarkini í Føroym frá 1967.* Tórshavn: Dimmalaetting.

Freeman, J. D. 1961. On the Concept of the Kindred. *Journal of the Royal Anthropological Institute* 91(pt. 2): 192–220.

Freidman, L. 1969. Legal Culture and Social Development. *Law and Society Review* 4:29–44.

Gaffin, Dennis. 1987. Everyday People as Living Legends: The Art of Social Control in a Faeroese Village. Ph.D. diss., State University of New York at Buffalo.

———. 1991. The Faeroe Islands: Clowning, Drama, and Distortion. In *Deviance: Anthropological Perspectives.* Ed. M. Freilich, D. Raybeck, and J. Savishinsky. Westport, CT: Bergin and Garvey. pp. 191–212.

———. 1993. Landscape, Culture, and Personhood: Names of Places and People in the Faeroe Islands. *Ethnos* 1–2:53–72.

———. 1994. People as Landmarks: The Geographic Identities of Faeroe Islanders. *Landscape* 32(2): 20–27.

———. 1995. The Production of Emotion and Social Control: Taunting, Anger, and the *Rukka* in the Faeroe Islands. *Ethos* (23)2: 149–72.

Glassie, Henry H. 1982. *Passing the Time in Ballymenone: Culture and History of an Ulster Community.* Philadelphia: University of Pennsylvania Press.

Gluckman, Max. 1955. *The Judicial Process Among the Barotse of Northern Rhodesia.* Manchester: Manchester University Press.

———. 1963. Gossip and Scandal. *Current Anthropology* 4(3): 307–316.

Goffman, Erving. 1967. *Interaction Ritual: Essays on Face-to-Face Behavior.* Garden City, NY: Doubleday.

Hall, Edward T. 1966. *The Hidden Dimension.* Garden City, NY: Doubleday.

Hammershaimb, Venceslaus Ulricus. 1846. Faerøiske trylleformularer. *Annaler for Nordisk Oldkyndighed og Historie* 1846:347–365. Reprinted in facsimile in Hammershaimb (1969), pp. 9–27.

———. ed. 1854. Faerøsk sproglaere. *Annaler for Nordisk oldkyndighed og Historie* 1854:233–316. Reprinted in facsimile in Hammerschaimb (1969), pp. 223–308.

———. ed. 1891. *Faerøsk anthologi.* 2 vols. Copenhagen: S. L. Møller (Møller & Thomsen). Facsimile edition 1969. Tórshavn: Hammershaimbs-grunnerin.

———. 1969. *Savn úr Anneler for Nordisk oldkyndighed og Historie og Antiquarisk Tidsskrift.* Tórshavn: Offset-Prent/Emil Thomsen.

Hansen, J. Símun. 1971. *Tey byggja land. 1. partur: Fugloyar sókn.* Klaksvík: privately printed.

———. 1973. *Tey byggja land. 2. partur: Svinoyar sókn.* Klaksvík: privately printed.

Harris, Marvin. 1983. *Cultural Anthropology* (3d ed.). New York: Harper & Row.

Haviland, William A. 1981. *Cultural Anthropology* (3d ed.). New York: Holt, Rinehart and Winston.

Heinesen, William. 1976. Caprices, Whims and Frolics: A Comment on Faeroese Weather. *Faroe Isles Review* 1(1): 4–8.

_____. 1980. *Filsni og Hampafólk: Tekningar malningar og litklipp.* Tórshavn, Faeroe Islands: Emil Thomsen.

_____. 1923. *The Wingéd Darkness and Other Stories.* Trans. Heðin Brønner. New York: Irvington Publishers.

Hermansson, Nanna. 1972. Nólsoy: En färöisk bygd i omvandling. Lund: Etnologiska institutionen, Lund Universitet. Mimeo.

Hiss, Tony. 1990. *The Experience of Place.* New York: Alfred A. Knopf.

Hjalt, Edward. 1953. *Sands søga.* Tórshavn: Varðin.

Hollos, Marida. 1976. Conflict and Social Change in a Norwegian Mountain Community. *Anthropological Quarterly* 49:239–257.

Hough, Michael. 1990. *Out of Place: Restoring Identity to the Regional Landscape.* New Haven: Yale University Press.

Hoydal, Karsten. 1976. The Development of Visual Art in the Faroes. *Faroe Isles Review* 1(2): 18–22.

Hoydal, Kjarten. 1993. Marine Resources and the Future of the Faroe Islands Community. *North Atlantic Studies* 3(2): 5–16.

Jackson, Anthony. 1979. Socioeconomic change in the Faroes. In *North Atlantic Maritime Cultures: Anthropological Essays in Changing Adaptations.* Ed. Raoul Anderson, pp. 31–64. The Hague: Mouton.

Jakle, John A. 1987. *The Visual Elements of Landscape.* Amherst: University of Massachusetts Press.

Jacobsen, Jørgen-Frantz. 1939. *Barbara.* Copenhagen: Gyldendalske Boghandel. Nordisk Felag.

Jakobsen, Jakob, ed. 1898–1901. *Faerøske folkesagn og aeventyr.* 2 vols. Copenhagen: Samfund til udgivelse af gammel norsk litteratur. Republished in 3 vols., 1964–1972. Tórshavn: H. N. Jacobsens Bókahandil.

Jakobsen, Jákup, W. U. Hammershaimb, and J. H. Schrøter. 1977. *Suðuroyarsagnir.* Tórshavn, Faeroe Islands: Einars.

í Jákupsstovu, Jákup. 1972. *Kor fiskimanna í Føroyum: Wage Determination and Working Conditions for Fishermen in the Faroe Islands.* Tórshavn, Faeroe Islands: Marius Ziska og Einars Prent.

Joensen, Hogna Debes, and J. P. Hart Hansen. 1973. Dráp og frasagnir um dráp í Føroyum. *Fróðskaparrit* (21): 72–85.

Joensen, Jóan Pauli. 1975. *Faerøske Sluppfiskere: Etnologisk undersøgelse af en erhvervsgruppes liv.* Tórshavn, Faeroe Islands: Føroya Fróðskaparfelag.

_____. 1976. Pilot Whaling in the Faroe Islands. *Ethnologica Scandinavica* (1976): 1–42.

_____. 1980. *Färöisk folkkultur.* Lund: LiverLäromedel.

_____. 1982. *Fiskafólk: Ein lysing av føroyska húshaldinum í slupptíðini.* Tórshavn: Føroya Sparikassi.

Joensen, Jóan Pauli. 1987. *Fra bonde til Fisker. Studier í Overgangen fra Bondesamfund til Fiskersamfund pa Faerøerne*. Tórshavn: Føroya Fornminnissavn. English summary (From Peasant to Fisherman: Studies in the Transition from a Peasant Society to a Fishing Society on the Faeroe Islands.) Ph.D. diss., University of Aarhus.

———. 1989. Socio-economic Transformation and Faroese National Identity. *North Atlantic Studies* 1(1): 14–20.

Joensen, Olivia. 1980. *Sjalmynstur*. Leirvík, Faeroe Islands: Forlagið Úti Á Bø.

Joensen, Poul F. 1963. *Seggjasøgur úr Sumba*. Tórshavn: Einars Prent og Forlag.

Johannesen, Marius. 1966. *Taettir I: Nólsoyar Páll*. Tórshavn: Tingakrossur.

———. 1969. *Taettir II: Hoyberatáttur, Brókatáttur, Lorvíkspáll, Ánaniasartáttur*. Tórshavn: Tingakrossur.

———. 1974. *Taettir III: Símunartáttur og 10 Adrir Taettir*. Tórshavn: Tingakrossur.

———. 1976. *Eitt Sindur um Kalsoyanna og Nakrar Sagnir Knýttar at Henni*. Tórshavn: Grønalid.

Johnston, George. 1975. *The Faroe Islander's Saga*. Canada: Oberon Press.

Kahn, Miriam. 1990. Stone-faced Ancestors: The Spatial Anchoring of Myth in Wamira, Papua New Guinea. *Ethnology* 29:51–66.

Kaysen, Susanna. 1990. *Far Afield*. New York: Random House.

Landt, Jørgen. 1810. A Description of the Feroe Islands. Translated from the Danish. London: Longman, Hurst, Rees and Orme. (Original 1800 ed. Copenhagen: Tikjøbs.)

Leenhardt, Maurice. 1947. *Do Kamo: Person and Myth in the Melanesian World*. Trans. Basia Miller Gulati, originally published in French. Chicago: University of Chicago Press.

Lind, Ivan. 1962. Geography and Place Names. In *Readings in Cultural Geography*. Ed. Philip L. Wagner and Marvin W. Mikesell, pp. 118–128. Chicago: University of Chicago Press.

Lockwood, W. B. 1961. *The Faroese Bird Names*. Copenhagen: Ejnar Munksgaard.

———. 1977. *An Introduction to Modern Faroese*. Tórshavn, Faeroe Islands: Føroya Skúlabókagrunnur.

Löfgren, Orvar. 1976. *Peasant Ecotypes*. Ethnologia Scandinavica, pp. 100–115.

Lutz, Catherine. 1990. Engendered Emotion: Gender, Power and the Rhetoric of Emotional Control in American Discourse. In *Language and the Politics of Emotion*. Ed. Catherine A. Lutz and Lila Abu-Lughod, pp. 69–91. Cambridge: Cambridge University.

Lynch, Kevin. 1973. Some References to Orientation. In *Image and Environment*. Ed. Roger M. Downs and David Stea. Chicago: Aldine.

Matras, Christian. 1933. *Stednavne Paa de Faerøske Norduroyar*. Copenhagen: H. H. Theiles.

Maybury-Lewis, David. 1984. Name, Person and Ideology in Central Brazil. In *Naming Systems: 1980 Proceedings of the American Ethnological*

Society. Ed. Elisabeth Tooker, pp. 1–10. Washington, DC: American Ethnological Society.

McDonald, Sharon, ed. 1993. *Inside European Identities: Ethnography in Western Europe.* Providence, RI: Berg Publishers.

Milliman, Lawrence. 1990. *Last Places: A Journey in the North.* Boston: Houghton Mifflin.

Montagu, Ashley, ed. 1978. *Learning Non-Aggression: The Experience of Non-literate Societies.* New York: Oxford University.

Moran, Emilio. 1982. *Human Adaptability: An Introduction to Ecological Anthropology.* Boulder, CO: Westview Press.

Morgan, Jane, Christopher O'Neill, and Rom Harre. 1979. *Nicknames: Their Origins and Social Consequences.* London: Routledge and Kegan Paul.

Müller, A. C. 1883. Whale-fishing in the Faroe Isles. In *Fish and Fisheries: A Selection of Prize Essays of the International Fisheries Exhibition, Edinburgh 1882.* Ed. Daniel Herbert, pp. 1–17. Edinburgh and London: William Blackwood and Sons.

Nadel, Jane Hurwitz. 1984. Stigma and Separation: Pariah States and Community Persistence in a Scottish Fishing Village. *Ethnology* xxiii(2): 101–115.

Nader, Laura, and Harry F. Todd, eds. 1978. *The Disputing Process—Law in Ten Societies.* New York: Columbia University.

Netting, Robert M. 1986. *Cultural Ecology.* (2d ed.). Prospect Heights, IL: Waveland Press.

Nolsøe, Mortan. 1977. The Faroese Dance: The Poetry. *Faroe Isles Review* 2(2): 29–33.

Norgate, Sydney. 1943. *"Kanska" or the Land of Maybe.* Tórshavn: H. N. Jacobsen.

Nørrevang, Arne. 1979. Land Tenure, Fowling Rights, and Sharing of the Catch in Faroese Fowling. *Fróðskaparrit* 27:30–49.

Oliver, Symmes. 1982. The Hills and the Plains: A Comparison of Two Kamba Communities. In *Culture and Ecology: Eclectic Perspectives.* Ed. John G. Kennedy and Robert B. Edgerton, pp. 142–157. Washington, DC: American Anthropological Association.

Olwig, Kenneth. 1993. Sexual Cosmology: Nation and Landscape at the Conceptual Interstices of Nature and Culture; or What Does Landscape Really Mean? In *Landscape: Politics and Perspectives.* Ed. Barbara Bender, pp. 307–343. Providence, RI: Berg Publishers.

Paine, Robert. 1970. Informal Communication and Information-Management. *Canadian Review of Sociology and Anthropology* (7)4: 172–188.

Parman, Susan. 1990. *Scottish Crofters: A Historical Ethnography of a Celtic Village.* Fort Worth, TX: Holt, Rinehart, and Winston.

Patursson, Jóannes. 1966. *Taettir úr Kirkjubøur søgu.* Tórshavn: Varðin.

Patursson, S. 1948. *Fuglameingi er landsvirði.* Tórshavn.

Pitt-Rivers, Julian A. 1971. *The People of the Sierra.* Chicago: University of Chicago Press.

Pocius, Gerald. 1991. *A Place to Belong: Community Order and Everyday Space in Calvert, Newfoundland.* Athens: University of Georgia.

Poulsen, Jóan Christian. 1947. *Hestsøga.* Tórshavn: Varðin.

Poulsen, Jóhan Hendrik W. 1979. Om brug af stednavne i faerøske familienavn. In *Språkform och språknorm (Skrifter utgit av Svenska Språknämnden* No. 67, pp. 190–196. Lund: Berling.

Rappoport, Roy. 1967. *Pigs for the Ancestors: Ritual in the Ecology of a New Guinea People.* New Haven: Yale University.

Rasmussen, Rasmus. 1909. *Bábelstornið.*

Rasmussen, R. 1950. *Føroysk Plantunøvn.* Tórshavn: Landsprentsmiðjan.

Redfield, Robert. 1960. Peasant Society and Culture. In *The Little Community and Peasant Society and Culture,* by Robert Redfield. Chicago: University of Chicago Press.

Robinson, Tim. 1986. *Stones of Aran: Pilgrimage.* Gigginstown and Dublin, Ireland. Lilliput Press in association with Wolfhound Press.

Rodman, Margaret C. 1987. *Masters of Tradition: Consequences of Customary Land Tenure in Longana, Vanuatu.* Vancouver: University of British Columbia Press.

_____. 1992. Empowering Place: Multilocality and Multivocality. *American Anthropologist* 94(3): 640–656.

Room, Adrian. 1983. *A Concise Dictionary of Modern Place-names in Great Britain and Ireland.* Oxford: Oxford University Press.

á Ryggi, Mikkjal Dánjalsson. 1940. *Miðvinga Søga.* 2d ed., corrected. 1965. Tórshavn, Faroe Islands: H. N. Jacobsens Bókahandil.

Shore, Bradd. 1982. *Sala'ilua: A Samoan Mystery.* New York: Columbia University Press.

Steele, Fritz. 1981. *The Sense of Place.* Boston: CBI Publishing.

Swan, James, ed. 1991. *The Power of Place: Sacred Ground in Natural and Human Environments.* Wheaton, IL: Quest Books.

Taussig, Michael T. 1980. *The Devil and Commodity Fetishism in South America.* Chapel Hill: University of North Carolina Press.

Tilley, Christopher. 1994. *A Phenomenology of Landscape: Places, Paths and Monuments.* Oxford/Providence: Berg Publishers.

Tuan, Yi-Fu. 1977. *Space and Place: The Perspective of Experience.* Minneapolis: University of Minnesota.

_____. 1991. Language and the Making of Place: A Narrative-Descriptive Approach. *Annals of the association of the American geographer.* 81(4): 684.

Vestergaard, Elisabeth. 1974. *En beskrivelse af religiøse ritualer i bygden Sand på Faerøerne og deres aendring eller ophør i løbet af de sidste hundrede ár.* Etnografisk Institut, Århus Universitet. Studenterfeldrapport no. 3 Århus: Moesgård.

_____. 1989. Space and Gender at the Faroe Islands. *North Atlantic Studies* 1(1): 33–37.

Vestergaard, Elsebeth. 1975. *Feðgarnir Miðgerða Poul og Poul Johannes.* Gøtu, Faeroe Islands: Estra Prent.

Vestergaard, Torben. 1974. *Faerøsk odelsbønder: En etnografisk analyse af resterne af et nordisk stammesamfund. Etnografisk Institut, Århus Universitet.* Studenterfeldrapport no. 2. Århus: Moesgård.

Wåhlin, Vagn. 1989. Faroese History and Identity—National Historic Writing. *North Atlantic Studies* 1(1): 21–32.

West, John F. 1972. *Faroe: The Emergence of a Nation*. London: C. Hurst.
_____. 1975. How Old Is the Faroese *Grannastevna? Fróðskaparrit* 23:48–59.
_____. 1980. *Faroese Folk-tales and Legends*. Lerwick, Shetland: Shetland Publishing.
_____. 1982–1983. *Beinta og Peder Arrheboe: A Case Study in Faroese Oral Tradition. Saga-Book XXI* (Pts. 1–2). University College, London: Viking Society for Northern Research.
Whorf, Benjamin. 1941. The Relation of Habitual Thought and Behavior to Language. In *Language, Culture and Personality: Essays in Memory of Edward Sapir*. Ed. Leslie Spier, pp. 75–93. Menasha, WI: Sapir Memorial Publication Fund.
Williamson, Kenneth. 1948. *The Atlantic Islands: A Study of the Faeroe Life and Scene*. London: Wm. Collins, Sons & Co. Ltd. 2d ed. 1970. With an additional chapter by Einar Kallsberg. London: Routledge and Kegan Paul.
Woodburn, James. 1982. Egalitarian Societies. *Man* 17:431–451.
Wylie, Jonathan. 1974. I'm a Stranger Too: A Study of the Familiar Society of the Faroe Islands. Ph.D. diss., Harvard University, Cambridge, MA.
_____. 1982. The Sense of Time, the Social Construction of Reality, and the Foundations of Nationhood in Dominica and the Faroe Islands. *Comparative Studies in Society and History* 24(3): 438–466.
_____. 1983. Ólavsøka, The Faroese National Holiday. *Ethnos* 48(1–2): 26–45.
_____. 1987. *The Faroe Islands: Interpretations of History*. Lexington, KY: University Press of Kentucky.
_____. 1989. The Christmas Meeting in Context: The Construction of Faroese Identity and the Structure of Scandinavian Culture. *North Atlantic Studies* 1(1): 5–13.
Wylie, Jonathan, and David Margolin. 1981. *The Ring of Dancers: Images of Faroese Culture*. Philadelphia: University of Pennsylvania Press.
Young, G. V. C. 1979. *From the Vikings to the Reformation: A Chronicle of the Faroe Islands up to 1538*. Douglas, Isle of Man: Shearwater Press.
Yngvesson, Barbara B. 1970. Decision-making and Dispute Settlement in a Swedish Fishing Village: An Ethnography of Law. Ph.D. diss., University of California, Berkeley.
_____. 1976. Responses to Grievance Behavior: Extended Cases in a Fishing Community. *American Ethnologist* 3:353
_____. 1978. The Atlantic Fishermen. In *The Disputing Process: Law in Ten Societies*. Ed. Laura Nader and Harry F. Todd, Jr., pp. 59–85. New York: Columbia University Press.
Zukin, Sharon. 1991. *Landscapes of Power: From Detroit to Disney World*. Berkeley: University of California Press.